Texas Confidential

TEXAS

Confid

ential

Sex, Scandal, Murder, and Mayhem in the Lone Star State

MICHAEL O. VARHOLA

Published by Clerisy Press
Printed in the United States of America
Distributed by Publishers Group West
First edition, first printing

CLERISY PRESS
PO Box 8874
Cincinnati, OH 45208-0874
www.clerisypress.com

Library of Congress Cataloging-in-Publication Data

Varhola, Michael O.
    Texas confidential : sex, scandal, murder, and mayhem in the Lone Star State by Michael O. Varhola; foreword by Jesse Sublett.
        p. cm.
    Includes bibliographical references.
    ISBN-13: 978-1-57860-458-6
    ISBN-10: 1-57860-458-3
    1. Crime–Texas–History–Case studies. 2. Sex scandals–Texas–History–Case studies.
    3.Scandals–Texas–History–Case studies. 4. Politicians–Texas–Conduct of life–History.
    I. Title.
    HV6793.T4V37 2011
    364.109764–dc23

                                2011019717

Edited by **DONNA POEHNER**

Cover designed by **STEPHEN SULLIVAN AND SCOTT MCGREW**

Interior designed by **STEPHEN SULLIVAN**

Layout by **ANNIE LONG**

Front and back cover photos appear courtesy of: Wikimedia Commons; photo of Anna Nicole Smith courtesy of Photofest, Inc.
Photos in *Texas Confidential* appear courtesy of:
Michael O. Varhola: pages 16, 19, 165, 263, 299, 310, 311, 312, 313, 333
Library of Congress: pages 29, 30, 33, 160, 169, 274–275
Wikimedia Commons: pages 35, 65, 81, 91, 121, 123, 127, 133, 139,179, 219, 282, 308, 321, 322, 324, 326, 346, 348, 351
NASA: pages 144, 316-317
Other photos appear courtesy of: p. 36, IMDB; p. 47, CityView; p. 52, U.S. Congress; p. 74, *New Braunfels Herald-Zeitung;* p. 90, Chester Harding; p. 95, Mexico City Museum; p. 10, National Photo Company Collection; p. 159, Joe Burgess; p. 175, J. H. E. Partington; p. 180, Paul Joseph; p. 204, © 1980 Larry D. Moore; p. 207, Austin Police Department; p. 208, Austin Public Library; p. 213, Gunnar Hansen; p. 217, Houston Police Department; p. 241, Anthony Frederick Augustus Sandys; p. 255, Laura McKenzie/*New Braunfels Herald-Zeitung;* p. 258, Laura McKenzie/*New Braunfels Herald-Zeitung;* p. 268, Jasleen Kaur; p. 271, Edward S. Curtis; p. 273, National Archives; p. 280, Frederic Remington; p. 289, Robert Stringer; p. 294, Matthew Rutledge; p. 295, U.S. Air Force; p. 296, Daniel Schwen; p. 309, Avon; p. 342, Diego Fernández

To the good people of Texas who have, over the years, been preyed upon by the villains of this volume and suffered the effects of their countless crimes.

Table of

SEX in the Lone Star State

CONTENTS

SCANDAL in the Lone Star State

MURDER in the Lone Star State

Table of

MAYHEM in the Lone Star State

CONTENTS

Foreword

EVERY SUMMER, WHEN THE MERCURY starts heading toward the100-degree mark, I ask myself, "Why do I live in Texas?" Walk outside on a typical July or August afternoon and the sun is like a hammer hitting you in the back of the head. Why stay in a place where the heat can kill you if you're not careful? Not that there aren't lots of other reasons to not be associated with a state that's number one in executions and dead last or close enough to it in education, environment, and other categories that would seem vital to the quality of life.

I have a theory, however, that extreme heat causes a kind of amnesia, with the result that once the summer heat wave ends, so does the memory of how awful it was. This may explain why the original inhabitants of the region did not move on to more hospitable climes after their first experience with the murderous months of mid-year.

One other thing that has kept me here, other than a seven-year stint in sunny Los Angeles, is the richness of material to write about. As a crime writer, Texas is a gift that keeps on giving. I confess I can't articulate a simple description of what exactly makes the Texas criminal environment special, but like pornography, I know it when I see it. Frontier traditions and a stubborn clinging to the bullshit myths of Texas' supposed independent streak have something to do with it, as do the collision of hardcore Christian repression, progressive ideals, and greed.

Texas narcissism is also a theme here, if not an explanation. Warren Burnet, the great Texas criminal attorney of Odessa, had a relevant comment about that. Responding to his fellow Odessans' boast that the town was bursting with friendly, virtuous, kindhearted people, Burnet said, "We've got the same cross-section of assholes here that they have everywhere else."

I was honored and thrilled to be asked to write the foreword for this book, and once I glanced at the table of contents, I felt as if I was flipping through folders in my own research files. I was cheered, for example, to see a mention of the Overton Gang of Austin. I've been working on a book about Timmy Overton and his merry band of fist-fighters, pimps, and safecrackers for several years now. It's been difficult but very rewarding to sift though all the stories about the Austin underworld of the 1950s through the 1970s. Part of the problem is that I've found enough material for several books.

The Veterans Land Scandal is another topic I'm pleased to see. A few years ago I was researching that story for a possible book project. The real estate scams perpetrated during that episode very often took advantage of African-American war veterans. A Cuero newspaper reporter named Ken Towery won a Pulitzer for his series of newspaper articles that blew the whistle on the scandal. When I interviewed Towery, however, I was repulsed by his own racist and ultra-conservative views. At the time I submitted an outline for the book to my agent, it had recently been revealed that President George W. Bush had lied to the public about the reasons that the U.S. invaded Iraq. My agent pointed out that the scandalous behavior of Texas politicians of the present would probably make those of the 1950s seem distant and trivial. It was hard to dispute his point, even though I'm not sure he was right. I still think it's a fascinating chapter in Texas history.

The chapter here on the band of scalp hunters, the Glanton Gang (which was actually only one of several such groups), helps evoke some of the bad juju that seems to have existed here since at least the years when the Comanche Indians were terrorizing the Plains, raiding and killing and stealing, then trading their booty with other groups, including white reprobates. The Comanche method has accurately been compared to outlaw motorcycle gangs, except that the Hell's Angles are pussies compared to the Comanche.

The Texas Rangers served as the tip of the spear for the white takeover of Texas territory from Native Americans. Talk about a license to kill, James Bond had nothing on the Texas Rangers. Texas school kids grow up hearing heroic legends about these frontier militia men, as sterling examples of rugged independence, virtue, and justice, who rescued white captives and protected white settlements by launching both punitive raids and preemptive attacks. Few of us hear about the atrocities committed by the rangers. A memoir by Captain Rufus Perry related his refusal to participate in the gang rape of Indian women and how, on one expedition, a fellow ranger hacked off the leg of a dead Indian to eat later.

Texas has many fine attributes, but the state has a lot to answer for. Lee Harvey Oswald may have assassinated President Kennedy, but (conspiracy theories notwithstanding) the city of Dallas always seemed complicit in the crime. If brain waves could kill, the toxic public sentiment there would've killed Kennedy before he stepped onto the tarmac at Love Field.

Coincidentally, the night before the assassination, the presidential party spent the night at Hotel Texas in downtown Fort Worth, right on the edge of what was still known as Hell's Half Acre, due to its reputation for vice. Back in the Roaring Twenties, Jim Thompson, the author of *The Killer Inside Me* and dozens of other pulp fiction classics, was a teenage bellhop working nights at the hotel and buzzing on cocaine and booze, attending high school during the day. Thompson helped procure hookers, booze, and dope for guests, and in addition to his tips, collected enough material for a few dozen pulp fiction novels. Later, Thompson worked as a roughneck and gambler in West Texas, places with rich oil reserves below ground and damned souls above.

Don't get me wrong, I don't think that crime is funny or that criminals are admirable. Mostly, criminal behavior is an indicator of the deep and often irreconcilable contradictions and injustices of modern society. I think crime is fascinating because of what it exposes, and because desperate people do desperate things, whether they are billionaire oil executives or crack dealers on the street. The big difference there is that the billionaire crooks and corporations usually do a lot more damage to society than the small-time operators. The latter, however, usually have more personality and better hair.

Jesse Sublett
Austin, Texas
May 2011

Preface

TO SAY THAT AUTHORING *TEXAS*
Confidential was a very personal experience
would be something of an understatement. In
the year leading up to the publication of this
volume, I read dozens of books and hundreds
of articles related to the subjects of sex, scandal, murder, and mayhem in Texas and travelled
from one end of the state to the other visiting
the sites associated with many of the chapters that follow. A number of things, however,
ended up making this project especially relevant and interesting to me on a personal level.

These have included covering the murder
trial of Janice Marie Vickers; being menaced
and stalked by her husband; interviewing

her attorney, Mark Clark, who warrants his own sordid chapter; socializing with one of the Enron executives convicted of fraud; and reporting on a local chupacabra sighting.

Two of the chapters also draw upon research I undertook several years before this book had even been conceived. One of these involved discovering in 2001 that a girl I had gone to school with had been convicted of murder and been sentenced to many years in the Texas prison system. The other involved author Robert E. Howard, to whose home and gravesite I made a pilgrimage in early 2003.

Going beyond the specific contents of this book, I have had a number of interesting encounters since moving to Texas in 2009 either tangential to the material I have included in it or, at least, evocative of it. These include interviewing a caterer who ended up being charged with more than a hundred counts of child pornography; having lunch and several rounds of drinks bought for me and another reporter by an attorney reputed to be a mouthpiece for the Mexican Mafia; being "profiled" by an almost open sociopath who presents himself as a federal agent, which he may or may not actually be; and being acquainted with someone involved in an apparent Medicaid scam.

Working as the news reporter and editor—the *Hilltop Reporter* in Comal County also affected my attitudes toward iniquity in the Lone Star State. I was verifiably lied to by at least some members of every single local board I covered, especially those associated with fire departments. Having the newspaper I helped run fold after just two years largely because of a lack of community support certainly did nothing to diminish the cynicism that seems to be an inevitable result of working as journalist.

There is a widespread perception, both in and outside of Texas, that the state's justice system is particularly severe, something that a little observation will reveal is only partially the case. It is true that a disproportionate number of black men have been given harsh sentences or put to death, and that a number of them have subsequently been proven innocent of the crimes for which they were convicted. Texas also has a history of coming down hard on drug offenses, and it is certainly true that much of the state's prison system is particularly grim.

Overall, however, the system is strikingly lenient toward violent crimes, especially those perpetrated by whites. Historically, it has set free an amazing number of criminals, often as a result of administrative issues like prison overcrowding, caused in part by over-incarceration for nonviolent crimes. Some of the state's most heinous criminals have not only gotten relatively light sentences, they have been released while they were still young enough to effectively continue their depredations.

Serial killer Kenneth Allen McDuff, for example, was given three death sentences but was released after just a little more than two decades in prison—and subsequently killed at least another eleven people. He was part of a broader wave of clemency that led to the release of a stunning 60,000 "low-risk" offenders and 127 convicted murderers, 20 of them former death row inmates. And confessed killer Janice Marie Vickers, whose murder trial I covered in 2009, received just seventeen years for what is generally known as First-Degree Murder—and simply Murder in Texas—meaning she will probably serve less than five years in prison for deliberately running over an old lady's head multiple times with a car.

So, to say that I have been personally moved by my involvement with this book would certainly be true. And, if I have done my job well, then you will also be moved by some of the stories in this book and find them to be as fascinating as I do!

Michael O. Varhola
Canyon Lake, Texas
May 2011

Acknowledgments

A GREAT MANY OF MY FRIENDS, family, and associates deserve recognition for the roles they played during the development of *Texas Confidential*.

Foremost among the people who are due thanks is my wife, Diane. Among other things, she traveled with me to a number of the sites associated with the various chapters, discussed the project to one extent or another on almost a daily basis, and carried the weight of household responsibilities so that I could devote the necessary time and effort to this project.

Karen Holmes, publisher of the *Hilltop Reporter*, deserves thanks both for providing a venue that allowed me to work as a journalist in Texas and for offering encouragement and information throughout the development of this book.

ACKNOWLEDGMENTS

Gratitude is due to the hosts, organizers, and affiliates of Psi-Fi Radio, a paranormal-themed show I appear on regularly. Donna Stewart, Sharon Kincaid, Laura Schier, and Clarence Rice encouraged me to discuss this book and some of its weirder chapters on the show. Fellow Texan Lydia Aswolf, host of the show Lydia's Literary Lowdown, also provided a platform for me to discuss my activities and provided ongoing encouragement during the progress on this book.

A group of people who deserve recognition for their help include the staff at Clerisy Press, including editors Jack Heffron and Donna Poehner, marketing and publicity specialists Kara Pelicano and Hillary Bond, and publisher Richard Hunt, all of whom provided critical support, guidance, and encouragement during the development of *Texas Confidential*. Thanks, too, to John Boertlein, author of two of the other books in the series of which this book is a part. The chapter "Walking Tall in the White House" in this volume was adapted from his book *Presidential Confidential*.

A number of fellow writers, editors, and publishers warrant some acknowledgment for their general encouragement and specific contributions. These include Dominick and Charlene Salemi of *Brutarian* magazine, for which I write "The X-Phile" column on the paranormal; journalist Theron Brittain, who covered the Vickers murder trial with me; newspaperman J.D. Prose, who has always set a standard in my mind; Chip Cassano, who introduced me to the works of Cormac McCarthy; author Gary Cartwright, whose books on Texas history and crime were invaluable resources for me; Jake Silverstein, editor of *Texas Monthly* magazine, whose research into the final days of Ambrose Bierce helped me with my own chapter on that subject; and crime author Jesse Sublett, who very generously agreed to write the foreword to this edition of the book at the last minute.

Several friends also followed the progress of this book and periodically provided comments or encouragement on various aspects of it, among them Rick Atkinson; Richard Balsley; Coleen Cox; Caroline Eveningstorm; Nikolas Orion French; Rebecca Gallagher; Robert Gruver; Denise Lindsey; Jon Reichman; Terri Rodabaugh; Roxie Ann Young Sasiela; William Thrasher; Chris Van Deelen; my parents, Mike and Merrilea Varhola; Pete Wyeth; and Stan, Charmaine, and Sean Swearingen.

A number of the proprietors of various sites I visited or people I encountered in the process of doing so deserve my thanks as well, and these include Mark Priest of Miss Hattie's Bordello Museum in San Angelo.

Various law enforcement personnel I have worked with over the past few years also warrant mention here, not necessarily because they directly assisted with this book but because they have generally been helpful in providing me with information related to my journalistic activities. They include Lieutenant Mark Reynolds of the Comal County Sheriff's Office, Chief Joe Hamilton of the Bulverde Police Department, and trooper Rick Alvarez of the Texas Department of Public Safety.

It is important to recognize the work of the many authors, editors, journalists, radio and television reporters, contributors to online sites, and others who created the vast body of published information that I drew upon for this book.

I would also like to thank all of the editors, colleagues, family members, business associates, and friends who patiently—or, in some cases, not so patiently—waited for me to fulfill my obligations to them while I was focusing so much of my attention on this project.

Finally, if there is anyone I have left out of these acknowledgments, I would like to sincerely beg their forgiveness and thank them for their help as well!

INTRODUCTION

"Everything is bigger in Texas," as the saying goes, and this certainly applies to the sleaze, iniquity, and violence that have taken place in the Lone Star State. This book is a selective overview of some of the most striking episodes of illicit sex, scandal, murder, and mayhem in Texas and the people who have perpetrated them and provides a glimpse of the state's seamy underbelly.

Anyone who frequently watches true crime shows—not to mention other television programs and movies—has likely been struck by how many episodes are based on incidents that occurred in Texas.

Part of this, of course, can be attributed to the fact that Texas is so much bigger than other states and is thus simply proportionately more likely to be the site of unsavory activity. It is ranked second after Alaska in terms of geographical size and second after California in terms of population and, as of this writing, has a growing population of more than 25 million. For sake of comparison, 268,820-square-mile Texas is 64 percent larger than California and 17,300 percent larger than Rhode Island, and within that vast area there are at least seven large, distinct, geographical areas—each as large as many other states—the Panhandle Plains, Prairies and Lakes, Piney Woods, Gulf Coast, South Texas Plains, Texas Hill Country, and Big Bend Country.

Geographically and culturally, Texas is a virtual subcontinent and nation unto itself.

And, exceptional among U.S. states, Texas was indeed its own nation, existing as an independent republic from 1836 until late 1845, when it became the twenty-eighth state. It also seceded from the United States and was one of the Confederate States of America from 1861 to 1865.

Its vast size and the commensurate number of crimes aside, there seems to be almost an assumption of good-old-boy malfeasance in Texas. An excerpt of an article from *The Handbook of*

Texas Online, a site operated by the Texas State Historical Association, succinctly points to this attitude:

"Texas went through one of its traditional and periodic governmental scandals in 1971–72, when federal accusations and then a series of state charges were leveled against nearly two dozen state officials and former state officials," the handbook says of the Sharpstown Stock Scandal (q.v.).

On a more metaphysical level, people have also always seen the devil in Texas, and his name appears in the names of desolate, isolated, or forbidding places throughout the state, a handful of examples being the Devil's Backbone, Devil's River, Devil's Sinkhole, and the Devil's Hollow. Other place names with a supernatural bent are also fairly common (e.g., Purgatory Road in Comal County). Perhaps the iniquity that has occurred in Texas has inspired people to see the devil in its landscape, or perhaps he really is present and has inspired much of the evil that has been perpetrated here.

Texans are not, nonetheless, an overly grim people, and there is a certain joviality associated with the Lone Star State, and much is made about how friendly its residents are (although one has to wonder if this may not just be an inside joke inspired by the fact that "Texas" itself is a Caddo Indian word meaning "friends").

Many residents of the Lone Star State may indeed be somewhat friendlier than the denizens of many other states in general. But while most Texans are in no way being disingenuous, what is often mistaken by outsiders and newcomers to the state as friendliness is, in fact, a very deliberate *politeness*. It would thus be more accurate to say that Texans tend to be a very courteous people (although this has its limits as well, of course).

In all likelihood, this deliberate politeness is a result of the state having historically been a chaotic, dangerous, frontier society, where civility served as a way to manage and forestall violence, and understanding this can help one go a long way toward understanding Texas and Texans.

"It starts when you begin to overlook bad manners," says Sheriff Ed Tom Bell, one of the protagonists in Cormac McCarthy's *No Country for Old Men*. "Any time you quit hearin Sir and Mam the end is pretty much in sight." And almost any local nightly newscast from a major U.S. city confirms this phenomena, via reports about urbanized folk who have been prompted to kill one another because one or more feel they have been "dissed," or not given the respect they believed was their due.

The contents of this book have been organized into four broad sections, one each devoted to the four topics in its subtitle, "Sex," "Scandal," "Murder," and "Mayhem." A great many of the chapters that appear in one section, however, could just as easily appear in one of the others, and a few of the most complex and lurid have substantial elements of all four. So, inclusion in one does not necessarily imply a dearth of the things that could qualify it to be in another.

With an eye toward including as much as possible in this volume, the various chapters tend to be relatively brief snapshots of episodes that could be expanded upon nearly indefinitely. Almost any one of the topics covered in this book could, in fact, be the subject of an entire book devoted completely to it (and many have, some of those books serving as references for this one). A number of the chapters in this book are composite pieces that include multiple entries of various sorts (e.g., porn stars, serial killers, gangs), and many also include a variety of lists and sidebars containing supplemental information pertinent to the topics being discussed.

There is much that is not included here and a great many potentially promising stories had to be rejected during the creation of this book for various reasons. One is that this volume could only be so big and contain so much material. Another is that many relatively new stories had still not fully played out by the time this book had to go to print (e.g., the probable murder trial of Houston Dr. Conrad Murray, who was treating entertainer Michael Jackson at the time of his death).

It bears mentioning that all of the events described in this book are the products of human iniquity, inadequacy, or incompetence, and that natural disasters, no matter how much mayhem they may have inflicted, are not included. So, the apocalyptic hurricane that ravaged Galveston in 1900 is not covered, nor is the 1886 storm that literally obliterated the coastal town of Indianola and removed it from maps of the state. The acts of people, not God or nature, are presented here.

And those people certainly comprise a colorful rogues' gallery of lunatics, corrupt politicians, prostitutes, murderers, and every other sort of scoundrel—to which has been added a smattering of UFOs, mythological beasts, zombies, and other paranormal oddities. Enjoy getting to know them and learning about the things they have done to earn their places on the seamy side of Texas history!

SEX

in the

Lone Star State

1

Texas Vice

PROSTITUTION WAS A FACTOR IN
Texas society from its earliest days, even before
it became a state or even an independent nation, and the Spanish had recorded its presence
in San Antonio at least as far back as 1817.
As settlers poured into the area and new towns
sprung up and grew throughout it, prostitutes
followed and set up business along with everyone else.

Military activity in the region was certainly one of the factors that encouraged prostitution. General Zachary Taylor's troops were well served by women of ill repute during the eight months they spent around Corpus Christi prior to the 1846 U.S. invasion of Mexico. Bawdy houses also sprang up around military camps in the years during, and after the Civil War (1861–65).

Encouraged by the boom in ranching, the arrival of the railroads, and the establishment of permanent military bases—and, ultimately, the arrival of the oil industry—permanent vice districts became a distinct phenomenon in cities from the 1870s onward. Some of the most significant of these included "Boggy Bayou" and "Frogtown" in Dallas, "The Concho" in San Angelo, "Guy Town" in Austin, "Happy Hollow" in Houston, "Hell's Half-Acre" in Fort Worth, the Postoffice Street district in *Galveston*, the "Sporting District" in San Antonio, "Two Street" in Waco, and the Utah Street reservation in El Paso. Many districts in smaller communities were also called Hell's Half-Acre or had names similar to those in larger cities (e.g., "Feather Hill," "Hog Town").

Often tacitly blessed by civic leaders as a means of segregating vice, these districts generally encompassed several city blocks, were located within a short distance of the downtown business area and railroad station, and included brothels, saloons, gambling dens, dance halls, burlesque theaters, and the little shanties used by many prostitutes.

Some streetwalkers in larger cities like San Antonio and El Paso had pimps, but most prostitutes were associated with brothels, where they were protected and managed by madams. The names of most of these have been lost to history but a few of them are known—at least by their working names—among them Blanche Dumont in Austin, "Miss Hattie" in San Angelo (q.v.), Mary Porter in Fort Worth, and Jessie Williams in La Grange (q.v.).

Cost for a session with a prostitute in the latter half of the nineteenth century depended on many factors but generally ranged from 25 cents at one end to $5 at the other. Depending on the demographics and purpose of a particular community, customers included cowboys, businessmen, convention goers, drifters, farm hands, laborers, ranchers, soldiers, oilfield workers, politicians, sailors, students, and gamblers.

Permanent vice districts became a phenomenon . . . these included:

Hispanic prostitutes were the norm in the early days but by the era of the Civil War had been joined by many white women as well and, by the 1880s, blacks.

"In Austin half or more of the prostitutes during the 1880s and 1890s were white, most of them born in the United States, while about 40 percent were blacks and some 7 percent Hispanics," wrote David C. Humphrey, author of several detailed articles on prostitution in Texas. "In Houston in 1917, 60 percent of the women who headed households of prostitutes in the vice reservation were Anglo, 35 percent black, and 5 percent Hispanic. Hispanic prostitutes were more common in San Antonio, El Paso, and Laredo, at army forts in West and South Texas, and generally in communities closer to the Mexican border. Anglo and black prostitutes lived and worked near each other in vice districts, but race had a significant bearing on how the districts operated. Whites predominated in brothels, while blacks predominated in cribs. Most bawdy houses maintained color separation in their employees, and Anglo houses refused as a rule to accommodate black men. On the other hand, many white men patronized black as well as white prostitutes."

Not all prostitutes were wholly devoted to their occupation, and some only turned tricks when they had to or also served in other capacities (e.g., as laundresses around military camps). Most were women in their twenties, but they ranged in age from their teens to their sixties. Many were itinerant, following the

Guy Town, Happy Hollow, and Hell's Half-Acre.

spread of the railroad or the establishment of new communities around railheads, ranchlands, and oilfields, or being driven out by periodic anti-vice campaigns.

Life was, in any event, rough for the majority of prostitutes in Texas, and most were constantly threatened by disease, violence, and municipal authorities and lived on the verge of poverty (although prostitution paid better than most jobs open to women, an enticement to widows and abandoned wives). Many also suffered from disorders like depression, abused drugs like cocaine, morphine, and opium, or attempted to commit suicide.

During the 1880s, the larger municipal vice districts probably had more than one hundred prostitutes working in them, a number that might have been twice as high for periods in even moderate-sized boomtowns, and which probably doubled or tripled by 1910.

While most Texas communities had ordinances on the books illegalizing prostitution, they generally did not overly enforce these and instead tried to control and isolate it, both because they considered it could not be eliminated and because it often had a significant impact on local economies (i.e., via rents, fines, money spent by patrons). And in the late 1880s and 1890s, Dallas, El Paso, Houston, and Waco tried legalizing prostitution within specified vice districts.

Campaigns led by clergymen, political reformers, and women's groups did manage to get a number of vice districts shut down during the years 1911 to 1915, notably in Amarillo, Austin, and Dallas. And, with the outbreak of World War I, opponents of prostitution gained an ally in Secretary of War Newton D. Baker, who wanted prostitution banned in communities where military bases were located so as to protect troops from venereal diseases. Fearing the loss of installations or that they might be put off-limits to troops, the cities of *Galveston*, El Paso, Fort Worth, Houston, San Antonio, and Waco complied with these demands in 1917 and shut down their vice districts.

During the 1920s and 1930s, prostitutes in Texas began to spread out of the vice districts and conduct their business from apartments, hotels, rooming houses, and roadhouses; to communicate with patrons via telephone; and to walk the streets to make themselves visible to people driving automobiles. Vice districts continued to operate during this era in many communities, including Beaumont, Borger, Corpus Christi, Corsicana, Dallas, El Paso, San Angelo, and San Antonio, but many of these deteriorated, becoming seedy and dangerous. Many brothels shut down and higher-end prostitutes became call girls.

During the late 1920s, however, Galveston had as many as nine hundred prostitutes working in its thriving vice district.

"Every big city in Texas had prostitution in the 1930s, but only in Galveston did it have identifiable, official boundaries, and tacit police protection," wrote author Gary Cartwright of the Postoffice Street district in his book, *Galveston*. "By day the street was mostly deserted . . . but it came alive after dark. Prostitutes dressed for the evening appeared in lighted doorways, or leaned against the sills of open windows, calling to the passing parade of seamen, dockworkers, soldiers, medical students, and conventioneers. Businessmen, trying to look nonchalant and appear as though they were just pricing the real estate, ducked furtively behind latticework screens that had been positioned in front of the houses for precisely that reason. Some houses had steep flights of steps, in various stages of disrepair, and doors with tiny stained-glass windows and peepholes. Black maids answered the doors and led customers to shabby parlors where they were permitted to buy watered-down whiskey for themselves, and colored water for the girls. They were urged to feed quarters into the music

Galveston had as many as nine hundred prostitutes.

box, and permitted a dance or two before being led upstairs. If the guests behaved, they were allowed to hang around afterward to dance and drink."

With the onset of the Great Depression in the 1930s, many more women were driven to sell themselves, pushing down prices, doubling or even tripling the number of women working the streets, and further damaging the viability of the vice districts and the brothels. Pimps became more common. Prostitution was sometimes targeted along with offenses like bootlegging, but enforcement remained uneven and many civic leaders continued to be tolerant.

During World War II (1941–1945), prostitution was once again attacked by the military leaders as a threat to the health of troops, and communities were pressured into shutting down their red-light districts under threat of being put off-limits to

Whores Galore

FOR A MORE DETAILED DISCUSSION OF TWO particular brothels in the Lone Star State, see the chapters in this section on "Miss Hattie's Bordello" and "The Best Little Whorehouse in Texas."

service members. By the time the war ended, the distinct, tolerated municipal vice districts had almost completely disappeared from Texas cities, and the general attitude of tolerance had been replaced with one of repression.

Galveston, San Antonio, and a few other cities maintained their districts well into the 1950s, but they were the exception to the rule, and some of the protected bordellos persisted even a few decades beyond this, remaining a feature of society in the Lone Star State much longer than they generally did elsewhere in the country. For the most part, however, prostitution had become dispersed over a much wider area and moved into motels and cheap hotels, massage parlors, cafes, bars, and the streets. The era of the Texas vice district as it had existed for a century had come to an end.

2

Miss Hattie's Bordello

FOR HALF A CENTURY, FROM 1902 until 1952, one of the best-known and most successful businesses in San Angelo, "the Oasis of West Texas," was Miss Hattie's Bordello. It was, in fact, the crown jewel in the local vice district known as the Concho, a neighborhood named for the river along which it was located.

Each of the girls who worked at Miss Hattie's Bordello had an area like this one for entertaining customers. Today, the site has been restored and is operated as a museum.

In 1867, the U.S. Army established Fort Concho in west central Texas as part of a network of posts designed to protect frontier settlers against the resident Comanche, Apache, and bandits. Its garrison included units of infantry and cavalry soldiers, among them the black troopers referred to as "Buffalo Soldiers" by the Indians.

A settler named Bartholomew J. DeWitt established the village of Santa Angela just outside the fort, at the juncture of the north and south forks of the Concho River, naming it after his late wife, Carolina Angela. This name was eventually shortened to San Angela and, in 1883, changed altogether and masculinized to San Angelo at the insistence of the U.S. Postal Service, ostensibly because this made it grammatically correct.

"As an early frontier town, San Angelo was characterized by saloons, prostitution, and gambling," says the Texas State

Historical Association. "Officers of nearby Fort Concho would not leave the garrison after dark." By any name, San Angelo was a rough place, and Miss Hattie's was by no means the first brothel to be established in it.

Many people settled in the area, however, and after San Angelo became the seat of Tom Green County in 1882 and the railroad arrived in 1888, the community became a regional transportation hub and grew quickly. As tuberculosis swept the country around the turn of the century, the warm, dry climate of the Texas plains also made it one of the venues that people flocked to in search of cures from the "consumption."

Around this time the woman who became known as Miss Hattie moved to San Angelo and married a local man named Mr. Hatton and the two of them purchased the building at 18 Concho Street. This beautiful structure had been built just a few years before, in 1896, and was located in what is now the historic heart of the downtown district of the city.

Their marital bliss was soon disrupted, however, when Mrs. Hatton discovered that she could not abide being married to a drinking man, and the two were soon divorced. As part of their settlement, Mr. Hatton received the lower level of the building they owned together, and the former Mrs. Hatton received the upper level, which could be accessed from a separate door at 18½ Concho Street.

It's not clear how much this lady's reputation was damaged by becoming a divorcee in this era or what options were available for supporting herself. What is certain, however, is that she tweaked her name to Miss Hattie and turned her part of the building on Concho Street into a high-end cathouse. It was, in fact, the first place in San Angelo to have running water.

Miss Hattie's Brothel soon became a fashionable spot for local cowboys, ranchers, and businessmen to unwind and blow off a little steam. Tricks started at just 25 cents for a turn with a typical girl and ranged upward to $2 for a visit with the most popular ones. And, while she was not willing to tolerate drinking by her own husband—or by the prostitutes who worked for her—Miss Hattie had no problems with her customers imbibing while they waited their turn with a girl, played cards, or chatted amongst each other.

Other girls who worked at the place over the years included Miss Juanita, whose job it was to sing, dance with, and otherwise platonically entertain the men while they were waiting for a girl; Miss Blue, who had everything from her wardrobe to her sheets in her namesake color and had the best room in the house, the only one with direct access to the bathroom; Miss Mabel, who worked at the brothel to support her husband while he recovered from tuberculosis and then moved back to New Mexico with him and the child she conceived by a customer; Miss Kitty, who eventually retired to a ranch left to her by an appreciative customer in his will (and whose descendants live on it to this day); Miss Rosie, whose room had a catwalk that would get used as an escape route during raids; and Miss Goldie, who eventually entertained just one particular client on condition that he remember her in his will and who had to work at the place into her thirties when he did not, becoming a flower seller when she was too old to turn tricks and eventually dying penniless.

Miss Hattie's establishment continued to thrive throughout the era of Prohibition, when it became linked to other brothels, speakeasies, and dens of ill repute through a network of subterranean tunnels that ran throughout the entire Concho district. And, during World War II, airmen and soldiers from nearby Goodfellow Field (now Goodfellow Air Force Base) spent their paychecks at the well-known whorehouse.

While Miss Hattie's operation was obviously illegal, it was also clearly well connected, and, even though it was periodically raided, locals joked that the police would come in the front door

Miss Juanita once used this parlor to entertain visitors to the brothel with music, dancing, and socializing while they were waiting for their turns with the various working girls.

and the county judge would run out the back. In 1952, however—some years after Miss Hattie herself had retired from the establishment—the decidedly unhumorous Texas Rangers finally raided the bordello and shut it down for good.

Even after it ceased to operate as brothel, and a new generation of residents forgot that it had even been one, 18 Concho Street continued to be known as "Miss Hattie's Building." In the decades after the girls left, it was variously empty, a sporting goods store, and an antique shop.

Then, in the early 1990s, its new owner discovered many of the original furnishings from Miss Hattie's stored in the upper rooms of the building and, upon investigation, learned what the place had been used for. They put some considerable effort into researching the history of the place and its inhabitants, restored it as best as they were able to its original appearance, and then opened it as a museum (the lower level, in keeping with its tradition of being used for legitimate commerce, is today a jewelry store).

And so today, six decades after it was shut down, Miss Hattie's is once again open to visitors—and, while they cannot enjoy the house in quite the same way as customers did back then, they can get a glimpse of what one of San Angelo's most popular and prosperous businesses was like in its heyday.

3

Porno, Texas Style

WHEN THEY SAY EVERYTHING IS bigger in Texas, sometimes they are talking about various naughty bits. Dozens of well-known pornographic actresses and actors have hailed from the Lone Star State, and some of these have had stories that were particularly sordid or interesting.

The Bedeviled Chloe Jones
(June 17, 1975– June 4, 2005)

In her short life, Chloe Jones's greatest claim to fame might be having received $15,000 for performing oral sex on actor Charlie Sheen, something she alleged in a 2005 interview— which, according to some, may have led to her demise.

Born Melinda Dee Jones on June 17, 1975, the blue-eyed blonde was raised about one hundred miles northeast of Houston in the town of Silsbee. After her father was killed in a 1982 traffic accident, she and her two sisters were exposed to the various perverts her mother shacked up with. By the time she was fourteen, she had been committed multiple times and experimented with acid, part of the chronic drug and alcohol abuse that would eventually ravage her from the inside out and lead to her untimely death.

Melinda eventually grew up into a disturbed but voluptuous, 5-foot 6-inch, 116-pound, 36D-22-32 young woman. In 1991, the sultry sixteen-year-old married a young Marine and made a go at a normal life, something that lasted about two years, until she started stripping and he filed for divorce.

Her career took off after that and she appeared in a several magazines, both nude and otherwise, including mainstream *Vanity Fair, Hustler, Swank, Playboy* on numerous occasions and, in April 1994, as the *Penthouse* "Pet of the Month." Around this time she married again—a nightclub manager named Michael Taylor—and had three children, a girl, Chloe, in 1996 (apparently by a man other than her husband), and twin boys, Austin and Tristan, in 1997.

In 2001, the industrious Jones kicked it up a notch and moved into the pornographic film industry, where she soon became relatively well known, signed contracts with two production companies, and acquired a professional reputation for being "difficult" and a prescription drug abuser. Three years of that was all Jones could handle and—also affected, perhaps, by her waning health—in 2004 she announced her retirement from the adult entertainment industry. At that point she had performed in eighteen films.

Jones apparently continued to trade on her looks and reputation, however, and to supplement her livelihood as an "escort" for men willing and able to pay a premium for sex. According to a March 2005 interview with the *National Enquirer*, these included Sheen, who she claimed to have fellated for a whopping fifteen grand in January 2005.

Jones, however, did not last too long after that and died just three months later, in June 2005 at age twenty-nine, with cause of death attributed to liver failure inflicted by an addiction to Vicodin and a lifetime of heavy drug and alcohol abuse. She was interred at Woodlawn Garden of Memories in Houston.

Less than a year later, in May 2006, the supermarket tabloid the *Globe* published an alleged interview with Jones's mother that quoted her as saying Sheen had made death threats against the starlet, had played a role in her death, and that she was considering filing a wrongful death suit against the actor. What is known for sure is that Donna Jones Noeller filed a lawsuit against the *Globe*, insisting she had never actually been interviewed and that her statements had been manufactured.

But the damage was done and some people believed the story—including, apparently, Sheen's wife, actress Denise Richards, who cited the actor's failure to deny any involvement in Jones' death as her basis for obtaining a restraining order against him.

The Devil in Georgina Spelvin
(March 1, 1936)

Not every Texas porn star is a train wreck waiting to happen, and some have managed to pace themselves and retire and go on to relatively normal lives after long and prosperous careers. One of these is certainly Georgina Spelvin, best known for her leading role in the 1973 classic *The Devil in Miss Jones,* widely considered to have significant artistic merit and be one of the best pornographic films ever made.

Born Michelle Graham in Houston on March 1, 1936, the future actress was struck by polio as a child but managed to gain enough mobility to train as a dancer and develop into a 5-foot 5-inch, 118-pound, 35-24-36, brown-haired, brown-eyed woman. She moved to New York City in the 1950s, where she started off as a chorus girl and was thereafter featured in Broadway produc-

"I wanted to be an opera singer but my voice wasn't good enough.

tions of *Guys and Dolls, Sweet Charity,* and *The Pajama Game.* She made the transition to pornography in 1957 with *The Twilight Girls* (aka, *Les Collegiennes*), a soft-core lesbian movie.

"At first, I wanted to be an opera singer but my voice wasn't good enough," she is quoted as having said. "My second choice was ballerina. After that, it was a series of compromises."

Soon after she moved exclusively into pornography, eventually adopting the screen name Georgina Spelvin, a variation on "George Spelvin," a traditional pseudonym used by stage actors (although she is also variously credited as Shelley Abels, Claudia

Clitoris, Tia Von Davis, Dorothy May, Merle Miller, Georgette Spelvin, Ona Tural, and Ruth Raymond).

Spelvin went on to become one of the most-well-known figures in the adult film industry, performing in more than seventy hard-core pornographic films by the time she retired in 1982. She also appeared in and did costume design for a handful of low-budget exploitation films, among them *I Spit on Your Corpse* (aka, *Girls For Rent*), and had minor roles in a number of mainstream films, including *Police Academy* and *Police Academy 3: Back in Training,* for which she was cast as a prostitute, as well as *Bad Blood* and *Next Year in Jerusalem,* and guest starred in a couple of television shows.

During her career as a pornographic actress, Spelvin won at least nine industry awards—including two for Best Actress, four for Best Supporting Actress, and three for pornography halls of fame—and was nominated for at least one other. Ironically, the

. . . My second choice was ballerina. After that, it was a series of compromises."

one for which she was nominated but did not receive was for her role in *The Devil in Miss Jones.*

After retiring from pornography, Spelvin went into desktop publishing and worked as a designer for the *L.A. Times* until 2004, when she retired again. Since then, she has appeared in a number of cameo roles, interviews, and music videos, and, in 2008, published an autobiography titled *The Devil Made Me Do It.*

Texas Porn Stars

FOLLOWING ARE MORE THAN TWO-DOZEN pornographic actors and actresses, most identified by their stage names, who have hailed from Texas. Years of birth (and death if applicable) are provided when known, followed by the communities from which they originally hailed or lived at some point if available.

- *Sunrise Adams* (Pickton)

- *Krista Allen* (1971; Houston, Austin; soft-core)

- *Candy Barr,* nee Juanita Dale Slusher (1935–2005; Edna, Victoria, Dallas)

- *Jessica Drake* (1974; San Antonio)

- *Katie Gold* (Dallas)

- *Jessie Jane,* nee Cindy Taylor (1980; Fort Worth)

- *Sindee Jennings* (1986)

- *Chloe Jones,* nee Melinda Dee Jones (1975–2005; Silsbee, Houston)

- *Jana Jordan* (1986; Houston)

- *Wendi Knight* (1975; Fort Worth)

- *Adrianna Lynn/ Adrenalynn* (1985; Allen)

- *Meggan Mallone*
  (1986; Houston)
- *Julie Meadows,*
  nee Lydia Lee
  (1974; Texarkana)
- *Nina Mercedez*
  (1977; Corpus Christi)
- *Britt Morgan*
  (1963; Tyler)
- *Bree Olson,*
  nee Rachel Marie Oberlin
  (1986; Houston)
- *Teagan Presley,*
  nee Ashley Ann Erickson
  (1985; The Woodlands,
  Houston)
- *Texas Presley*
  (1981; Austin)
- *Jesse Santana*
  (1986; Houston)

- *Georgina Spelvin,*
  nee Michelle Graham
  (1936; Houston)
- *Sydnee Steele,*
  nee Amy Jaynes
  (1968; Dallas)
- *Shay Sweet,*
  nee Kristy Lynn Castle
  (1978; Fort Worth)
- *Taylor Vixen*
  (1983; Dallas)
- *Honey Wilder*
  (1950;
  Panhandle region)
- *Tyla Wynn,*
  nee Nancy Spencer
  (1982; Lubbock)
- *Christian XXX*
  (1974; San Antonio)

4

Walking Tall in the White House

LYNDON BAINES JOHNSON, THIRTY- sixth President of the United States, always seemed proud of his womanizing ways. He had sex, inside and outside the White House, with secretaries, aides, and just about any other woman who would agree.

LBJ was constantly on the lookout for women willing to help satisfy his seemingly insatiable sexual desires.

Lady Bird Johnson, wife of philandering President Lyndon Baines Johnson, was just one of the many women who shared his bed with him.

Johnson was quoted as saying he had "more women by accident than Kennedy did on purpose"—a formidable claim, especially as he certainly lacked JFK's looks, charm, and sophistication—and enjoyed bragging about his sexual appetites and prowess in true "Texas fashion."

Despite his promiscuity, LBJ had at least two long-lasting affairs (and a thirty-nine-year marriage, of course).

The first affair lasted nearly three decades, from 1938 until 1965, with a lady named Alice Glass. Alice was the mistress and later the wife of Texas millionaire Charles E. Marsh, publisher of the *Austin American-Statesman*, who also had newspaper interests across the nation. Lyndon and Alice first met in 1937 at Marsh's Culpepper, Virginia, estate. Alice was twenty-three years younger than Marsh and found young Johnson quite irresistible.

At one time, Alice believed Lyndon would divorce his wife to marry her, but she realized the affect a divorce would have on Lyndon's political career, and the couple settled for a long-term, adulterous affair, sometimes meeting at the Mayflower Hotel in Washington, D.C., sometimes at Marsh's estate. It is unlikely the

Johnson had "more women by accident than Kennedy did on purpose."

affair could be kept secret from Lady Bird Johnson or Charles Marsh, but both seem to have resigned themselves to it.

Ironically, the liaison ended around 1965 over political disagreement. Alice opposed the Vietnam War and apparently wanted no more to do with its then-commander-in-chief. She even burned Lyndon's love letters in protest.

In 1948, twenty-three-year-old Madeleine Brown was an advertising buyer for radio in Texas. She met Johnson at a reception hosted by Austin radio station KTBC, which Johnson owned. According to Brown, shortly after another event she and LBJ hooked up at an Austin hotel for a sex session. Afterward, KTBC's station manager acted as intermediary in setting up sexual encounters for the pair. Lyndon and Madeleine would meet at different hotels in Texas anytime Johnson was there on business or making a campaign visit.

In 1950, Madeleine told Johnson she was pregnant with his child. Steven Brown was born in 1951. However, on the birth certificate Brown listed her estranged husband as the father.

The affair ended in 1969 at the Shamrock Hotel in Houston in a dispute over Steven's paternity. Steven was more than six feet tall and seemed to resemble Lyndon. Madeleine claimed she tried to persuade LBJ to acknowledge being Steven's father for more than two hours, but he would not consider the notion because of Lady Bird and his two daughters.

Shortly after LBJ died in 1973, Texas lawyer Jerome T. Ragsdale contacted Brown to say plans had been made to continue to provide for her and Steven. Ragsdale had been providing financial support, including a house, to Madeleine since Steven's birth.

In 1987, Steven Brown filed suit against Lady Bird Johnson and the LBJ estate for $10.5 million, claiming unjust denial of his inheritance and his name. The lawsuit never made it to trial, however, as it halted when Steven died of lymphatic cancer.

In 1997, Madeleine Brown published an account of her affair with LBJ titled *Texas in the Morning: The Love Story of Madeleine Brown and President Lyndon Baines Johnson.*

The luxurious Mayflower Hotel in Washington, D.C., was one of the love shacks where LBJ pursued a long-term affair with Alice Glass.

5

The Best Little Whorehouse in Texas

Rumor spreadin' around, in that Texas town
'bout that shack outside La Grange
and you know what I'm talkin' about.
Just let me know, if you wanna go
to that home out on the range.
They gotta lotta nice girls. . . .

— ZZ Top, *"La Grange"*

WHETHER OR NOT IT WAS ACTUALLY "the best little whorehouse in Texas" is probably a matter of personal opinion, but there really was a brothel in the southeastern town of La Grange that inspired first a Broadway musical and then a film.

A picture of the notorious Chicken Ranch probably taken shortly before it was shut down for the last time in 1973.

One is probably safe assuming, however, that singer Dolly Parton—who played the madam of the establishment in the 1982 movie *The Best Little Whorehouse in Texas*—was somewhat more charming and savory than the woman known as "Mrs. Swine," the widow who opened La Grange's first cathouse in 1844.

In the early days, the whorehouse was run out of a hotel next to a saloon and staffed by three young women from New Orleans who used the lobby for meeting and getting to know their clients and rooms upstairs for entertaining them in private. Mrs. Swine's establishment thrived for nearly two decades, until the eve of the Civil War, when the locals finally had enough and drove her and her working girls out of Fayette County—for

The story of the Chicken Ranch inspired first a Broadway play and then a film, both titled The Best Little Whorehouse in Texas.

being loyal to the Union and unwilling to swear loyalty to the Confederacy!

Prostitution in La Grange continued in the years following the war, mostly operating out of the local saloons, but there is not much information available until after the turn of the century. Then, in 1905, a woman known as "Miss Jessie" purchased a small house on the banks of the Lower Colorado River, about two-and-a-half miles from the center of La Grange, and turned it into a bordello.

Whatever her morals, Jessie Williams was a canny business-woman, and she managed to keep her establishment relatively respectable by banning drunks and protected by welcoming lawmen and politicians. This gave her early warning of a local anti-vice campaign and prompted her to sell her house and move her operations to just outside of La Grange. There, on a ten-acre lot located just off of the highway running from Houston to the state capital of Austin, Miss Jessie continued with her business as usual in a small farmhouse.

These sorts of connections allowed the brothel to remain in this final location and to operate illegally but with impunity for nearly seventy years and to become a veritable regional institution. In 1917, during World War I, Miss Jessie even began to advertise her establishment by having some of the girls who worked for her send letters and packages to servicemen.

Between spreading the word and the proliferation of automobiles, which allowed more people to easily make the trek out to the increasingly popular institution, the brothel enjoyed a boom in business. Miss Jessie even had to expand her house, adding rooms as needed until it had fourteen rooms and a number of outbuildings. Its entrance was in the rear, and there was nothing overt to indicate what it was used for.

Miss Jessie is said to have stringently policed her establishment, patrolling the halls when patrons were in the house and intervening if any were out of line, going so far as to chase them out with an iron bar. She also prohibited the girls in her employ from getting tattoos, drinking, or frequenting bars in town and required them to get examined by a doctor on a weekly basis.

It also could not have hurt that the madam was on good terms with county sheriff Will Loessin. According to local lore, he would drop by every night to trade gossip with Miss Jessie and find out if she had gotten wind of any criminal activity from her clients. Numerous crimes were reportedly solved as a result of this exchange of information. Miss Jessie also fostered goodwill amongst the people of La Grange by alternating which businesses she purchased goods and services from and contributing to local causes.

When the Great Depression struck in 1929, men had less money to spend (and more women were forced into prostitution, increasing supply), so Miss Jessie had to first lower her prices and then go over to a barter system altogether in order to stay in business. It was during this time that the clever procuress began to charge one chicken for each sex act performed by a customer. As the volume of poultry at the establishment proliferated and Miss Jessie began selling eggs and chickens to supplement the income of the house, the brothel became known as the Chicken Ranch, a nickname it would keep for the rest of its existence.

A new sheriff named T.J. Flournoy took office in 1946 and reportedly had a phone line installed directly from his office to

One base even reportedly provided a helicopter to

the Chicken Ranch so that he could continue to use it as a source of information but not have to be bothered driving out to it every night. He also began fingerprinting, photographing, and running background checks on the girls Miss Jessie hired to work at the bordello.

Miss Jessie was getting on in years and around this time started to suffer from arthritis, so in 1952 she turned the day-to-day management of the brothel over to a younger resident named Edna Milton. The cathouse continued to flourish under her direction and throughout the 1950s employed sixteen prostitutes.

After Miss Jessie died in 1961, Miss Edna bought the ranch and, while she continued with many of the traditions her predecessor had started, renamed it "Edna's Fashionable Ranch Boarding House."

The 1950s and 1960s were certainly the heyday of the establishment, and the women stayed busy and worked hard, each of them entertaining from five to twenty customers each a day. On weekends, there was generally a line of men at the door, many of them students from Texas A&M University or personnel from one of the local military facilities. One base even reportedly provided a helicopter to ferry troops to and from the Chicken Ranch. And students at Texas A&M University made sending their freshmen there as an initiation into an informal tradition (ostensibly because so many of the girls who worked there had attended the school).

At its peak, the ranch brought in more than a half million dollars annually. During this period the girls typically charged $15

ferry troops to and from the Chicken Ranch.

for fifteen minutes, had all of their living and medical expenses covered, and remitted three-quarters of what they earned to management (although at some particularly lucrative points they were allowed to keep as much as $300 a week beyond this).

The permissive attitude of La Grange law enforcement toward the Chicken Ranch did not extend to the state level. In November 1972 the intelligence team of the Texas Department of Public Safety covertly watched the place over a two-day period, during which they observed some 484 people entering it. It was hard for anyone to deny what was going on at the ranch and, at the prompting of the DPS, local law enforcement was forced to briefly shut it down.

In July 1973, however, the existence of the Chicken Ranch became public knowledge when Marvin Zindler, an investigative news reporter for Houston television station channel 13, KTRK-TV, launched an exposé of it.

"Action 13 received an anonymous complaint about two alleged houses of prostitution," Zindler said in his initial broadcast. "The complainant said the houses were operating openly in our neighboring towns of Sealy and La Grange. It's illegal to operate a house of prostitution in Texas. And past history shows they cannot function without someone in authority protecting them."

Zindler himself was not playing it completely straight with the public but stuck to his story for twenty-five years. He finally came clean in the late 1990s and admitted that his anonymous source was really Tim James, chief of organized crime division in the office of Texas Attorney General John Hill. Hill, who who was reportedly concerned that the ranch was part of a ring being run by mobsters, had asked Fayette County District Attorney Oliver Kitzman to shut it down. Knowing that his constituency wanted the brothel to stay open, however, Kitzman declined to take action. James then contacted Zindler in the hopes that the high-profile reporter could bring to bear enough public attention to get the ranch shut down.

Zindler interviewed Kitzman in the course of his exposé, and the county attorney admitted to knowing about the brothel but gave as his reason for declining to shut it down that "we have never had any indication by anyone that these places are a problem to law enforcement." The journalist also spoke with Flournoy, who had served the county as sheriff for twenty-seven years, and he asserted that he had never received bribes to keep the ranch open and that it was in no way affiliated with organized crime.

Zindler then approached Texas Governor Dolph Briscoe, who was prompted to launch his own brief investigation of the brothel. It revealed no evidence of mob links, but he and Attorney

General Hill nonetheless ordered that the Chicken Ranch be shut down for good.

Sheriff Flournoy stepped up to do his part for the cathouse and, carrying a petition signed by three thousand people opposed to its closure, went to Austin to speak with Governor Briscoe. The politician refused to meet with the sheriff and, on August 1, 1973, the Chicken Ranch closed its doors for the last time and a Texas tradition came to an end.

6

Going Down to Get Ahead

IN 1976, JOHN ANDREW YOUNG (1916–2002) had been a career politician for three decades and was on his eleventh term in the U.S. House of Representatives when a woman who had worked for him accused him of pressuring her to have sex with him. Even worse, she said, the married father of five had compensated her at taxpayers' expense by giving her substantial pay raises.

Colleen Gardner, a young woman who had, as it were, worked on the Democratic congressman's staff since 1970, said she had reluctantly had sex with her boss on numerous occasions after giving in to his relentless advances.

Gardner was, in fact, suspiciously well paid for someone who had admitted that "maybe four days out of the week I had nothing to do." When she began working in Young's office, Gardner received an annual salary of $8,500, good for a novice staffer, but before long had it increased to $25,800. To put that in perspective, only 27 of the 464 staff members of the Texas congressional delegation earned more, and most of them were senior personnel like chiefs of staff.

Woefully underemployed, Gardner asked for more work, and Young cheerfully obliged, making her primary duty sitting with him in his private office and chatting "about sex for hours and hours."

Talk is cheap and Young decided to kick it up a notch, and the two reportedly met at nearby motels—where Young registered under the assumed name of "George Denton"—at least thirty-two times over a sixteen-month period.

"I'd deny it if it were true, but the fact is, I didn't," Young said in response to the pay-for-play allegations. But, unable to refute a messy paper trail that led straight from Capitol Hill to multiple sleazy motel rooms, the senior congressman had no choice but to admit both that he had rented them and used a false name to do so. He claimed he had done so, however, in pursuit of his official duties—namely, for purposes of meeting with Department of Defense employees who wanted to give him confidential information about illicit activities at the Pentagon.

A Department of Justice investigation concluded before the end of 1976 failed to prove a connection between Young's affair with Gardner and her exorbitant pay.

Young's wife, Jane, however, was not quite as concerned with the technicalities of the case as were the federal government investigators and, on July 13, 1977, fatally shot herself in the head.

Ever the trooper, Young worked through his grief and ran for reelection in the June 1978 primary but was defeated and left the office he had held for twenty-two years in 1979. He thereafter worked as a consultant until his death in early 2002, upon which he was buried with honors at Arlington National Cemetery, across the Potomac River from Washington, D.C., in Arlington, Virginia.

7

Paying for It, Lying About It —And Getting Away With It

NOBODY LIKES TO ADMIT THEY HAVE paid too much for something, and it is certainly the kind of thing people fib about every day without fear of dire consequences. But when the FBI is conducting a background investigation on someone being appointed to public office and asks him how much money he gave to his mistress, it is a bad idea to lowball the amount. That is what the honorable Henry Cisneros did, and it caused him untold problems, tarnished a presidential administration, and cost the American taxpayers a lot of money.

Cisneros was one of the shining stars of the Democratic Party, having served four successful terms as the mayor of San Antonio and as a key advisor to Bill Clinton during his 1992 presidential campaign. Clinton rewarded Cisneros for his efforts by appointing him U.S. Secretary of Housing and Urban Development, and he was confirmed in this position on January 22, 1993. He was, by all accounts, as passionate and competent in his new post as he had been in his previous ones.

U.S. Attorney General Janet Reno, however, learned that Cisneros—labeled, along with Clinton, a "skirt chaser" during the campaign—had lied to the FBI about the amount of money he had paid to his mistress, a woman named Linda Medlar (aka Linda Jones). In March 1995, Reno secured the appointment of Independent Counsel David Barrett to investigate these allegations. Although he was married, the fact that Cisneros had a mistress was not that much of an issue, as this had been fairly widely known for some time.

Cisneros had been involved with Medlar since 1987, when she was a volunteer staffer for his mayoral campaign, and soon thereafter he began to support her. According to subsequent court records, from 1988 to 1992 Cisneros gave her a total of $250,000, and then continued to pay her even after becoming the chief of HUD, a whopping $79,500 in 1993. After a point, this money was intended to keep Medlar quiet and keep her from making any embarrassing public revelations.

While Cisneros was certainly guilty of poor judgment, his girlfriend was, by all accounts, an emotionally disturbed gold digger. In 1994, Medlar sued the mayor for breach of contract, fraud, and failing to support her, eventually screwing him out of another $49,000 (although she had been shooting for $250,000). She also sold secret recordings she had made of conversations with Cisneros to the Fox television program *Inside Edition*, which it subsequently aired, leading Attorney General Reno to unleash Barrett.

Former mayor of San Antonio Henry Cisneros had something to smile about after the six-year, $22 million investigation into his activities was brought to a close with a judicial order that kept its findings secret.

to the FBI and was fined $10,000 but did not receive prison time or even probation. And some sixteen months later, in January 2001, Clinton pardoned his buddy as one of his last official acts in the Oval Office.

Prosecutors had granted Medlar immunity in exchange for testifying against her former sugar daddy. Being a dumb, greedy whore, however, she lied to them and ended up getting charged with multiple counts of bank fraud, conspiracy to commit bank fraud, and obstruction of justice as a result of a bank fraud scheme she had entered into with her sister and brother-in-law in an attempt to conceal the source of the money she had received. She pleaded guilty to twenty-eight charges and was sentenced to time in prison.

His girlfriend was an **emotionally disturbed** gold digger.

Independent Counsel Barrett was by no means pleased with the outcome for Cisneros and persisted in his inquiries, broadening them to include a look into allegations that the Clinton administration, the Justice Department, and the IRS had obstructed his investigation. Year after year, he continued his witch hunt, right up until 2005, when a number of Democratic senators decided that the *$22 million* he had spent up to that point was more than enough and tried to pull the plug on the investigation. He continued, however, until the Special Division of the Court of Appeals, which supervises independent counsels, eventually ordered him to bring to an end the six-year investigation—by far the longest independent counsel investigation in U.S. history.

Meanwhile, Cisneros and Clinton had, in fact, been trying to obstruct the investigation, and their lawyers took legal steps to have as much as possible of Barrett's final report suppressed before it could be released to the public. By the time the report was eventually revealed in January 2006, an estimated 120 pages had been removed from it as a result of judicial orders, and exactly what they may have contained remains a mystery to this day.

"An accurate title for the report could be, 'What We Were Prevented from Investigating,'" Barrett said in a press release about it. "After a thorough reading of the report, it would not be unreasonable to conclude, as I have, that there was a cover-up at high levels of our government, and it appears to have been substantial and coordinated. The question is, 'Why?' And that question, regrettably, will go unanswered. Unlike some other cover-ups, this one succeeded."

8

Below the Bench

BY ALL ACCOUNTS, U.S. DISTRICT Court Judge Samuel B. Kent was exceptional among jurists not just in Texas but in the country overall and is notable for having made legal history in a number of ways. Unfortunately, the most significant way was becoming the first federal judge to be charged in federal court with sex crimes.

"Your wrongful conduct is a huge black X," said Judge Roger Vinson to Kent when sentencing him to nearly three years in prison for a variety of charges related to a decade of his sexual predation, boozing, and cronyism. " . . . a stain on the judicial system itself, a matter of concern in the federal courts."

After being nominated by President George H.W. Bush on August 3, 1990, and confirmed by the U.S. Senate the following month, Kent became the sole judge presiding over the Galveston Division of the U.S. District Court for the Southern District of Texas on October 1, 1990. This broad jurisdiction covered the coastal Texas counties of Brazoria, Chambers, Galveston, and Matagorda.

Hints of Kent's legal downfall emerged in 2001, when the Chief Judge of the Southern District of Texas reassigned eighty-five of his cases because they were being handled by an attorney, Richard Melancon, who was a close personal friend of the rogue judge.

Six years later, in August 2007, an even more ominous hint of things to come occurred when the Chief Judge of the Southern District of Texas ordered that Kent would not be hearing any cases from September 2007 until January 2008. During this period of suspension—hardly an uncommon situation for judges—Kent did not perform any official duties, his cases all being parceled out to other judges, but continued to draw his substantial annual salary of $169,300. And what started out as a four-month leave of absence ultimately turned into a permanent hiatus from the bench.

In late December of 2007, the Fifth Circuit announced that there was an ongoing criminal investigation by the Department of Justice into allegations of sexual misconduct that had been made against Judge Kent by his former case manager, Cathy McBroom, and secretary, Donna Wilkerson. The following month he was transferred to the Houston division of the Southern District of Texas.

Donna Wilkerson, the secretary of the dishonorable Samuel B. Kent, is shown here testifying before the U.S. House Judiciary Committee Task Force on Judicial Impeachment on June 5, 2009.

Near the end of August 2008, a federal grand jury indicted Kent on three counts of attempted aggravated sexual abuse and abusive sexual contact, all related to the complaints of misconduct that had been made against him the previous year. Kent made his mark with these charges, becoming the first federal judge to be arraigned in federal court for sex crimes.

As it turned out, he had been involved in even more sex crimes than was initially apparent, and in January of 2009 the grand jury indicted him on three additional charges: abusive sexual contact, aggravated sexual abuse, and, naturally, obstruction of justice.

Perhaps as a result of having greater-than-usual insights into the judicial process, Kent took steps to keep it from moving forward, and on February 23, 2009—the day that jury selection was set to start—he agreed to retire as judge and pleaded guilty to one count of obstruction of justice for lying to the judicial committee investigating the allegations against him. He also admitted to non-consensual sexual contact between 2003 and 2007 with the two women who worked for him.

Despite his generous offer to retire, however—which would have entitled him to draw his hefty paycheck for life—it was by no means clear whether he could be permitted to do so; the minimum age of retirement for a federal judge was sixty-five and, at the time, Kent was just fifty-nine. One exception to this age requirement applied to judges who had become permanently disabled while performing their duties, and the increasingly and infuriatingly cute Kent claimed that applied to him—as a result of defending himself against the charges leveled against him!

In order to have this claim recognized, Kent needed to receive certification from the Chief Judge of the Fifth Circuit that he was, indeed, disabled, and then petition the President of the United States to honor it. In May 2009, however, the United States Court of Appeals for the Fifth Circuit denied Kent's request for disability status and instead recommended that he be impeached.

"A claimant should not profit from his own wrongdoing by engaging in criminal misconduct and then collecting a federal retirement salary for the disability related to the prosecution," wrote Chief Judge Edith Jones, who furthermore observed that Kent did not appear to actually be in any way disabled.

On May 11, Kent was sentenced to thirty-three months in federal prison on the charge of obstructing justice in the investigation of sexual abuse accusations (the former charge alone might have gotten him a full twenty years in the pen). On June 15, the ostensibly disabled Kent reported to the Federal Medical Center in Devens, Massachusetts, to begin serving his sentence (although in November of that year he was moved to a state prison in Florida). He was also ordered to participate in an alcohol-abuse program and to pay a $1,000 fine and a total of $6,550 in restitution to his two victims.

The leaders of the House Judiciary Committee, Congressmen Lamar Smith of Texas (R) and John Conyers Jr. of Michigan (D) also demanded that Kent resign immediately or face impeachment. Kent responded by submitting his resignation on June 2, 2009—but with the proviso that it would not take effect for a full year! This enraged the members of the committee, and eight days later they unanimously voted to send articles of impeachment to the full House of Representatives. On June 19, the legislature passed these articles, making Kent the first federal judge to be impeached in twenty years.

On June 25, Senate officials traveled to the Massachusetts penal facility where Kent was being held in order to serve him with the formal summons to his impeachment trial, and when they arrived, he presented them with a new letter of resignation, this one bearing an effective date of June 30. President Barack Obama accepted Kent's resignation on the day it became effective, and on July 20 the House of Representatives requested that the Senate end Kent's trial, which two days later it agreed to do.

Upon his resignation taking effect, Kent ceased to draw the salary that he had maneuvered to keep following his downfall as a judge.

9

Now *All* Sex is Fine in Texas

FOR THOSE WHO ARE INTERESTED, anal and oral sex between consenting adults of all genders is now legal in the State of Texas— but only since 2003, when the U.S. Supreme Court stepped in with the landmark *Lawrence v. Texas* case to tell the state where it could stick its intrusive sodomy laws.

Like the sodomy laws that existed in a dozen other U.S. states until the first decade of the twenty-first century, those in Texas originated with the ilk of pious people who think their own religious beliefs entitle them to tell other people what to do. Most states had repealed their laws of this sort in the 1970s—which generally prohibited consensual anal and oral sex between homosexual and sometimes also heterosexual people—but a handful of the most die-hard bastions of conservative sentiment continued to retain theirs.

Such laws do not get put to the test on a regular basis, and even Texas police departments probably never had Sodomy Squads dedicated to enforcing them, but they do periodically get thrust into the public arena.

On the night of September 7, 1998, just outside of Houston in Harris County, Sheriff's Deputy Joseph Quinn, gun in hand, entered the unlocked apartment of fifty-five-year-old John Geddes Lawrence and encountered him and thirty-one-year-old Tyron Garner engaged in consensual anal sex. The deputy had been dispatched to the apartment in response to a report of a "crazy" man with a gun involved in a robbery or domestic disturbance. Struck by the enormity of what was actually going on in the home, the deputy, naturally, proceeded to arrest both of the offenders.

Ironically, the false report of an ongoing crime had been called in by forty-year-old neighbor, Robert Royce Eubanks, a boyfriend of Garner's who, motivated by jealousy, had been harassing the two backdoor lovers. But, because the police were not aware that the report was false, probable cause to enter the residence was never a factor in the case that proceeded from the incident. Eubanks later pled guilty to filing a false police report and served fifteen days in jail as a result.

Lawrence and Garner were jailed and charged with violating Chapter 21, Section 21.06 of the Texas Penal Code, the state law dictating "Homosexual Conduct," which prohibited "deviant sexual intercourse with another individual of the same sex." Under this law, oral and anal sex between members of the same gender were classified as a Class C misdemeanor.

The two men were freed after they posted $200 bail and, two-and-a-half months later, they pleaded no contest to the charges against them before Justice of the Peace Mike Parrott.

Lawrence and Garner exercised their right to a new trial before a state criminal court, however, and there asked the judge to dismiss the charges against them on the basis of the Fourteenth Amendment of the U.S. Constitution's guarantees of equal protection and privacy. Their claim was that the Texas law was unconstitutional in that it both prohibited certain sex practices between same-sex couples but not heterosexual ones and was

The U.S. Supreme Court stepped in to tell the state where it could stick its intrusive sodomy laws.

intrusive. When the criminal court rejected this argument, the two men once again pleaded no contest and reserved their right to file an appeal, upon which the court fined them $200 each, along with $141.25 in court costs.

In November 1999, the appellants presented arguments on the grounds of both equal protection and the right to privacy to a three-judge panel of the Texas Fourteenth Court of Appeals.

Two of the judges ruled in their favor, finding that the sodomy law violated the 1972 Equal Rights Amendment to the Texas Constitution, which bars discrimination based on race, color, creed, national origin, or sex. The full court, however, ultimately overturned this decision, voting 7–2 to uphold the constitutionality of the state law and denying both the privacy and equal protection arguments that had been brought before it.

In April 2001, Lawrence petitioned the Texas Court of Criminal Appeals, the highest appellate court in the state for criminal matters, but it declined to review it.

Nearly two years later, however, in December 2002, the U.S. Supreme Court agreed to hear *Lawrence v. Texas*, prompting a wide variety of organizations to file *amicus curiae* briefs on behalf of both parties. In its deliberations, the justices had to consider whether the petitioners' criminal convictions under the Texas law violated the Fourteenth Amendment guarantees of equal protection, liberty, and privacy.

On June 26, 2003, the Supreme Court decision rendered its highly publicized decision, in which it voted 6–3 to strike down the Texas law. Five of the justices—Stephen Breyer, Ruth Bader Ginsburg, Anthony Kennedy, David Souter, and John Paul Stevens—maintained that this law violated due process guarantees, and one, Sandra Day O'Connor, found that it violated equal protection guarantees. In its deliberations, the high court rejected the legal arguments presented by the state of Texas, essentially dismissing them as matters of taste rather than law.

"The Texas statute furthers no legitimate state interest which can justify its intrusion into the personal and private life of the individual," the high court stated in its decision. It did, however, also specify the limitations of its decision.

"The present case does not involve minors," it said. "It does not involve persons who might be injured or coerced or who are situated in relationships where consent might not easily be refused. It does not involve public conduct or prostitution. It does not involve whether the government must give formal recognition to any relationship that homosexual persons seek to enter."

And, while the case had originated in Texas, the Supreme Court decision had the additional effect of invalidating the sodomy laws in twelve other states and overruled a 1986 ruling it had made in *Bowers v. Hardwick,* in which it had upheld the Georgia state sodomy law, and was applauded by proponents of gay rights.

"Bowers was not correct when it was decided," the court stated. "And it is not correct today."

10

A Risky Proposition

TEXANS ARE BIG INTO RIGHTS— unless they involve sex, gays, or other people in general. And sometimes, the effort to control what other people do can backfire. That is what very nearly happened with Proposition 2, a poorly written amendment to the state constitution that one can almost imagine being scratched out by shoeless rednecks on the lid of a cracker barrel.

Proposition 2 was one of nine items on the statewide Constitutional Amendment Election ballot held on November 8, 2005, and was among the seven approved by Texas voters, of whom 76.25 percent voted for and 23.74 percent against it (with Travis County, where the state capital of Austin is located, being the only county to oppose it).

Passage of this proposition created an amendment to the Texas Constitution intended to limit marriage in Texas to traditional male-female relationships and prohibit alternative legal arrangements of a similar sort. In short, even though same-sex marriages, plural marriages, and civil unions were already prohibited under state law, the backers of the proposition saw fit to push through a showy and redundant modification to the state constitution.

This amendment reads:

(a) Marriage in this state shall consist only of the union of one man and one woman.

(b) This state or a political subdivision of this state may not create or recognize any legal status identical or similar to marriage.

Opponents of the proposition, however—including the nonprofit group Save Texas Marriage—assert that by leaving out key words, legislators are technically invalidating even traditional marriage, because section "b" negates section "a."

"A greedy insurance company, tricky divorce lawyer, or a liberal Austin activist judge can easily use these words to overturn traditional marriage and cause people to lose health insurance, tax breaks, and pensions," said San Antonio's Beacon Hill Presbyterian Church's Rev. Tom Heger in an automated telephone call that went out to about two million households statewide, with an emphasis on seniors.

Those in favor of the amendment indignantly noted that this appeal was merely a "smokescreen" intended to confuse voters on the issue.

Four years after the amendment passed, it again received statewide attention, when a candidate for Texas attorney general once more attacked it on the merits of its grammar. In November 2009, Barbara Ann Radnofsky stated her belief that, because marriage is, by definition, identical to itself, the amendment does in fact outlaw *all* marriage in the state. Whether this stance

Texans are big into rights—unless they involve sex, gays, or other people in general.

harmed or helped her cause, she did not win the election.

The amendment was also challenged on the basis of its intended purpose of targeting certain segments of the population. On October 1, 2009, Dallas District Judge Tena Callahan struck it down on the grounds that it denied same-sex couples equal treatment under the Fourteenth Amendment to the U.S. Constitution. This was in response to a lawsuit filed by a same-sex Dallas couple whom had married in Massachusetts in 2006 but were attempting to get divorced in Texas, as Massachusetts only permits state residents to file for divorce.

Texas Governor Rick Perry and state Attorney General Greg Abbott appealed the lower court ruling to the Fifth Court of

Appeals in Dallas, in an attempt to get the decision nullifying the amendment overturned. They got their way, and on August 31, 2010, the higher court reversed the ruling on the basis that the Texas constitutional ban on same-sex marriage does not violate the Equal Protection Clause of the Fourteenth Amendment to the U.S. Constitution.

To date, no judge in Texas has gone on to use the shoddy wording of the upheld amendment to invalidate the traditional institution of marriage favored by three-quarters of the state's voters. And, while that will likely never happen, no credit is due to the people who drafted the problematic piece of legislation in the first place.

11

Anna Nicole Smith

BEFORE SHE WAS A CELEBRITY OF questionable virtue, Texas native Anna Nicole Smith was a woman of no apparent virtue at all.

Born Vickie Lynn Hogan in November 1967 and raised by various combinations of relatives between Houston and the little east Texas town of Mexia, Smith was pretty much doomed to a life of sordid obscurity from an early age. She dropped out of high school her sophomore year, ended up working at a chicken restaurant in Mexia, and, in 1985 at age seventeen, married sixteen-year-old fry cook, Billy Wayne Smith, and had a child by him (and briefly changed her name to Nikki Hart).

Within a couple of years, Smith left her child lover for Houston where, after a handful of other menial jobs, she started dancing at Gigi's, a local strip club. She also began to parlay her fleshy charms into a career as a model of sorts (Guess, Lane Bryant), ostensible sex symbol, questionable actress, and decidedly unwholesome media personality, gaining national

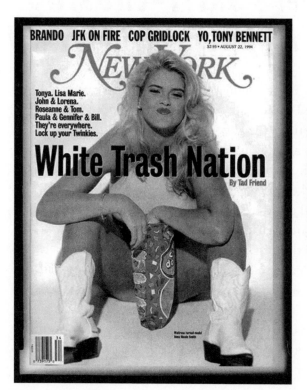

New York magazine summed up Anna Nicole Smith pretty succinctly when it made her the cover girl of its August 22, 1994 issue.

attention when she appeared in *Playboy* in 1992 (where she was identified as Vickie Smith) and became its Playmate of the Year in 1993. During this time Smith began trying to emphasize her similarity to bombshells Marilyn Monroe and Jayne Mansfield (both of whom died young and in tragic circumstances, as would Smith).

In October 1991, while stripping at Gigi's (now known as Pleasures), Smith also met drooling old oil tycoon J. Howard Marshall, a man more than sixty-two years her senior who courted, lavished gifts upon, and repeatedly proposed to her.

Marshall's sons, unable to curtail their father's **skirt-chasing** during his life, were certainly not

With an innate understanding for the needs of social mobility, Smith responded to these advances by divorcing her estranged husband and accepting the eighty-nine-year-old Marshall's withered hand in marriage. From the start, people with small, dirty minds—along with nearly everyone else, for that matter—said the young sex worker had married the mogul for his money, but she denied this and protested that it was a case of true love.

Smith and the octogenarian Marshall never actually lived together during their thirteen months of highly publicized marriage but, upon his death in August 1995, she immediately sought half of his $1.6 billion estate, which she said her husband had verbally promised her in exchange for marrying him.

Marshall's sons, E. Pierce Marshall and James Howard Marshall III, unable to curtail their father's skirt-chasing during his life, were certainly not willing to give any deference to the wearers of those skirts after his death, and a lengthy and sordid legal battle ensued almost immediately. It went on for the rest of Smith's life and involved various judgments for and against her and jurisdictional disputes between Texas, California, and federal courts. And, in a strange twist that no one could have predicted when it was filed, Marshall v. Marshall actually reached the U.S. Supreme Court over a question of federal jurisdiction.

Difficulties followed Smith throughout the rest of her life, to include having to file for bankruptcy as a result of an $850,000 judgment against her for sexually harassing an employee; the

willing to give any deference to the wearers of those skirts after **his death.**

tragic drug-overdose death of her son, Daniel, in September 2006; and the scandal over the inappropriate means by which a friend who was an official for the government of the Bahamas had obtained citizenship for her in his country.

There was also the paternity dispute and custody battle over her daughter, Dannielynn, who was born the same month her son died. Fatherhood was variously attributed to or claimed by photographer Larry Birkhead, attorney Howard K. Stern, Zsa Zsa Gabor's husband Frédéric Prinz von Anhalt, former body-guard Alexander Denk, or a frozen sample of sperm collected from Marshall prior to his death.

These travails, Smith's increasingly bizarre behavior, and her dramatic weight gain brought unwanted media attention, ridicule, and stress to Smith, particularly over what would be the last six months of her life.

Probably living on borrowed time from the start, Smith died February 8, 2007, nine months short of her fortieth birthday, from an overdose of nearly a dozen prescription drugs—several of them sedatives—at a hotel in Hollywood, Florida. What did not die with her, however, was the battle over her billionaire former husband's estate, which was still not resolved at the time of her death. E. Pierce Marshall died as well before it could be resolved, and at this writing it continues on behalf of his widow and Smith's young daughter.

12

Sex Toys Now Legal in Texas!

SINCE NOVEMBER 2008, PEOPLE IN Texas have had the right to sell or purchase sex toys of various sorts as desired. Prior to that, however, the Lone Star State explicitly reserved the right to regulate morality and to prosecute people who did not measure up to its lofty standards—which it periodically did.

In 1973, even as swingers, wife-swappers, and disco threatened to destroy the moral fiber of the nation, the Texas Legislature passed the Obscene Device Law, a section of the Texas Penal Code that dealt with obscenity. In part, it also prohibited the sale or promotion of "'Obscene device[s]' mean[ing] a device including a dildo or artificial vagina, designed or marketed as useful primarily for the stimulation of human genital organs."

Only rarely did prosecutors in Texas presume to enforce the statute but it did happen on a number of significant occasions.

In 2004, Joanne Webb, a former schoolteacher and mother of three, faced up to a year in prison for selling a vibrator to two undercover police officers who infiltrated a private party posing as a married couple.

"It was not a secret in Burleson, a small town near Fort Worth, that Webb sold vibrators, edible creams, and racy lingerie," CNN reported on the incident. "But not everyone was

A former **schoolteacher** and mother of three

happy about it. . . . A few prominent citizens with strong Christian beliefs were angered by Webb and her activities and asked police to investigate."

Webb was ultimately acquitted and the undercover officers were reprimanded for their puritanical fervor.

In 2007, police raided Somethin' Sexy, a lingerie shop in Lubbock, and confiscated items determined to be illegal under the Texas obscenity law and arrested the clerk working there at the time, who thereafter had to register as a sex offender.

According to the local district attorney's office, a device met the test for obscenity if someone *intended* to use it for a sex toy but was okay if they did not.

"If the seller is selling it as a novelty, and the buyer is buying it as a novelty to make fun of, then it probably has not reached the level of an obscenity," said Assistant District Attorney John Grace, who said a candle was a non-obscene candle if it was promoted for use on a birthday cake, but that the same candle was an obscene sex toy if it was sold for use as a dildo. Based on that thread of logic, purchasing a normal candle and using it as a sex toy would violate the law, while purchasing a vibrator and jamming it on a cake would not. Intent was, in any event, an explicit component of the law.

"A person commits an offense if he ... possesses with intent to wholesale promote any obscene material or obscene device," Section 43.23 of the code stated. "A person who possesses six

faced up to a year in prison for selling a **vibrator.**

or more obscene devices ... is presumed to possess them with intent to promote the same." This section specified higher penalties for violators, forcing sellers of items covered under the act usually to market them as "educational items" or "novelties."

A number of companies that dealt in sexual devices in Texas, operating under the names Dreamer's, Le Rouge Boutique, and Adam & Eve Inc., responded to the state's heavy-handed interest in the matter by claiming that the statute was unconstitutional and filing suit accordingly.

On February 12, 2008, a three-judge panel of the Fifth Circuit Court of Appeals, on appeal from the United States District Court for the Western District of Texas, agreed with the sex toy merchants and overturned the statute by a vote of 2–1. This panel maintained that "the statute has provisions that violate the Fourteenth Amendment of the U.S. Constitution."

"Because of *Lawrence v. Texas* . . . the issue before us is whether the Texas statute impermissibly burdens the individual's substantive due process right to engage in private intimate conduct of his or her choosing," the majority opinion stated (*see the chapter "Now All Sex is Fine in Texas" for more on this case*). "Contrary to the district court's conclusion, we hold that the Texas law burdens this constitutional right. An individual who wants to legally use a safe sexual device during private intimate moments alone or with another is unable to legally purchase a device in Texas, which heavily burdens a constitutional right."

Texas had presented to the court that it had the right to regulate the morality of its citizens and to discourage "prurient interests in autonomous sex and the pursuit of sexual gratification unrelated to procreation." The court of appeals, however, was not having it.

On October 29, 2008, the Texas Attorney General's Office notified the Fifth Circuit Court of Appeals that it would not file a writ of certiorari with the U.S. Supreme Court and was dropping the matter, making it legally safe for sex toy merchants to sell their wares in Texas.

13

Mark of Shame

ON FEBRUARY 7, 2011, A JURY IN NEW Braunfels, Texas, sentenced local attorney Mark A. Clark to seven years in prison for trying to induce a twelve-year-old girl to pose for him in sexy clothing at his office the previous summer.

Attorney Mark A. Clark was not thanking heaven for little girls when justice finally caught up with him and he was sentenced to seven years in prison for trying to take indecent liberties with a minor.

During the trial, the girl emotionally testified that in June 2010 Clark had offered to pay her $1,000 to model provocative clothes, including a see-through shirt, and that he had also made a number of highly suggestive remarks to her. She was the daughter of a former client Clark was representing in a child custody case, and the girl testified that he also offered to waive her mother's legal fees.

The girl had gone to the office to help with paperwork and, in preparation for this, had French-braided her hair, put on what she described as her "Alice in Wonderland" dress, and made the lecherous lawyer a plate of chocolate chip cookies.

Clark had some treats for the girl, too, and started off by offering her some alcoholic "hard lemonade." A subsequent police search of his office revealed a hidden stash of items that included more hard lemonade and some vodka, champagne glasses, a breast pump with hoses, condoms, cell phones, KY Jelly, a sex toy, a box of feminine douches, corsets, fishnet stockings, lacy underwear, and bikinis.

"His cat was sitting in his lap and he was petting it," said the girl, who was thirteen at the time of the trial. "He said the cat would let him pet it and pet it, and he would just stop whenever it wants him to, and that's how he wished I would be."

Another witness testified that, four years earlier when she was seventeen and pregnant, she had come to Clark, her father's attorney, to seek advice about getting child support from the father of her unborn child. She said that Clark had offered to pay her to secretly accompany him to a motel room and pose for pictures in lingerie, which she refused to do. When she reported the incident to New Braunfels police they opted not to look into her allegations.

"They said they couldn't do anything because they had no proof," she said.

According to statements made in court and to police eight years earlier by yet more witnesses, Clark had accosted a fourteen-year-old girl at a snow cone stand in 2002, slipping a note with his phone number and a $5 bill into her pocket. She told her mother, Diane Zavala, who, in the guise of her daughter, called the number.

"What are you doing?" Zavala testified Clark said. "You want to come over to my house?"

Not Just a Pervert ...

PRIOR TO BEING CONVICTED AS A SEXUAL PREDATOR, Mark A. Clark was a pretty good defense attorney and defended convicted murderer Janice Vickers in 2009. See the chapter in the "Murder" section of this book titled "A Texas Murder Trial."

After cursing out Clark over the phone, Zavala and her daughter reported the incident to the police and then met with a prosecutor from the county criminal district attorney's office. A young Comal County assistant district attorney named Melissa Rowcliffe also got wind of the incident and pushed her bosses to pursue the case. Despite the efforts of both women to have Clark charged and prosecuted, however, then-Comal County District Attorney, Dib Waldrip—now a district judge—declined to do so.

The fact that Clark's father, Fred Clark, had been the county judge twenty years earlier, gone on to serve two terms as a county court-at-law judge, and remained a prominent figure in the community was by no means irrelevant to the attorney's predatory actions being swept under the carpet.

"It is an **aberrant** behavior you have found him guilty of

The fifty-five-year-old defense attorney could have received a sentence of as much as twenty years for "attempted sexual performance" of a minor, the second-degree felony for which he had been convicted (he had also been charged with but not convicted of attempted aggravated sexual assault of a child). Such a sentence was actually fairly heavy for an offense of this sort and, furthermore, bucked what Comal County's chief felony prosecutor called the county's "good ol' boy" system—a system that protected Clark in the past.

Even during the sentencing phase of Clark's trial, his defense attorney attempted to sway the penalty imposed by the jury by trotting out influential friends of the family. This rogues gallery included former Bexar County Commissioner Tom Stolhandske, real estate appraiser Gary Meyer, Comal County defense attorney Wade Arledge, and Judge Robert Pfeiffer, a former Comal County District Court judge who had gone to school with Clark's parents from kindergarten through graduation in New Braunfels.

Pfeiffer recommended the defendant be given probation for his crimes and, along with Clark's defense attorney, cited state budgetary problems as a reason for letting his family friend remain free.

"It costs (Texas) lots and lots of money to keep them locked up," Pfeiffer testified, citing his concerns that doing so would help to "break the state budget." He did not, however, make a statement about the potential impact upon the community of allowing known sexual predators to remain free within it.

"It is an aberrant behavior you have found him guilty of . . .

. . . *an irrational behavior, a **bizarre** behavior.*"

It is, if you will, an irrational behavior, a bizarre behavior, and it breaks our law," Clark's defense attorney, Joe James Sawyer, said while trying to convince the jury to let his client off with probation. "It bears consideration he will no longer be able to practice law and, for the rest of his life, he will be a registered sex offender."

That was not good enough for prosecutor Sammy McCrary, who made a passionate plea for the jury to impose the maximum two-decade prison term.

"We have a pretty good ol' boy system in Comal County," McCrary said, emphasizing that because Clark was an attorney and the son of a judge "people have looked the other way" for many years. "It won't be some judge who's friends with (his) daddy making the decision . . . It will be the twelve of you."

Following his conviction, the Texas State Bar Association also took action against Clark and, on February 23, suspended him and ordered that he contact all of his current clients to inform them of his conviction and return any payments for services not yet rendered. As a result, he will likely never again be allowed to practice law in Texas.

"The continual possession by (Clark) of a license to practice law in Texas constitutes a substantial threat of irreparable harm to clients or prospective clients," read the order of suspension. "Respondent is ordered to immediately refund to such clients any unearned fees paid in advance," as well as all files, papers, and other property belonging to current and former clients.

Like many convicted criminals in Texas—including his former client, convicted killer Janice Vickers (q.v.)—Clark could end up serving as little as a quarter of the time to which he was sentenced and be out in less than two years. The girl he was convicted for propositioning will be just fifteen years old at that point.

SCANDAL

in the
Lone
Star
State

1

Jean Lafitte

PIRATE JEAN LAFITTE WAS CERTAINLY one of the most fascinating, dashing, and enigmatic figures of the early nineteenth century in America. He is believed to have been born between 1776 and 1782, but no one is sure exactly where—France, Spain, Haiti, or even New York all being possibilities. He fought against the British alongside Andrew Jackson in the Battle of New Orleans during the War of 1812, motivated in large part to obtain a reprieve for piracy and smuggling. And he became such an embarrassment to the United States government

Jean Lafitte

that it forced him to leave an area that was only adjacent to one of its territories. But the last place he is verifiably known to have lived and tried to carve out a fortune for himself was in Texas.

In 1805, the year after the United States acquired Louisiana from France, Lafitte obtained a warehouse in New Orleans for purposes of moving contraband and stolen goods, including slaves, smuggled into the area by him and his brother, Pierre. Two years later, however, the United States passed the Embargo Act of 1807, the provisions of which made it difficult for Lafitte to conduct his smuggling activities. This prompted him to move his base of operations to Barataria Island in the delta south of New Orleans.

Just beyond the reach of authority, Lafitte enjoyed great success with his new smuggling port, which quickly turned into a boomtown. He eventually decided to expand his activities into direct piracy, and began to build a small fleet and personally prey upon ships in the Gulf of Mexico, primarily ones sailing to and from Spanish colonies in the region.

By 1814, U.S. authorities had grown weary of Lafitte's flouting of the law, prompting them to begin taking legal action against him and ultimately conducting a raid in force against his

The Diary of Jean Lafitte

IN 1948, AN ANTIQUARIAN OF SORTS NAMED JOHN Andrechyne Laflin approached the Missouri Historical Society with a French-language document he claimed was a diary kept by Jean Lafitte over the period 1845–1850, decades after it was believed he had been killed. The historical society, however, would not authenticate this claim.

Laflin then approached a Louisiana author named Stanley Arthur, who subsequently wrote the historical novel *Jean Laffitte: Gentleman Rover*, based on the diary and published in 1952. Laflin himself published an English-language translation of the diary six years later, but declined to allow anyone to examine the original manuscript on which it was based.

Then, in 1969, Laflin sold the journal to a professional document dealer, who had the ink and paper used in it analyzed and determined them to have originated in the

base on Barataria Island, where they seized his goods and vessels. Fortunately for Lafitte, the United States was at war with Great Britain, and the pirate negotiated pardons for himself and his men in exchange for them helping to defend New Orleans when the British invaded the poorly protected city in January 1815.

Lafitte soon after returned to his criminal ways, however, and was before long thoroughly unwelcome in Louisiana. So, he and his brother moved once again, westward, to Galveston Island, at that point part of the vast Spanish territory that would subsequently become first part of Mexico and then Texas (and which had long been used as a base by pirates). There, at the east mid-1800s. Soon after, an archivist for Bexar County, Texas —the county where the city of San Antonio is located— declared that the manuscript was authentic and the work of Jean Lafitte.

In 1980, the owner of the journal donated it to the Sam Houston Regional Library and Research Center in Liberty County, in East Texas, finally making it available for examination by independent researchers. Many of these noted a similarity between the writing in the journal and Laflin's own handwriting, observations that were given all the greater credence in light of allegations that the antiquarian had forged letters ostensibly written by David Crockett (q.v.), Andrew Jackson, and Abraham Lincoln.

Today, most authorities on the matter consider the diary to be a fake, but there are some who still believe otherwise. Only Lafitte, and maybe Laflin, know for sure.

end of the island he established the colony, privateer base, and admiralty court of Campeachy, ostensibly under the authority of the Mexican republican government that was at that time fighting for independence from Spain. This claim may not actually have been true and, in any event, he and his brother were in fact acting as paid spies for Spain at this time.

"Campeachy resembled a boomtown, a single main street lined with houses, taverns, gambling parlors (equipped with billiard tables), and the inevitable Yankee boardinghouse," author Gary Cartwright says in his *Galveston.* "At the edge of the bay were an arsenal, a dockyard, and a ship's repair shop, all stocked with the best examples of nineteenth-century technology." He built a two-story, fortified, red building that served as his headquarters.

Operating out of Galveston, Lafitte and the pirates under his command continued to attack shipping of all nations in the Gulf of Mexico, transporting captured goods back to their base and selling it there or in New Orleans. Slaves were among the goods he captured from the Spanish and subsequently offered for sale, and at one point his slave market was the largest in the entire Western Hemisphere. In 1818 the United States did pass a law prohibiting the importation of slaves into the country but, in cooperation with men like Jim Bowie (q.v.), Lafitte exploited loopholes that allowed him to profitably continue this end of his business.

*Lafitte had once **again** become an **embarrassment** to the United States.*

Lafitte had once again become an embarrassment to the United States, in large part because of the diplomatic strain his piratical activities were causing between it and Spain. And when one of the captains under his command attacked an American merchant vessel in 1821, a U.S. Navy warship, USS *Enterprise,* was dispatched to drive him and his men from the island.

Lafitte met with the commanders of the U.S. expedition and agreed to leave without a fight. He and his men burned most of Campeachy, loaded as much loot as they could onto their three best vessels, and, on May 7, 1821, sailed out of Galveston Bay.

Precisely what happened to Lafitte after he sailed away from Galveston remains a mystery. There are stories of him continuing his activities as a pirate, and some historians believe he persisted in these until being killed while trying to capture a Spanish convoy in 1823. Other accounts describe him rescuing Napoleon Bonaparte from the island of St. Helena and living to a ripe old age in Louisiana. Yet others claim he was murdered by his own men soon after leaving Galveston. But the place where he reached the pinnacle of his success and is known to have last inhabited is Texas.

2

Rogues of the Alamo

EVEN HEROES HAVE PASTS, AND JUST about everyone associated with the Texas Revolution of 1835–1836 in general and the Battle of the Alamo in particular had something they would have just as soon have remained hidden. That is not altogether surprising, however, when one considers the things that might have prompted a man to go to a teeming wilderness like Texas with an eye to carving out from it a new and better life. Skeletons in some of their closets include slave mongering, brawling, and the abandonment of wives and children. A handful of the most famous follow.

HOUSTON, SANTA ANNA, AND COS.

A nineteenth-century political cartoon depicts some of the major players in the Texas Revolution.

James Bowie, who died fighting for the freedom of Anglo-Americans in the Texas Revolution, was not quite so dedicated to the liberty of others if there was a profit to be made. Bowie and his brothers made several trips during the period 1818–1819 to Galveston Island, at the time the largest slave market in the Western Hemisphere, and there bought blacks captured by privateers like Jean Lafitte who preyed on Spanish shipping. Such slaves could be purchased wholesale at $1 a pound, or about $140 each, and then resold in Louisiana for as much as $1,000 apiece, and Bowie and his brothers made $65,000 in just two years from the trade.

"Though the slave trade had been outlawed in the United States, there was a loophole that allowed smuggled slaves confiscated by the government to be sold at auction like any other contraband," historian Gary Cartwright says in his *Galveston*. "The law also rewarded informers with payments equal to half the value of whatever was seized. Bowie delivered the slaves to a customs officer, becoming in effect an informer against himself. When the slaves were sold at auction, Bowie bought them back and resold them to planters at a price agreed on in advance."

In the course of his adventures, Bowie also acquired a reputation as a fierce knife fighter and—whether or not he actually invented or even carried the sword-like weapon that now bears his name—definitely gained national fame for his role in what became known as the Sandbar Fight. This armed brawl outside of Natchez, Mississippi, on September 19, 1827, exploded in the

Bowie grabbed him, pulled him to the ground, and *fatally* disemboweled him.

wake of an organized duel that ended with its antagonists shaking their hands and walking away.

Bowie was considered to be the most dangerous man in the faction he was part of, and some of the men opposing it tried to kill him right away. One of them shot him in the hip and then hit him in the head with the emptied pistol so hard that it broke, knocking Bowie to the ground. Sheriff Norris Wright of Rapides Parish, Louisiana, with whom Bowie had a running feud, took advantage of his enemy's predicament and also took a shot at him but missed, upon which Bowie returned fire and may or may not have struck Wright. The sheriff then attacked the prone Bowie with a sword cane and ran him through, embedding the blade in his body. When Wright planted his foot on Bowie's chest to dislodge his weapon, Bowie grabbed him, pulled him to the ground, and fatally disemboweled him. Bowie was both shot and stabbed at least once more each before the fracas was dispersed but survived his injuries and was lauded in newspapers that covered the incident.

Bowie's luck ran out for the last time a little less than nine years later, and he was killed, at age thirty-nine, while commanding the volunteer forces at the Battle of the Alamo on March 6, 1836.

David Crockett was an American legend in his own time and was certainly the most famous defender to perish at the Alamo. While he was the subject of all sorts of embellishments and fictions even in his lifetime, the biggest controversy surrounding him concerns his final day on Earth.

According to many accounts of the battle, between five and seven Texans survived the final assault on the Alamo and surrendered to the Mexican soldiers under General Manuel Fernández Castrillón, who initially spared them. His commander, the infamous General Antonio López de Santa Anna, was reportedly incensed by this clemency and ordered the half-dozen-or-so prisoners executed immediately.

Many have dismissed this episode as an attempt to emphasize the viciousness of Santa Anna, but many see it as an aspersion cast against Crockett—perhaps the iconic hero of the Alamo, who is sometimes depicted making his final stand by using his rifle as a club against onrushing Mexican troops. And statements made by witnesses to the aftermath of the attack dispute this version of events. One of these was a former American slave attached to the conquering forces, who claimed to have seen Crockett's body

David Crockett, the iconic hero of the Alamo, was a legend in his own time.

surrounded by no less than sixteen dead Mexicans, one of whom had the frontiersman's knife stuck in him.

James W. Fannin, a thirty-two-year-old West Point dropout from Georgia, was the commander of a Texan force occupying the old Spanish fort in Goliad, somewhat less than one hundred miles southeast of San Antonio during the siege of the Alamo.

Lieutenant Colonel William B. Travis, commander of the Alamo garrison, expected that his fellow commander would march to his assistance and sent one desperate letter after another to Fannin, explaining the increasingly hopeless situation for him and his men and begging for reinforcements. And right up until the end, the defenders of the Alamo thought Fannin might actually show up; on the night of March 3, just days before the final assault on the mission, David Crockett and a handful of companions slipped out of the fort in order to search for Fannin and his men in the surrounding area.

Fannin made one half-hearted attempt to lead a relief force to the Alamo but ultimately gave up on the idea of risking his own command for the sake of the Alamo defenders; long before

Most of the most famous people associated with the 1836 Battle of the Alamo had some skeletons in their closets.

he had gotten the last of Travis's desperate letters, he had abandoned any idea of marching to his aid.

Fannin's own ultimate contribution to the war effort was to surrender his forces at the Battle of Coleto and to become one of the victims of the infamous Goliad Massacre. He was killed March 27, 1836, exactly three weeks after the last defenders of the Alamo had perished. Had he gone to their assistance, his life certainly would not have ended up being too much shorter, if he had been killed at all—and the history of the revolution might have been very different indeed.

Sam Houston served as commander-in-chief of the Texan revolutionary forces from March 1836 onward and went on to serve two terms as president of the republic of Texas.

In April 1832, three years before the Texas Revolution began, Houston was in Washington, D.C., where he was working to expose frauds being perpetrated by government agents against Cherokee Indians in Arkansas. While he was there, Ohio Congressman William Stanbery gave a speech to Congress in which he accused Houston himself of corruption in the supplying of provisions to the Cherokee. When Stanbery declined to reply to Houston's correspondence about these slurs, Houston confronted him on Pennsylvania Avenue and, even as the congressman tried to shoot him, proceeded to beat him into submission with a hickory cane.

Congress had Houston arrested and charged with the attack, and he countered by pleading self defense and hiring attorney Frances Scott Key—author of the "Star-Spangled Banner"—to defend him. He was found guilty but, through the intervention of influential friends who included James K. Polk, received only a reprimand. Unmollified, Stanbery sued Houston in civil court and obtained a $500 judgment against him. Houston responded by ignoring this decision and departing for Mexico.

James C. Neill, a colonel in the revolution, was a veteran of the War of 1812 and one of the Texans' older and most experienced field commanders, being especially proficient in the use of artillery. On February 3, 1836, Neill was the officer in charge of the Alamo when young Lieutenant Colonel William B. Travis arrived at the fort and reported to him.

Nine days after Travis got there, Neill responded to a report that his family was ill and promptly turned command of the Alamo over to his second-in-command, promising to be back within twenty days (twenty-two days later, when Mexican troops overran the fort, Neill had still not returned).

There are no reasonable suggestions that Neill was motivated by cowardice, especially as he had fought hard throughout the Texas Revolution, both before and after the Battle of the Alamo. His biggest priority was certainly not the military mission he had sworn to uphold, but had it been, his experience and command presence might have been what was needed to turn the crushing defeat at the Alamo into something else.

Neill survived the Texas Revolution and lived until 1845, long enough to see Texas give up its hard-won independence and become the twenty-eighth U.S state.

Louis "Moses" Rose, a veteran of the Napoleonic Wars who signed on with the Texan military forces fighting to overthrow Mexican control of the region at age fifty-one, has gone down in history with the unenviable title "Coward of the Alamo."

According to the most common account, Rose was a French Jew who had served as a lieutenant in Napoleon's army and participated in campaigns that included the ill-fated invasion of Russia, receiving the *Légion d'honneur* for heroism in 1814. Following Napoleon's defeat and exile, Rose immigrated to Nacogdoches,

"By God, I wasn't going to die!"

Texas, where he was living when the Texas Revolution began in 1835. He apparently signed on as a volunteer and was in the Alamo under the command of James Bowie in March 1836.

Two or three days before the Mexicans under Santa Anna made their final assault on the Alamo, Lieutenant Colonel William B. Travis realized that the situation was likely hopeless and gave the defenders a choice of whether to leave or to stay and die. According to a story carried out by Rose himself, Travis drew a line in the sand with his sword and asked anyone willing to stay to come across it, and Moses was the only fighter present not to do so. On March 5, 1836, he supposedly climbed over the wall of the fort and slipped through the Mexican lines to safety.

"By God, I wasn't going to die!" was reportedly his reply when years later he was asked why he departed the doomed fort before it finally fell.

William B. Travis, commissioned as a lieutenant colonel and the de facto commander of the regular military forces defending the Alamo in March 1836, was committed to the establishment of an independent Republic of Texas. He was somewhat less committed to his family, however, and in 1831, two-and-a-half years into his marriage, abandoned his wife, son, and unborn daughter in Alabama in order to begin a new life as a lawyer in Texas.

Travis became a prominent member of the Texan military forces raised during the revolution against Mexico and was made commander of the Alamo right before the siege of it began. On March 6, 1836, the twenty-six-year-old officer was killed during the final day of the battle.

Mexican General Santa Anna, never lacking in ego, styled himself "the Napoleon of the West."

Severino López de Santa Anna y Pérez de Lebrón, better known merely as Santa Anna, is unequivocally the villain of the Alamo but should not escape scrutiny on that account.

One of the supporters of Mexico's independence from Spain in 1821, Santa Anna went on to serve as president of Mexico elven times over a twenty-two-year period (and to hold the title "general" many times over his forty-year career). He was not in favor of independence for Texas, however, and took stern measures to curtail the civil, political, and religious rights of Anglo-American settlers in the region. Santa Anna also displayed an unbecoming bloodthirstiness toward the Texas revolutionaries and, advice from his commanders notwithstanding, was eager to raise the "no quarter" flag in battle and to massacre prisoners of war. His military failures and limitations notwithstanding, he eagerly styled himself "the Napoleon of the West," and embraced extravagant, self-aggrandizing pomp and ceremony as much as any third-world despot ever has.

Santa Anna at age fifty took a fifteen-year-old girl as his **bride.**

Santa Anna was also a confirmed and lecherous womanizer and, at age fifty, took a fifteen-year-old girl as his bride. While he did not have any children with her, he recognized four illegitimate offspring in his will—and is believed to have had at least three more.

3

"Ma" and "Pa" Ferguson

BACK BEFORE THE TERM "POWER
couple" would have meant anything to people,
that is exactly what "Ma" and "Pa" Ferguson
were. Unfortunately, they abused the power they
controlled over their tumultuous careers in Texas
politics and their names became a byword for
government malfeasance.

James Edward "Pa" Ferguson Jr. was, by all accounts, a self-made man. Even though he was born to a good family and had many opportunities, he was expelled from school at age twelve and four years later left his home in Bell County and drifted around the West doing odd jobs. Upon his return to Texas, he studied law and was admitted to the bar, ultimately became the attorney for the city of Belton, started a couple of banks, and managed several local political campaigns. And, on December 31, 1899, he married Miriam A. "Ma" Wallace, four years his junior, who would be his partner in crime, as it were, for the rest of his life.

In 1914, charismatic "Pa" Ferguson won his first term as governor of Texas, running as a Democrat on an anti-prohibitionist platform and taking office in January 1915. During his initial two-year term as governor he strengthened education in Texas and helped to make the prisons self-sustaining, and in 1916—despite rumors of impropriety in his administration—he was reelected.

Early in his second term, however, Ferguson vetoed the appropriations for the University of Texas in retaliation for its refusal to dismiss a number of faculty members he disliked. This prompted his enemies in the state legislature to impeach him, with the House of Representatives preparing twenty-one charges against him. The Senate convicted him on nine of these—five related to the misapplication of public funds, three to his quarrel with the university, one that he had received $156,500 in currency from an undisclosed source, and one that he had failed to properly enforce and respect the banking laws of Texas—and declared he be removed as governor and be ineligible to hold public office in the state.

These impediments notwithstanding, Ferguson ignored the legislature and ran for governor again in 1918! He was, however, defeated in the Democratic primary by his former lieutenant governor, William P. Hobby, who went on to become the next governor of Texas.

Trying to kick it up to the next level, in 1920 Ferguson ran in the U.S presidential election as the candidate of his own American Party. He was only on the ballot in Texas, however, where he garnered 47,968 votes—some 9.86 percent of the votes cast in Texas and a mere 0.18 percent of those cast nationwide. Warren G. Harding won the election, and Ferguson was left in the dust by at least four of the other losers.

Ferguson made a bid for the U.S. Senate in 1922 but was defeated in that attempt as well. It was at this point that he decided to start forging a political career for his wife.

In 1924, Miriam Ferguson followed in her husband's footsteps and was elected Governor of Texas, becoming one of the first two women elected to the executive office of a U.S. state (Nellie Tayloe Ross of Wyoming, who also followed her husband into her state's gubernatorial office, was elected the same year).

"Ma" Ferguson—whose nickname was probably inevitable when one considers her middle initials, the matronly aspect her supporters tried to cultivate, and her husband being referred to as "Pa"—ran on a platform that was opposed to Prohibition and the Ku Klux Klan and which was intended to clear her family's name. The former first lady of Texas hedged her bets by assuring voters that she would be relying on the advice of her husband and that the state would get "two governors for the price of one."

Two governors may have been more than the Lone Star State could handle, and political dissension and allegations of corruption dogged her throughout her first term in office.

One of the main subjects of complaint against "Ma" (and "Pa") Ferguson concerned the granting of construction contracts by the state highway department, which critics claimed were given to their friends and political allies in exchange for kickbacks.

Ferguson was also accused of accepting bribes of cash and land in exchange for granting pardons, which "Ma" Ferguson did at the rate of about one hundred convicts a month. State expenditures also increased somewhat on her watch, despite promises to reduce them by $15 million, and her campaign vows to get an anti-mask law passed against the KKK were foiled by the courts.

These problems were not enough for her political enemies to get her impeached, as they had done to her husband, but did

Two governors may have been more than the Lone Star State could handle.

lead to "Ma" Ferguson being defeated in the 1926 gubernatorial election.

"Ma" Ferguson did not run again for governor in 1928, but when the Texas Supreme Court rejected "Pa's" own attempt to run again in 1930, she ran again herself but once again lost. This was not necessarily a bad thing for her, however, as the full weight of the Great Depression struck during the term of victor Ross Sterling, who received the inevitable acrimony of the voters.

In 1932, "Ma" Ferguson threw her hat into the gubernatorial ring again, condemning the ostensibly corrupt way that incumbent Sterling was running the state highway commission and promising to cut state spending and lower taxes (i.e., played all the cards that had been played against her administration six years earlier).

By this time, "Ma" Ferguson had learned to keep her head down more so than before, and she was not the object of as much acrimony during her January 1933 to January 1935 term, the ominous prognostications of her opponents notwithstanding. "Ma" Ferguson was conservative on fiscal matters and, even

One of "Ma" Ferguson's redeeming values was her attempt to pass anti-mask laws that were aimed at the Ku Klux Klan.

though she remained liberal with regard to the number of convicted criminals she opted to parole or pardon, this lessened the burden on the state and engendered much less criticism than it had previously.

Shortly after "Ma" Ferguson's second term as governor ended, the couple experienced severe financial problems and lost their ranch near Belton and thereafter decided to take a five-year hiatus from politics. In 1940, she once again ran for high office in the state of Texas, but by then she was past her prime, and the Ferguson name had not been in the forefront of people's minds for some time. Her grand promises garnered a respectable number of votes but she was nonetheless handily defeated. The role of the Fergusons in public life had come to an end.

In 1944, "Pa" Ferguson succumbed to a stroke at age seventy-three, upon which his wife retired to private life in Austin. She lived another several years, until 1961, when she herself died of heart failure at age eighty-six. Today, the two of them are interred beside each other at the State Cemetery in Austin.

4

The Veterans' Land
Board Scandal

IN 1954, ROLAND KENNETH TOWERY,
the thirty-two-year-old managing editor of the
tiny *Cuero Record* newspaper, looked into a
tip he had received that a number of prominent
Cuero-area businessmen had been entertaining black and Hispanic laborers after hours at
a local club.

"Down in this country, white people just don't set up big parties for colored field hands," Towery observed. When he looked into the rumors, he learned that the workers were veterans and that the businessmen were signing them up to buy land under a program established by the state the year after the war ended. They were even paying the caretaker of the establishment $10 for every veteran he could inveigle into signing one of the applications.

Eight years earlier, the Texas legislature had passed the Veterans' Land Act, a measure intended to help World War II veterans obtain property at affordable prices. Under this measure, the state appropriated $100 million between 1946 and 1951 that it used to purchase land in order to resell it to veterans who could obtain it with forty-years loans at a 3 percent interest rate.

Two conditions applied to such purchases, odd when considered in light of each other. One was that loans to individual veterans could not exceed $7,500; the other was that the blocks

"Down in this country, white people just don't

of land sold to them had to be at least twenty acres. Because twenty or more acres could not generally be obtained for $7,500, veterans were allowed to participate in block sales in which they would pool their resources to purchase the land. The law also stipulated a 5 percent down payment on purchases and that the land could not be resold for at least three years.

It was the block purchase provisions that speculators like those in Cuero had found a way to abuse, and, unfortunately, the working-class veterans being drawn into the program by them—many of who were effectively illiterate—did not even know they were buying land. Some were led to believe that they were applying for some sort of veterans' compensation from the state, while others actually thought that they were receiving free land. Most were paid between $10 and $300 for their signatures. Meanwhile, the speculators used the veterans' signed applications to obtain and pocket the land grant money, in some cases transferring land to the veterans and in some cases not.

A veteran of World War II, Towery had been captured by the Japanese during their conquest of the Philippines, suffered various tropical maladies while a prisoner of war, and spent about half the time between 1945 and 1951 recuperating in veterans' hospitals. He had, in short, bled for his country and was not going to stand by while others who had done the same were taken advantage of. He was also a diligent journalist.

Wanting more information, Towery approached DeWitt County Attorney Wiley Cheatham (yes, incredibly, that really was his name). When he did, he learned not only that the official had been investigating reports of irregularities in the land

set up big parties for colored field hands."

program since August of the previous year, but also that local veterans had been receiving bills from the state for payments on land they were not even aware they had purchased. Cheatham spoke on condition that Towery hold off running anything in the newspaper until his own office could get a better sense of what was going on. After the county attorney failed to get any cooperation from state officials in Austin, however, he told the journalist to publish whatever he deemed appropriate.

Towery went to the state capital himself and started to get a sense of just how widespread the land grant problem was when he went to talk to General Land Office Commission Chairman

Bascom Giles, "the father of the Veterans' Land Bill." Giles immediately denied involvement in any fraudulent activity—even before the reporter suspected this was the case—and the commissioner both blamed local speculators for the irregularities and dismissed complaints against him as "politics" and the machinations of political opponents.

Towery turned what he had been able to learn into a feature story replete with charges of fraud and bribery and, on November 14, 1954, splashed it across the front page of the *Cuero Record*. He continued to single-handedly investigate the situation and ran a number of follow-up stories on it.

This public unveiling of the scandal induced Texas Attorney General John Ben Shepperd to step up an investigation he had begun the previous year, and prompted the state auditor's office, the Senate General Investigating Committee, the Texas Department of Public Safety, and the governor himself to launch their own investigations. It also sparked interest among the state's big urban newspapers, which remained oblivious or indifferent to the scandal up to that point.

The attention directed at the situation soon uncovered fraud in nine south Texas counties—including DeWitt, Lavaca, Victoria, Dimmit, Uvalde, Zavala, and Bexar, for which San Antonio is the seat—and led to charges of fraud and conspiracy to defraud veterans being filed against numerous members of the General Land Office. Democratic opponents of the Republican regime running the state at that time also used the scandal to cast aspersions of corruption against Governor Allan Shivers and Shepperd, both of whom—along with Giles—were ex officio members of the state Veterans Land Board.

Ultimately, Giles was convicted of conspiracy to commit theft of $83,500 in state funds. He was heavily fined, forced to forfeit around $80,000 as the result of civil suits brought against him, and was sent to prison. He served a little less than two years of a six-year sentence at the Texas State Penitentiary at Huntsville. He was the first Texas state official to be imprisoned for a crime committed while in office.

Nineteen other people were also charged with defrauding both the state and individual veterans, and two of them also served some time in prison for their role in the episode. Civil suits forced the speculators to both buy back the land they had sold under the program and maintain the payments on it, which allowed the state to recover most of the illegally obtained funds.

With an eye toward preventing future abuses of this sort, the Texas state legislature took steps to close the loopholes in the land grant program. And, in 1955, Towery was recognized for his efforts when he was awarded a Pulitzer Prize for his distinguished reporting.

5

King of the
Wheeler-Dealers

IN THE LATE 1950S, TEXAS FINANCIER
Billie Sol Estes launched a Ponzi scheme
of such epic proportions that it ultimately
shook the Kennedy administration and forced
numerous members of the U.S. Department of
Agriculture to resign in embarrassment.

During that era, the "King of the Wheeler-Dealers" was involved in the anhydrous ammonia industry. Estes used his knowledge of the business to produce mortgages on nonexistent anhydrous ammonia tanks by convincing local farmers to purchase them, sight unseen, on credit. He then leased these tanks from the farmers for the same amount as the mortgage payment—paying them a fee for their troubles—and used the fraudulent mortgage holdings to obtain loans from banks outside the Lone Star State (knowing that they would be unable to easily check on the tanks).

During this time, the U.S. Department of Agriculture began controlling the price of cotton through the specification of quotas to farmers. A loophole in this program was an acreage allotment that could not normally be transferred from the land with which it was associated but which could be conveyed if the original land was taken by eminent domain.

Estes took advantage of this by developing a system for buying large numbers of cotton allotments from farmers who had lost land as a result of eminent domain, convincing them to purchase land from him in Texas and transfer their allotments there. Estes would then lease the land and allotments back from the farmer at a rate of $50 an acre.

A stipulation in these agreements delayed the first mortgage payment for the first year and, when the first one came due, the farmer would intentionally default and the land would revert to Estes. He had, in effect, bought the cotton allotments with the fees from the leases. Because these sales and mortgages were based on fraud, however, transfer of the cotton allotments in this way was illegal.

These and a variety of other schemes perpetrated by Estes ultimately collapsed in the early 1960s, and the federal government launched a massive investigation of the wheeler-dealer's activities that at one point involved the efforts of seventy-six FBI agents.

The wheeler-dealer's activities . . . involved the efforts of seventy-six FBI agents.

A *Time* magazine article from 1962 succinctly summed up his activities.

"Billie Sol [Estes] never smoked or drank," the *Time* article reads. "He considered dancing immoral, often delivered sermons as a Church of Christ lay preacher. But he ruthlessly ruined business competitors, practiced fraud and deceit on a massive scale, and even victimized Church of Christ schools that he was supposed to be helping as a fundraiser or financial adviser. He pursued money relentlessly but, despite energy, ingenuity, cunning, and a dazzling gift of salesmanship, ended up not only broke but hopelessly in the red—by $12 million according to his own figures, by $20 million according to Texas' Attorney General Wilson."

In 1964, Estes was convicted on charges related to the fraudulent ammonia tank mortgages and was sent to prison. The following year, however, this conviction was overturned in *Estes v. Texas* by the U.S. Supreme Court, which found by a vote of 5–4 that it had been impossible for him to have a fair trial due to the presence of broadcast journalists and television cameras in the courtroom.

As of this writing, eighty-seven-year-old Estes is alive and well in Granbury, Texas, a cogent answer to naïve assertions that what goes around comes around.

6

The Sharpstown
Stock Scandal

ON JANUARY 18, 1971, TEXAS Democrats gathered in the state capital of Austin to celebrate their victories in the 1971 election and to inaugurate their new top officials. They might not have felt quite so festive, however, if they had known what was going on two hundred miles to the north, in Dallas.

There, attorneys for the U.S. Securities and Exchange Commission were filing a lawsuit in federal court alleging stock fraud against a number of influential Texans, including Houston banker and real estate developer Frank W. Sharp, former Democratic state attorney general Waggoner Carr, and former state insurance commissioner John Osorio. The suit also included Sharp's corporations, including the National Bankers Life Insurance Corporation and the Sharpstown State Bank. By the time the events they were initiating had played out, the state government would be shaken to its core, and a number of promising political careers would be destroyed.

While it was not filed against them, the civil suit also alleged that several other people, among them Governor Preston Smith, state Democratic chairman and state banking board member Elmer Baum, Representative Tommy Shannon of Fort Worth, House Speaker Gus Mutscher Jr., and Mutscher aide Rush McGinty had, effectively, accepted bribes.

State government would be shaken to its core.

According to the SEC, Sharp had used his Sharpstown State Bank to grant more than $600,000 in loans to state officials, who then used the money to purchase stock issued by his National Bankers Life Insurance Corporation. This artificially inflated the value of the stock, and when the buyers then sold it, they enjoyed an overall profit of about $250,000.

Even worse, the SEC said, granting of the loans had been contingent upon the governor arranging to have considered at a special session of the legislature in September 1969 some banking bills that would benefit Sharp's businesses. Legislators Mutscher and Shannon then quickly got the bills passed. (Smith did later double-cross Sharp by vetoing the bills but only after he and his cronies had profited from the sale of stock they had bought with the loans they had received.)

In response to the charges, the state officials named in the suit maintained it was simply a coincidence that they had received loans from Sharp and used them to purchase stock from him after helping see through the passage of the banking bills that had helped him. That did not sound very plausible to the public, however, especially as it learned about how victims of the scam had been damaged so that the perpetrators might profit. Strake Jesuit College Preparatory, for example, lost $6 million as a result of buying the resold stock at up to $26 a share upon the advice of Sharp.

As a result of such revelations, everyone named in the SEC suit was damaged politically by the ongoing attention to the episode (which was eventually dubbed "the Sharpstown Scandal," after a planned community outside of Houston that had been developed by Sharp). And any chance that the furor would die down was prevented by the efforts of the "Dirty Thirty," a diverse coalition of state representatives who banded together against the participants in the scandal.

State prosecutors were motivated to act as well and, in early 1972, tried Mutscher, Shannon, and McGinty on charges of conspiracy to accept a bribe from Sharp. The trial took place in Abilene, a change of venue from the capital due to the widespread negative publicity the incident had been receiving. On March 15, a jury found "the Abilene Three" guilty, and the following day, Judge J. Neil Daniel sentenced them each to five years of probation. Sharp himself was charged separately with violating federal banking and securities laws and, upon being convicted, was sentenced to three years of probation and assessed a $5,000 fine.

While no other elected officials were convicted in the scandal, the political fallout was significant, and a struggle ensued between the conservative Democrats then dominating the state government and their less-conservative Democratic and Republican opponents, who used calls for reform to their advantage. During the 1972 election, incumbents not involved in the scandal distanced themselves from those who were, and a whole raft of reform candidates came forward to challenge them. Every one of the candidates associated even peripherally with the scandal was defeated or opted not to seek reelection, and half of the state's representatives and a greater-than-usual number of its senators were replaced, almost all by "reform" candidates. Governor Smith and his lieutenant governor, Ben Barnes, had their political careers ruined, as did a number of other state officials with formerly bright careers.

In 1973, the final direct consequences of the scandal occurred when newly constituted legislature—with encouragement from the new governor, lieutenant governor, and attorney general—passed a sweeping series of reform laws. These included, among other things, compelling candidates to reveal more details about their campaign finances, making most governmental records open to public scrutiny, expanding the requirements that policy-making agencies conduct open meetings, forcing revised disclosure regulations on paid political lobbyists—and, naturally, requiring state officials to disclose the sources of their income.

7

The Duke of Duval County

BY THE TIME GEORGE BERHAM PARR became the pageboy of his father, Archer, in the Texas Senate in 1914, at the age of thirteen, he had become the heir apparent to the corrupt and powerful Democratic Party political machine that controlled Duval County. He went on to absolutely control politics in his south Texas county, to suborn them in adjacent counties such as Jim Wells, and influence them on a state and even national scale.

The Parr family had long been prominent in Duval County, where it owned substantial amounts of ranchland and enjoyed a boost in its fortunes when oil was discovered in the area. George Parr eventually owned two large ranches, the local San Diego State Bank, was a partner in dozens of business throughout the region, and was one of the first landowners to actively exploit the labor of illegal aliens.

Core to the Parr family's power base was a system of patronage that catered to the impoverished and poorly educated working class Hispanic majority population of the county and achieved its ends through bribery, graft, fraud, illegal donations, and violence. These tools were used to produce large numbers of both legal and illegal votes—from people living and dead—to gain control over all key county positions and to sway the out-

President Harry S. Truman
pardoned him, allowing
him to participate

come of state elections. George himself served variously as both sheriff and judge of the county from 1926 onward.

While the Parr family had long exerted undue influence over county politics from its seat, the town of San Diego, Archer and George felt sufficiently confident to take this to an entirely new level by overtly appealing to the growing number of Mexican-American residents. This further marginalized the white, relatively educated class of independent farmers and ranchers who had long held power in the county and, by the mid-1930s, driven away many of them and largely disenfranchised the rest.

Archer Parr had, in fact, long been known as "El Patron" by

Spanish-speaking residents for his practice of providing money, jobs, and favors in exchange for their unwavering political support. The charismatic George followed in these footsteps, communicating with his constituents in their native language, sharing money from the county and school district coffers with his supporters, and assuming the mantle of "El Patron" upon his father's death in 1942. Neither of his brothers had much of a taste for politics, although they had both served in a number of prominent county positions, and there was never much question that George would be his father's successor.

Even before George Parr became known as the Duke of Duval County, his activities had attracted the attention of the federal government, and in 1934 he was convicted of tax evasion and served a nine-month term in prison that ended in 1937. He continued his activities relatively unabated upon his release, however—and completely so after 1946, when Democratic Pres-

in politics just as if he had never been **a convicted criminal**.

ident Harry S. Truman pardoned him, restoring his civil rights and allowing him to once again participate in politics just as if he had never been a convicted criminal. It was soon after this that he began to be known as the Duke.

"His most celebrated scheme decided the outcome of the United States Senate race between Coke R. Stevenson and Lyndon B. Johnson in 1948," the Texas State Historical Association says. "With Stevenson the apparent winner, election officials in Jim Wells County. . . reported an additional 202 votes for Johnson a week after the primary runoff and provided the future president with his eighty-seven-vote margin of victory for the whole state. Amid charges of fraud, the voting lists disappeared." Many of the names on those lists are believed to be those of dead people.

By 1950, Parr's antics had made him a number of powerful enemies, including Texas Governor Allan Shivers and state Attorney General John Ben Shepperd (q.v.)—who was, ironically, a political advisor to Johnson at this time—and the state and federal governments launched an investigation into the Duval County machine. Ultimately, some 650 indictments at various levels of jurisdiction were brought against Parr family members and their cronies. Under the protection of Johnson, however, at that point a powerful U.S. Senator, the Duke himself evaded all attempts to successfully convict him of crimes that included bribery, corruption, fraud, racketeering—and even murder.

At around this time, the Freedom Party, led by World War II veteran Jake Floyd, began to challenge the corrupt Parr political machine and even managed to seize from it some key posts, including that of district judge. The Duke retaliated by sending one of his henchman to assassinate Floyd, an attempt that went woefully wrong when the killer mistakenly gunned down Buddy Floyd, the target's son. Two other Parr opponents were also murdered.

Governor Shivers responded by declaring war on the Parr machine and launched an intensive state investigation of it in 1954. Even though the Duke was charged with embezzlement of county funds, he beat that rap, too, and despite the legal and political pressure brought to bear on them, he and his cronies maintained control of both Duval and Jim Wells Counties.

Parr continued with business as usual for another fourteen years, but when the Johnson administration collapsed in 1968, he lost his most powerful political ally. Even as elements within the machine attempted to usurp control of it, Johnson himself urged the Duke to abdicate, and by the early 1970s, he had turned over control of the apparatus to his nephew, Archer Parr III. This was the beginning of the end for Parr and, in 1974, he was finally convicted of a crime for which no one was willing to protect or pardon him and sentenced to ten years in prison for federal income tax evasion.

On April 1, 1975, the seventy-four-year-old Duke of Duval County was found dead by his own hand at the Parr family ranch. With his death the machine he had perfected collapsed. Its effects were still felt, however, for some time to come. Despite their best attempts, the remaining white yeoman farmers in the county were unable to once against wrest control of its politics. And the wealthy and powerful Parr family played kingmaker in a number of elections even into the 1990s and managed to keep Duval County a Democratic bastion in what is now a largely Republican state.

8

Charlie Wilson's Whore (And More)

IT IS AMAZING IN A STATE AS TIGHTLY wrapped and conservative as Texas has become that an elected official with a taste for booze, drugs, and hookers who *also* helped arm an enemy America has fought for more than a decade could become a virtual folk hero. But that is the case with Congressman Charlie Wilson, who gained even national adoration after the release of the 2007 film *Charlie Wilson's War*, based on a book of the same name by author George Crile III. Being played by Tom Hanks probably did not hurt one bit.

Congressman Charlie Wilson was instrumental in providing Afghan military leaders with weapons and training that they used first against the Soviet Union and then the United States.

Trinity native "Good Time Charlie" served in Congress for twelve terms, from 1973 to 1996, as the representative from the second congressional district of Texas. During that time, his activities prompted investigations by government entities that included the House Committee on Ethics, the Federal Election Commission, the Department of Justice, and the FBI. He even served as a state representative from 1961 to 1973, and it was during this period that he began to forge his reputation as a party animal. Somehow, however, the fun-hating authorities never really had the vice-loving Wilson dead to rights, and while there were often allegations of smoke, there was rarely proof of fire.

A good example of this is a picture of Wilson sitting on a bed with a nude Mexican prostitute, ostensibly in a bordello, which was described in Wilson's hefty, 463-page FBI file. She was just

Federal prosecutors launched an investigation of what

one of Charlie Wilson's whores, of course, and he is reported to have spent time with many others.

In 1969, Wilson had his first substance-abuse-related run-in with the law when he was arrested for driving under the influence of alcohol. Wilson refused to take a blood test, and after his doctor revealed that he had prescribed him certain drugs, the charges against the state representative were soon changed to driving under the influence of drugs. Wilson later said that he "barely" avoided a DUI and for a time had to attend Saturday-morning classes about the evils of drinking whisky. They failed, by all accounts, to sink in, and a number of similar incidents occurred over the following decades (including a drunken fender bender on the Key Bridge in Washington, D.C., in the 1980s).

Three years later, however, the incident came back to haunt Wilson when the mugshots from his arrest appeared on widely distributed but anonymous campaign fliers during his 1972 congressional campaign. Wilson was also reportedly concerned that the photo of him with the Mexican prostitute would turn up on its own anonymous flier.

In 1976, "Good Time Charlie" became known for awhile as "Timber Charlie," when he was accused of plotting with Texas lumber tycoon Arthur Temple—a former employer of Wilson— to induce Congress to create the "Big Thicket National Biological Preserve." This bill directed the purchase of nearly ninety thousand acres in southeast Texas, much of it owned by Temple,

and **whom** Wilson had done in the **Fantasy Suite** of Caesar's Palace.

for a whopping $70 million. An investigation determined that the complaints against Wilson were politically motivated and it eventually fizzled.

In 1980, federal prosecutors launched an investigation of what and whom Wilson had done in the Fantasy Suite of Caesar's Palace during a visit to Las Vegas (commemorated in an iconic scene in the film *Charlie Wilson's War* in which Tom

Wilson, an inveterate party animal, was investigated by the federal government for a weekend he spent with a couple of drug-laden hookers in the Fantasy Suite at Caesar's Palace in Las Vegas.

Hanks cavorts in a hot tub with two hookers clad in nothing but high heels). One of the concerns of the weeks-long but fruitless investigation was with whether or not Wilson had partaken of cocaine during his bacchanal.

"The girls had cocaine, and the music was loud. It was total happiness. And both of them had ten long, red fingernails with an endless supply of beautiful white powder," Wilson was quoted as saying in the book *Charlie Wilson's War*. "The feds spent a million bucks trying to figure out whether, when those fingernails passed under my nose, did I inhale or exhale, and I ain't telling," Presumably, however, if he had not illegally snorted cocaine, he would have just come right out and said he had not.

In 1993, the Department of Justice looked into allegations that Wilson had made improper use of campaign funds and given inadequate financial disclosures. Most of the errors associated with this were traced back to "Charlie's Angels," the good-looking but not necessarily competent women that Wilson hired to staff his office. Wilson admitted error in the face of these allega-

"The girls had **cocaine**, and the music was loud. It was **total happiness**."

tions, and they were dismissed after his campaign paid a $90,000 fine to the Federal Election Commission.

The many minor scandals in which he was involved, however, were largely overshadowed by the great achievement of his career, namely his pivotal role in Operation Cyclone, which ran from 1979 to 1989, primarily during the Reagan administration. This was the largest-ever CIA covert program and was created to support the *mujahideen* in their war of resistance against the Soviet Union by providing them with military advisors, Stinger anti-aircraft missiles, and other weapons. Wilson used his role on the House Appropriations Subcommittee on Defense to have the CIA provided with massive amounts of "black" money and at one point even visited the war-torn region himself.

This was great as far as it went but, like many American initiatives, was ultimately shortsighted. True, the USSR, the boogeyman of the Cold War, was defeated in Afghanistan and collapsed shortly thereafter, and it is certainly possible that Charlie Wilson played a disproportionate role in the demise of the evil empire.

But, the fact is, the United States never really fought the Soviet Union directly, just mutually postured and supported proxy wars around the world. As of this writing, the United States has actually been fighting in Afghanistan a full decade, against enemies that might not even exist today if they had not been strengthened materially, morally, and organizationally by Operation Cyclone. Much of the aid provided during the course of the operation went to a character named Gulbuddin Hekmatyar, an Islamist hardliner who is now a senior Taliban leader, a supporter of al-Qaeda, and one of the top three leaders in the insurgency against the U.S. forces.

Charlie Wilson retired from public life in 1996 and died in February 2010 at his home in Lufkin, Texas, age seventy-six, but his legend certainly did not die with him. And, contrary to conventional wisdom on such matters, he both managed to avoid getting punished for the various peccadilloes that agitated his detractors, and to actually get praised for the things he did that were most harmful.

9

The Enron Scandal

FOR AN UNPRECEDENTED SIX YEARS
in a row, *Fortune* magazine named Enron
Corporation "America's Most Innovative
Company," and in 2000 the company claimed
staggering revenues of just over $100 billion.
The following year, however, the massive corporation would declare bankruptcy, and it would
be revealed that it had applied its vaunted in-
novation to deliberately perpetrating one of the
greatest financial frauds in history, an episode
that became known as the "Enron Scandal."

Enron maintained a lavish office complex in Houston that was ultimately sold off to help settle its massive financial liabilities.

Following the creation of the corporation through the merger of several subsidiary businesses in the mid-1980s, Kenneth Lay, the former CEO of one of those companies, became head of what became known as Enron and relocated it to Houston. Enron ultimately employed some twenty-two thousand people, directly traded nearly three-dozen commodities, exchanged futures for several others, and became one of the most prominent communications, energy, utilities, pulp and paper, and online services corporations in the world. Through its global holdings it had a huge network of natural gas pipelines and constructed and operated thirty-eight power plants throughout the world. It established lavish offices, millions of dollars flowed into the pockets of its officers, and it laid claim to being the seventh-largest company in America.

The massive conglomerate was heavily in debt from the start and almost immediately it began selling off keys assets, including a major petrochemical company, and taking on a variety of silent partners with portfolios similar to its own. This made the company less diversified but did nothing to offset its problems.

Then, in 1990, Enron began establishing a large number of limited-liability, special-purpose companies to shift debt so that it would not appear in the accounts for the parent corporation, allowing it to continue to grow its stock price and maintain an investment-grade credit rating. Enron CFO Andrew Fastow led the team that created these offshore entities and established a system by which he, his family, and his friends enjoyed hundreds of millions of dollars in revenues at the expense of the corporation and its stockholders.

The company also took full advantage of the wave of utility deregulation that was beginning to sweep the United States beginning in the 1990s and thrived in the environment of reduced government oversight.

In late 1999, under the leadership of president and chief operating officer Jeffrey Skilling, Enron launched an online trading system that allowed people to trade commodities directly with the corporation. At its peak, some $6 billion worth of commodities *a day* were being moved through the network.

"Enron generated huge revenue numbers—but relatively scant profits—by buying and selling the same goods over and over," wrote Dan Ackman for *Forbes* magazine in his 2002 article "Enron the Incredible." "Some of this trading was done between Enron and its supposedly independent partnerships. Each individual trade was accounted for as revenue at its full value."

By the turn of the millennium Enron had, by all accounts, become the golden child of analysts, the financial media, and even its own employees, and was being given a pass by oversight entities like the Financial Accounting Standards Board. During this period some people did begin to question Enron's policies and what appeared to be an increasingly precarious house of cards, prompting the company to start aggressively attacking its detractors.

In April 2001, Wall Street analyst Richard Grubman questioned Enron's odd accounting practices during a conference call with Skilling.

"Well, thank you very much, we appreciate that," Skilling said. "Asshole."

Insult quickly led to injury in the case of other detractors.

"For investors looking for 'performance' bonds, Enron may not be the ideal choice," wrote Daniel Scotto, a financial analyst for BNP Paribas SA, in a report on the company in August 2001. Enron pressured the banking group to punish Scotto for this, and they promptly placed him on a twelve-week leave and then fired him the day it ended.

In August 2000, the price of Enron stock reached a high of $90. Enron's inner circle knew that this level was unsustainable and, even as the company publicly encouraged people to continue buying stock and predicted a high-water mark of $140, its executives began to secretly dump their own. Lay himself unloaded more than $90 million worth of stock at this time.

Twelve months later, the price of Enron stock had dropped to just $42 a share and, by October 2001, to just $15, and the collapsing, cash-strapped corporation was immersed in a largely unsuccessful campaign to sell off many of its overseas assets in an attempt to drum up capital.

Toward the end of the year, Enron began to fall apart, and it was publicly revealed that many of the company's profits and assets were not just exaggerated but, in some cases, did not even

Enron stock *crashed*, plummeting to just *pennies a share.*

exist! Losses, debts, and other liabilities had been fraudulently shifted to the offshore, special-purpose subsidiaries, and, overall, the corporation had systematically misrepresented its financial activities on a massive, unprecedented scale. Another large corporation stepped in to purchase Enron but, after examining its books, retreated quickly and fired the CEO who had been guiding them in the acquisition.

As the magnitude of the scandal was revealed, the price of blue-chip Enron stock crashed, plummeting to just pennies a share, a financial disaster with worldwide effects.

In December 2001, Enron filed for bankruptcy protection. Over the ensuing years the mega-corporation reorganized and then emerged from bankruptcy in 2004, became a mere shell when it sold its last remaining business in September 2006, and then changed its name to Enron Creditors Recovery Corp. in 2007.

"Enron Creditors Recovery Corp.'s sole mission is to reorganize and liquidate the remaining operations and assets of Enron following one of the largest and most complex bankruptcies in U.S. history," the company states on its Web site as of this writing.

Fallout from the episode was profound and widespread, and in the wake of its collapse, Enron became a symbol of corporate corruption. Enron shareholders lost a staggering $74 billion in the years leading up to the corporation's collapse. More than twenty thousand former Enron employees lost their pensions and, after filing a class-action suit, received settlements of approximately $3,100 each.

Enron's actions also precipitated the California energy crisis of 2000–2001; caused attention to be brought to bear on the activities and financial practices of many other corporations; prompted Congress to pass the Sarbanes–Oxley Act of 2002, in which "the company's perceived corporate governance failings are matched virtually point for point;" drove the Securites and Exchange Commission to change stock exchange regulations; and effectively destroyed the formerly prestigious Arthur Andersen accounting firm, which had been complicit with Enron in its fraudulent dealings and was found guilty of obstruction of justice. While Enron CEO Kenneth Lay dodged justice by dying—whether actually or apparently—most of his partners in crime had to face the music in one form or another. Not surprisingly, some of them managed to make cushy plea deals in exchange for turning on each other or to avoid the hazards of jury trials. Some of the top players follow but many others were charged in the scandal.

Dan Boyle, Enron vice president of energy finance and services, was charged with conspiring to mischaracterize the sale of three Nigerian energy-generating barges to make it seem as if the company had received more revenue than it actually had. In May 2005, he was sentenced to three years and ten months in prison and fined $320,000.

Richard Causey, formerly with disgraced accounting firm Arthur Andersen, joined Enron in 1991, and eventually became executive vice president and chief accounting officer. He helped Enron to hide its debts by manipulating financial records. Between 1998 and 2001, he was paid more than $4 million in salary and bonuses and received more than $14 million from the sale of Enron stock. He was indicted for conspiracy and wire fraud and, after pleading guilty, was given a five- to seven-year prison term. As of this writing, he was scheduled to be released from the federal penitentiary in Bastrop, Texas, in October 2011.

A Bad Lay

KENNETH LAY WAS CHAIRMAN AND CHIEF EXECUTIVE officer of Enron from 1985 until January 2002—except for a few months in 2000 when he was just chairman—when he was forced to resign following the collapse of the corporation.

As the CEO of Enron, Lay received an exceptional compensation package, worth $42.4 million in 1999, and between 1998 and 2001, he personally sold more than $300 million in Enron stock and stock options (although in 2006 he claimed that he was about a quarter–million dollars in the hole and had spent most of his fortune on his legal defense).

In July 2004, a grand jury indicted Lay on eleven counts of wire fraud, securities fraud, and making false and misleading statements. His trial began in Houston on January 31, 2006, after four-and-a-half years of preparation by federal prosecutors and despite protests from his defense attorneys that he would not be able to get a fair trial in the city where crimes had affected so many thousands of people.

Lay was short-tempered and confrontational during much of his testimony and argued that Enron's collapse was the result of a conspiracy by rogue executives, unscrupulous traders, and the news media. This alienated the jury and, on May 25, 2006, it found Lay guilty of six of the charges against him; a judge found him guilty of four more in a separate bench trial and dismissed the final charge.

Each of these counts carried a prison sentence of up to ten years, and legal experts commenting on the case

Ken Lay had close connections to the ever-shady Bush family.

predicted that the former CEO would likely receive twenty-to-thirty years in prison when he was sentenced on October 23, 2006.

Less than six weeks after his trial, however, while vacationing in Snowmass, Colorado, the sixty-four-year-old Lay died of an apparent heart attack. He was quickly cremated and his ashes reportedly buried in a hidden location in the mountains. A week after his death, some twelve hundred guests, including former President George H. W. Bush, attended a memorial service for him at First United Methodist Church in Houston.

Because he died prior to exhausting all of his appeals, on October 17, 2006, the federal district court judge who had presided over the case abated Lay's conviction, meaning that under the law it is as if he had never been indicted, tried, or found guilty. Additionally, claimants can no longer

A Bad Lay (continued)

seek punitive damages against a deceased defendant in civil court.

Some of the circumstances of Lay's death have led to conspiracy theories that he is still alive, and these include its occurrence in a remote area, the fact that it happened after his conviction but before his sentencing, the quick cremation of his body, irregularities on his autopsy report, and his close connections with the ever-shady Bush family.

David Duncan ran Arthur Andersen's Enron account starting in 1997 and admitted that he ordered Enron-related documents shredded in October 2001, two days after he learned about a federal probe. He pled guilty to charges of obstruction of justice and faced up to ten years in prison. Once the Arthur Andersen conviction was overturned in 2005, however, he withdrew his guilty plea.

Dave Delainey, chairman and CEO of Enron Energy Services, was charged with participating in numerous schemes to mislead the public about the true state of Enron's profitability. He was sentenced to two-and-a-half years in prison for insider trading, for which he could have faced ten, and forced to pay nearly $8 million in restitution.

Andrew Fastow, an underling of Jeffrey Skilling, joined Enron in 1990 and became its chief financial officer. He was the mastermind behind the secret partnerships Enron used to hide debt, inflate revenue, and enrich himself. He was charged with conspiracy, insider trading, making false statements, money laundering, securities fraud, and wire fraud and initially received a ten-year sentence that a federal judge ultimately reduced it to six, plus two years probation. He was also fined $23.8 million. As of this writing, he was scheduled to be released from the federal penitentiary in Pollock, Louisiana, in December 2011.

Lea Fastow, wife of Andrew Fastow, was the assistant treasurer at Enron and served as executive assistant for one of the company's off-the-books partnerships that pillaged money from Enron shareholders. She was indicted by a federal grand jury for conspiracy to commit wire fraud and money laundering and four counts of filing false income tax returns. She pled guilty to submitting a fraudulent income tax return and served a year in prison.

Ben Glisan Jr., also formerly with Arthur Andersen, joined Enron in 1996 and became its treasurer in 2000. He turned a $5,800 investment into a $1 million profit through one of the company's off-the-books partnerships. He pleaded guilty to fraud and was sentenced to five years in prison.

Kevin Hannon was former chief operating officer for Enron Broadband. Both the Securities and Exchange Commission and the Department of Justice charged that he had been involved in a scheme to fraudulently inflate the value of Enron Broadband stock, which he had sold at prices inflated by $8 million. He cooperated with prosecutors and was sentenced to two years in prison, two years probation, and fined $150,000.

Joseph Hirko was also alleged by the SEC and DOJ to have been involved in a scheme to fraudulently inflate the value of Enron Broadband stock, which he had sold at prices inflated by $35 million. He pleaded guilty to one charge of wire fraud and was sentenced to sixteen months in prison, likely much less than if he had rolled the dice and faced a jury trial.

Kevin Howard faced a criminal indictment relating to a video-on-demand partnership with Blockbuster, "Project Braveheart," which illicitly booked $111 million in nonexistent revenue. He pled guilty to one count of falsifying books and records and, in part because he did not personally profit from his fraud, was sentenced to just one year of probation, to include nine months of home confinement.

Mark Koenig, former head of Enron investor relations and who presented false financial statements on behalf of the company, pleaded guilty to aiding and abetting securities fraud and was sentenced to eighteen months in prison, two years probation, and fined $50,000. He had faced up to ten years in prison.

Michael Kopper joined Enron in 1994, and became a key lackey to Andrew Fastow, with whom he helped set up many of the off-the-books partnerships used by the company. After cooperating with prosecutors and pleading guilty to money laundering and conspiracy to commit wire fraud he was sentenced to three years and one month in prison, plus two years of probation, and fined $50,000.

Lawrence Lawyer, an employee of Enron Capital Management, helped Michael Kopper form the RADR partnership in 1997, which prosecutors said was created to secretly enrich Enron executives through the sale of the company's interests in wind farms. He neglected to report nearly $80,000 in kickbacks he had received over a four-year period and was sentenced to two years probation (rather than the three-year maximum he had faced).

Kenneth Rice, like Hannon and Hirko, was also alleged by the SEC and DOJ to have been involved in a scheme to fraudulently inflate the value of Enron Broadband stock, which he had sold at prices inflated by $53 million. He was sentenced to twenty-seven months in prison and ordered to turn over some $15 million in assets.

Paula Rieker, former number-two executive in Enron's investor relations division and afterward corporate secretary to Lay, was charged with criminal insider trading. She had purchased 18,380 shares of Enron stock for $15.51 a share and then sold them for $49.77 a share in July 2001, a week before the public learned about a $102 million loss she was already aware of. In October 2006 she was given two years probation after pleading guilty and becoming a witness for the prosecution. She had faced up to ten years in prison. "Rieker stayed on Enron's payroll several months after the company filed for bankruptcy," the AP reported. "She received $130,000 in bonuses designed to entice needed employees to stay and signed papers that said she had not illegally traded stock."

Jeffrey Skilling, an Enron executive who briefly served as the company's CEO in 2000, was charged with insider trading and with taking part in widespread schemes to mislead investors and government regulators about the company's earnings. Between 1998 and 2001, he was paid more than $14 million in salary and bonuses and received $200 million from the sale of Enron stock. He was convicted of one count of conspiracy, one count of insider trading, five counts of making false statements to auditors, and twelve twelve counts of securities fraud and sentenced to twenty-four years and four months in prison; he is serving his time at the prison in Englewood, Colorado. He was also fined $45 million.

10

Rathergate

ON SEPTEMBER 8, 2004, DURING THE Wednesday broadcast of the CBS investigative news program *60 Minutes*, veteran correspondent Dan Rather presented four documents that were critical of President George W. Bush's service in the Texas Air National Guard in the early 1970s. These documents were purportedly written by Bush's former commander, the late Lieutenant Colonel Jerry B. Killian.

Dan Rather's decision to release unverified documents on the air wrecked his four-decade career with CBS.

"We are told [they] were taken from Lieutenant Colonel Killian's personal files," Texas native Rather stated, noting that their authenticity had been verified by experts working for the network. Coming less than two months before the 2004 presidential election, the contents of the documents were a potential bombshell and continued to enflame the ongoing controversy over Bush's questionable military service during the Vietnam War.

CBS's source for the documents was a Lieutenant Colonel Bill Burkett, a former officer with the Texas Air National Guard, who ultimately told so many stories about how he had obtained them that at least a few had to be lies. He had provided six documents allegedly obtained from Killian's files, including the four presented on the air, and provided them to *CBS News* producer Mary Mapes.

As it turned out, however, CBS had not actually bothered to verify the veracity of the documents Burkett had provided at all, and their authenticity was questioned almost immediately. A main point of criticism was that the documents, which had supposedly been prepared on a typewriter in the 1970s, just happened to look exactly as if they had been created in a contemporary version of Microsoft Word using default settings. Numerous typography experts and other media organizations subsequently

The documents were a potential bombshell.

launched their own investigations into the genuineness of the documents and concluded that they were forgeries.

For a full two weeks, CBS maintained what was later characterized as a "strident defense" of its actions. But as its position became more and more absurd—and phrases like "Memogate" and "Rathergate" were increasingly bandied about—it finally came clean and admitted to the sloppy error it had made in using the documents. Indeed, even after it bothered to really engage the services of forensic document experts, CBS could do little to refute the third-party conclusions as to the illegitimacy of the papers, as Burkett had supposedly destroyed the originals after faxing them to the network. It was thus impossible to prove their authenticity.

Sixteen days after its original broadcast, CBS came clean in an on-air admission of error.

"If I knew then what I know now, I would not have gone ahead with the story as it was aired, and I certainly would not have used the documents in question," Rather asserted.

That was almost certainly an understatement, as Rather and the other network personnel involved in the scandal had not yet felt the full effects of the backlash. Several months later, news producer Mapes was fired, several senior news executives were forced to resign, and Rather himself appeared to have been irreparably damaged by the incident. In March of 2005, he stepped down from his position as news anchor and, in 2006, after forty-three years with CBS, left the network for good.

Rather and Mapes continue to defend their actions.

"Nobody has proved that they were fraudulent, much less a forgery," Rather said of the Killian documents on *Larry King Live* in September 2007. "The truth of this story stands up to this day."

11

A Spacewoman Scorned

FOR A DECADE, U.S. NAVY OFFICER
and astronaut Lisa Marie Nowak was one of
the shining stars of America's space program,
until early 2007, when she dropped from the
heavens in an incident that was as strange and
chilling as it was sordid.

Nowak was commissioned in 1985 upon her graduation from the U.S. Naval Academy and, over the ensuing eleven years, enjoyed a progressively successful military career as an aviator, logging more than fifteen hundred flight hours in nearly three dozen types of aircraft.

In 1996, Nowak was selected for the NASA Astronaut Corps and assigned to the Johnson Space Center in Houston, Texas. Over the following decade she honed her skills as a robotics mission specialist and, in July 2006, flew aboard the space shuttle *Discovery* as a flight engineer on a mission to the International Space Station. During this mission Nowak was charged with operating the robotic arms aboard both her craft and the space station and logged thirteen days in space. This was, in every way, the highpoint of her career, and her fall to earth came soon afterwards.

In 1988, Nowak (*nee* Caputo) married Richard T. Nowak, a classmate of hers from the Naval Academy who went on to work at the Johnson Space Center, and the couple had three children, a son in 1992 and twin daughters in 2001.

In 2004, Nowak became involved with a recently divorced fellow astronaut named William Oefelein, and the two went on to have a two-year affair that was, as she later said, "more than a working relationship but less than a romantic relationship." Toward the end of 2006, however, Oefelein started to break off the relationship with Nowak, even as he initiated one with a lower-ranking Air Force officer named Colleen Shipman who was assigned to the 45th Space Wing at Patrick Air Force Base in Florida.

Shipman started spending weekends in Houston with Oefelein and, in turn, Nowak started stalking her, sometimes wearing a variety of disguises and costumes to do so. This weird *ménage a trois* lasted about two months before Nowak decided to take it to the next level.

On the evening of Sunday, February 4, 2007, Nowak drove

Is she or isn't she ... wearing an adult diaper? Only deranged astronaut Lisa Marie Nowak (and her stalking victim) know for sure.

out of Houston for Florida, with an eye to arriving at Orlando International Airport ahead of Shipman, who would be flying back home from Houston just in time to get ready for work. Equipment she loaded into her car included both latex and leather gloves, a wig, a hooded trench coat, an umbrella, black sweats, rubber tubing, plastic garbage bags, $585 in cash, her computer, pepper spray, a BB gun, an eight-inch folding knife, a two-pound hammer, and sixty-nine orange pills of an indeterminate sort. Equipment she loaded onto herself included a set of astronaut diapers so that she would not need to lose time making unnecessary stops during the nine-hundred-mile overnight drive. She also had with her a floppy disk containing images of an unidentified woman in different states of undress engaged in various acts of bondage.

Nowak made it to the airport about an hour ahead of Shipman, lurked around in the baggage claim area in a disguise until her rival's flight came in from Houston and she collected her luggage, and then followed her out to the parking lot. Shipman noticed someone following and then running up to her, so

Equipment she loaded onto herself included a set of astronaut **diapers.**

she locked herself in her car, upon which Nowak successively slapped the window, attempted to open the car door, asked for a ride, and began crying. And, when the younger woman rolled down the window a little to speak with her stalker, Nowak fired pepper spray at her, prompting her to drive off.

The parking lot attendant called the police, and when they arrived, they observed Nowak stuffing some of her equipment into a trashcan. They arrested her, initially charging her with battery, attempted kidnapping, attempted vehicle burglary with battery, and destruction of evidence—and, soon after, attempted first-degree murder with a deadly weapon.

It ultimately took more than two-and-a-half years' worth of motions, hearings, medical and psychiatric evaluations, postponements, appeals, announcements of insanity defenses, findings of police misconduct, setting of trial dates, and ultimately a plea deal to bring the case to its conclusion. NASA, however, moved quickly to distance itself from the scandal, and in early March 2007 the agency terminated Nowak's assignment to the astronaut corps. Nowak and her husband separated around the same time and were subsequently divorced (while Oefelein and Shipman, after being discharged from their respective services, were married).

Nowak **lurked around** *in the baggage claim area in a* **disguise.**

On November 10, 2009, Nowak finally agreed to a plea deal with prosecutors and pled guilty to charges of felony burglary of a car and misdemeanor battery, for which a judge sentenced her to one year of probation and the two days she had already served in jail.

Naval officials had waited for Nowak's kidnapping case to be resolved before taking action of their own and had assigned her to Naval Air Station Corpus Christi, Texas, where was tasked with helping to develop training materials. In August 2010, a panel of three U.S. Navy admirals recommended that Nowak be discharged from the service and that her rank be reduced from captain to commander. As of this writing, Nowak was still on active duty, and the Secretary of the Navy was considering whether or not to accept the panel's recommendation.

12

The Love of Money . . .

IT IS TRULY SAID THAT LOVE OF MONEY
is the root of all evil, and this unbecoming
fondness has tainted the reputations of innumerable politicians the world over, Texas included.
Some of the Lone Star politicos whose greed has
gotten the better of them follow (with their Democratic or Republican party affiliations provided
in parentheses).

Albert Garza Bustamante (D) was convicted in

1993 on two counts of accepting bribes and racketeering and was sentenced to forty-two months in prison, of which he served nearly three years, followed by a stint in a halfway house.

In 1992, investigators began looking into allegations that the eight-year Texas congressman—and former Bexar County Commissioner and Judge—had taken a bribe from a food-service company that was seeking to have a contract renewed with the Air Force (San Antonio, Bustamante's home town, is also home to a number of major Air Force bases). Bustamante was also investigated for receiving a no-risk loan as a bribe as part of a deal involving a San Antonio television station.

Bustamante claimed that he was targeted by the FBI for having helped three Hispanic agents sue the bureau for discrimination and that it then harassed him and his family in a multi-million-dollar investigation that went on for several years. He is, in any event, widely believed to have lost his bid for reelection in 1992 because of what the probe into his activities revealed. His supporters subsequently blamed redistricting and a media conspiracy orchestrated by his opponent, rather than the criminal convictions and prison sentence, for Bustamante's failure to retain his office. It is just as well either way, as he would have had trouble performing his official duties from a prison cell.

Bustamante was also one of the congressmen involved in the 1992 House Banking Scandal (described below).

Ronald D. Coleman (D) was one of more than 450

congressmen involved in what became known variously in early 1992 as the House Banking Scandal, Congressional Check-Kiting Scandal, or Rubbergate, in which members were allowed to overdraw their accounts at the House bank without penalty. Just about everyone was doing it, but *USA Today* identified Coleman as one of the worst twenty-two, having written 673 checks without sufficient funds to cover them over a twenty-three-month period, causing his account to be overdrawn by a staggering $275,848. The seven-term congressman from Texas served from 1983 to 1997, and his involvement in the scandal has been credited with his decision not to seek reelection thereafter.

Tom DeLay (R), styled by some as "the Boss Tweed of the Republican Party" and "the Meanest Man in Congress" and best known to many as the stiff old white guy who staggered around a few episodes on season nine of *Dancing with the Stars,* represented various Texas congressional districts from 1985 to 2006.

In 2005, DeLay resigned as House Majority Leader, a post he had held for two years, because of a campaign finance investigation that led to criminal charges of money laundering being leveled against him. In 2010, he was finally convicted on those charges and sentenced to three years in prison (but, as of this writing, is free on bail pending the results of his appeal).

The high-profile case that finally ended his congressional career notwithstanding, it was not the only one of DeLay's financial improprieties.

. . . Best known to many as the stiff old white guy who staggered around a few episodes of *Dancing with the Stars.*

In 2004, the House Committee on Ethics admonished De-Lay for improperly supporting a personal interest in the way he voted on the Medicare Prescription Drug Act of 2003. The same year, DeLay was alleged to have solicited and received campaign contributions in return for legislative assistance, improperly used official resources for political purposes, and used corporate political contributions in violation of state law.

Going back to 1997, DeLay is alleged to have improperly linked official actions to contributions made to his campaign and to have bestowed favors upon his brother, a registered lobbyist. After sending a private letter to DeLay advising him against creating the impression that he was willing to grant political access in exchange for campaign contributions, however, the House Committee on Ethics dismissed the complaint.

John V. Dowdy (D), a congressman from the 7th District of Texas from 1953 to 1967 and then from the 2nd District of Texas until 1973, was accused of accepting a bribe of $25,000 to intervene in the federal investigation into a Maryland construction company. In 1971, while he was still serving as a member of the House of Representatives, Dowdy was convicted on two counts of conspiracy, one count of transporting a bribe over state lines, and five counts of perjury. In response to his conviction, the House passed a resolution stating that members convicted of serious crimes should voluntarily refrain from voting. Dowdy did not thereafter seek reelection.

In 1973, after he had retired from Congress, the U.S. Court of Appeals for the Fourth Circuit in Richmond, Virginia, overturned Dowdy's bribery and conspiracy convictions. His convictions for perjury stood, however, and he served time in prison for them.

A number of right-wing political groups and publications agitated on Dowdy's behalf, claiming that he had been framed as part of a "vicious" conspiracy between the U.S. Department of

Justice and "a clique of housing racketeers" who wanted to derail the congressman's subcommittee investigation into fraud at the U.S. Department of Housing and Urban Development. Nothing, however, came of these ructions.

Martin Frost (D), notable as the highest-ranking Jewish member of Congress up to the point that he served, represented the voters of Texas's 24th District, located in the Dallas area, from 1979 to 2005. In 1994, he was alleged to have both improperly used his congressional staff for redistricting work and shaken them down for campaign contributions. The House Committee on Ethics found him guilty of technical violations of campaign regulations, and Frost agreed to appropriate reimbursement.

Charles "Charlie" Wilson (D), one of the most famous of all Texas congressmen and the hero of a film about his personal war against the Soviet Union, was in 1993 alleged to have made improper use of campaign funds and given inadequate financial disclosures. Wilson admitted error in the face of these complaints, which were dismissed after his campaign paid a $90,000 fine to the Federal Election Commission.

(Wilson is only briefly mentioned here but is the subject of his own chapter in this section as a result of his love for whisky, cocaine, and hookers and his staunch support of the Taliban.)

James C. Wright Jr. (D), a Texas congressman who served thirty-four years in the House of Representatives and as Speaker of the House from 1987 to 1989, was investigated toward the end of his tenure by the House Committee on Ethics. In a report it released in 1989, the committee charged that Wright had used bulk purchases of his book, *Reflections of a Public Man,* as a device for earning speaking fees in excess of the allowed maximum. It also contended that Wright's wife, Betty, was given

a job and other benefits in order to avoid the limit on gifts to elected officials.

Wright was also alleged to have had an improper relationship with a constituent with whom he shared an interest in a gas well, intervened on a matter before the Department of the Interior on behalf of a Texas petroleum company, made improper use of a condominium in Fort Worth, and exerted undue influence with officials of the Federal Home Loan Bank Board on behalf of four Texas businessmen.

Tainted by these allegations, Wright was increasingly ineffective as a political leader and, in June of 1989—ahead of any punishment Congress might have imposed on him, resigned first as Speaker of the House and then as a congressman.

Republican Newt Gingrich had filed the original charges against Wright and used the subsequent investigation into the activities of the senior legislator as a springboard for his own career. The acrimony caused by the incident and the cynical way Republicans like Gingrich used it intensified the partisan infighting on Capitol Hill that has persisted to this day.

13

Friday Night Lies

THROUGHOUT THE 2009–2010 SCHOOL year, all eyes in Odessa, Texas, were on a young man everyone knew as sophomore Jerry Joseph, a standout player on the Permian High School basketball team and a recent illegal immigrant from Haiti. (If Odessa Permian sounds familiar, it is probably because of the fame it has gained as the venue for the television show *Friday Night Lights,* which focuses on the school's football program.)

Joseph's personal fame was enhanced when he was featured in a local news story that broke after the devastating earthquakes that struck his homeland in January 2010.

On Tuesday, May 11, however, Ector County Independent School District Police and U.S. Immigration and Customs Enforcement arrested Joseph and revealed that he was instead Guerdwich Montimere, a twenty-two-year-old naturalized citizen who had been passing himself off as a minor for more than a year and was seven years older than many of his classmates.

"A twenty-two-year-old being in our schools is very much a concern," said ECISD Police Lt. Mark Rowden. "That's why this has been an ongoing investigation, that's why we have not dropped it, that's why we were not going to let go until we had found the truth."

Montimere had, in fact, graduated from Dillard High School in Fort Lauderdale, Florida, three years earlier in 2007, a fact revealed by the Fort Lauderdale *Sun-Sentinel* newspaper a week before his arrest. He had, naturally, played basketball there as well.

Rather than sign up for some college classes or do anything else a normal person might expect,

Rumors started to circulate in late April that Montimere might have been older than he was saying and not who he was claiming to be. When authorities looked into them, ICE discovered that he had used fake documents and an assumed name to get into the school system.

Montimere relocated to Odessa in February of 2009 and moved into the dorms at the University of Texas of the Permian Basin with a friend, who at the time he claimed was his half-brother. Rather than sign up for some college classes or do anything else a normal person might expect, the twenty-one-year-old instead went to Nimitz Junior High School, presented a Haitian birth certificate that indicated he was just fifteen, and enrolled as a freshman.

A little kid that looks and plays basketball like a full-grown man is a rare asset to be sure. When Montimere's friend left Texas in the summer of 2009, Permian High School boys' basketball coach, Danny Wright, let the young phenom move in with him. A judge made it official when he granted guardianship of Joseph to his coach.

The sweet deal soured on Tuesday, April 27, when school administrators received an anonymous email message that revealed Joseph/Montimere's true identity and supported its contentions with photographs of him from Florida. "Joseph" denied having ever heard of Montimere, and pending their investigation, law enforcement officials were bound to treat him as who he said he was.

Who he really was was revealed by a fingerprint match with his original immigration papers, which directly contradicted the fake papers he had provided to the school district and led to his arrest. Montimere admitted to the deception at that point.

the twenty-one-year-old instead went to Nimitz Junior High School.

Since the scandal broke, embarrassed school district officials have been adamant that they acted appropriately and had no choice under state law but to allow him to enroll when presented with authentic-looking documents.

"ECISD followed all legal requirements in keeping Joseph enrolled in school until his true identity was confirmed. . . . denying enrollment to children who are illegal aliens is against the law . . . [and] a student shall not be denied enrollment solely because they fail to provide proof of identity or education records from a previous school," the school district said in a statement. "Nimitz and Permian followed policy and procedures in enrolling and educating this student."

Once he was verifiably outed, Montimere was initially charged with presenting false identification to a peace officer and that would be bad enough. Unfortunately, it seems the ersatz high-schooler was hitting more than the basketball court and that he had been availing himself of the benefits of jockdom and been dating at least one under-aged girl. Add statutory rape to his rap sheet.

Even worse—at least from the point of view of the Permian fans!—every game Montimere is forfeiting, the minimum penalty for fielding an over-aged player.

"The next question is what repercussions will be felt by the PHS basketball team," the school district said in a statement. "The boys went 16–13 this season, including a loss in the bi-district round of the playoffs. ECISD athletic officials have stayed in touch with University Interscholastic League officials throughout this episode . . ."

Montimere has pleaded "not guilty" to three counts of tampering with government documents, one count of identity theft, and two counts of sexual assault, and, as of this writing, is awaiting trial in Ector County.

MURDER

in the

Lone
Star
State

1

The Border Reivers

AUTHOR CORMAC MCCARTHY IS certainly best known for those novels of his that have been adapted to the big screen, among them *No Country for Old Men*, *All the Pretty Horses*, and *The Road*. His masterpiece, however, and perhaps one of the greatest American novels of the twentieth century, is *Blood Meridian* and, like many of his other stories, is set along the lawless and dangerous border separating Texas and Mexico. Subtitled *The Evening Redness in the West*, this book is a fictionalized account of the historic Glanton Gang, a bloodthirsty

The bloody Glanton Gang fought its last battle on the banks of the Gila River in 1850.

Originally contracted to help curtail the problem with marauding bands of warlike Apache, the Glanton Gang eventually applied its scalp-taking to peaceful agricultural Indians and Mexican peasants.

pack of scalp-hunters that terrorized the border region in the late 1840s and served as a mercenary unit tasked with exterminating local Indians.

Early on in the history of the Republic of Texas, John Joel Glanton had acquired a reputation as a scoundrel and a murderer. Born in South Carolina in 1819, his family worked their way southwest, and, according to some accounts, he was a teenaged outlaw in Tennessee before their arrival in Texas.

By 1835, Glanton was living with his parents in Gonzales, Texas—about seventy-five miles east of San Antonio—and was engaged to be married to an orphan girl with whom he had fallen in love. Their plans for a happy future were dashed, however, when she was abducted, tomahawked to death, and scalped by raiding Lipan Apaches, an incident that would color the remainder of Glanton's short, dark, and bloody life.

On October 2 of that year, Glanton became involved in the Texas Revolution and, in the course of it, narrowly escaped being one of the victims of the infamous Goliad Massacre. He apparently committed some crimes of his own during the conflict, because President Sam Houston was reputed to have banished Glanton from Texas (although this pronouncement, if it was ever actually made, does not seem to have been very effective).

After the revolution, Glanton served for a time as part of the Texas Ranger company that protected San Antonio and, for a decade starting in 1839, participated in a number of wars, paramilitary operations, and feuds throughout Texas. During this time he gained a reputation as a scalawag and a murderer, in one case killing an unarmed civilian and stealing his horse and in another shooting a comrade.

In 1849, Glanton obtained a contract from the government of the Mexican state of Chihuahua to kill hostile Apaches—taking their scalps as proof, each redeemable for the substantial sum of $50—and assembled for these purposes the gang of ruffians that would bear his name.

According to Samuel Chamberlain, a U.S. Army deserter who signed on with Glanton's gang and years later published an account of his activities in it, the gang consisted of "Sonorans, Cherokee and Delaware Indians, French Canadians, Texans, Irishmen, a Negro, and a full-blooded Comanche" and numbered about three dozen strong. This rogues' gallery included the notorious Judge Holden, a diabolical character who had numerous atrocities attributed to him before and during his tenure with the Glanton Gang, to include the brutal rape and murder of a ten-year-old Mexican girl.

Initially, the Glanton Gang's mercenary scalping venture was quite profitable, but by 1850 the pool of hostile Indians in the vicinity of Chihuahua had largely been depleted. In no way dissuaded by this, the gang proceeded to start killing peaceful Indian farmers and Mexican peasants and turning their scalps in for bounties. The local government was not fooled by this brutal ruse for long, however, and they responded by placing a bounty on Glanton's scalp.

Driven from their old hunting ground, Glanton and his gang fled into the neighboring Mexican state of Sonora, where they promptly struck a deal with the government there to suppress hostile Indians in the area. And, as they had before, the gang supplemented their income by murdering and scalping the local inhabitants and descended to outright banditry, sacking villages, abducting and raping women and girls they found attractive and killing (and, naturally, scalping) those they did not. They even disguised themselves as Indians for some of their depredations.

Glanton's gang generated a lot of enmity, and in the course of these activities had to flee superior numbers a number of times and began to suffer casualties, as many as twenty in one particularly desperate battle with a large group of Apaches.

In early 1850, the remnants of the gang moved northward and, in early summer, captured a ferry crossing on the Gila River, not far from its junction with the Colorado River in what is now Arizona, and drove off the Yuma Indians that operated it (except for the women that they opted to keep). From this base of operations, they profited from running the ferry, periodically murdered and robbed travelers, extorted the local peasantry for supplies and killed a number of them, and began to build a stone fort.

This lucrative concession, however, did not last long. The Yumas retaliated, attacking the gang and killing most of them. A handful of the reivers managed to escape but Glanton himself was slain in the melee—and his scalp taken for the substantial bounty that had been placed on it.

2

The Nueces Massacre

BEGINNING IN THE 1840S, THOUSANDS of German immigrants left their homeland for Texas, fleeing repressive government and limited economic opportunities and seeking to make a new life for themselves and their families. Many of them settled in or near the Hill Country, founding such towns as New Braunfels, Fredericksburg, and Comfort.

When Texas began contemplating seceding from the Union in 1860, on the eve of what would become the U.S. Civil War, a majority of the German immigrants were opposed to this for any number of reasons. Most were adamantly loyal to their new country and many—being intellectuals, liberals, and people who benefited from the fruits of their own labors—were also opposed to the institution of slavery.

A number of the Hill Country counties in which many of the Germans lived, including Bexar, Gillespie, Kendall, Kerr, and Medina, voted against secession, and the Confederate government of Texas responded by placing the area under martial law.

The Treue Der Union *monument in Comfort, Texas, bears the names of the German settlers massacred by Confederate troops along the banks of the Nueces and Rio Grande Rivers.*

Treüe der Union

AFTER THE CONCLUSION OF THE CIVIL WAR, THE remains of many of the Germans killed on the banks of the Nueces and Rio Grande Rivers were relocated to the town of Comfort, where a monument to them was erected. It was dedicated on August 10, 1866, on the four-year anniversary of the Nueces Massacre and is inscribed with the words *Treüe der Union*—"Loyalty to the Union." It is the only German-language monument to the Union in the South where the remains of those killed in battle are buried and one of only a half-dozen burial sites where a U.S flag—an 1866 version with thirty-six stars—flies at half-staff in perpetuity.

Revisionist histories about the universal desire of Southerners to do battle with the Yankee oppressors notwithstanding, the Confederacy could not induce nearly enough men to take up arms in its cause—slave-owners generally being exempt from doing so—and its states had to institute drafts early on in the conflict. When Texas followed suit in the spring of 1862, its German citizens were among those who objected.

Seeking to avoid being conscripted into fighting for a cause they were morally opposed to, some Germans fled across the border to Mexico. In early August 1862, a group of more than sixty German Texans from the Hill Country, many from around the town of Comfort, left their families behind and headed for Mexico under the leadership of a Major Fritz Tegener. A number of them were members of a civil defense organization called the Union League, which had been organized to protect against Indian raids and Confederate depredations.

By August 9, the Germans had covered about 150 miles and were encamped on the west bank of the Nueces River, in Kinney County, about thirty miles from the border with Mexico. In the early morning darkness of August 10, however, a unit of ninety-four Confederate cavalrymen, under a Lt. C.D. McRae, attacked their camp, which was not well guarded or established in a strong defensive position. Caught off guard, some thirty-four of the Germans were killed and nine of them badly wounded in the ensuing skirmish; two of the Rebel troopers were killed and eighteen of them wounded, among them McRae. In the aftermath of the battle, the Confederate troops gathered up the nine wounded German prisoners and then executed them.

Some two dozen of the Germans managed to escape during the battle. About half of them managed to make it back home; eight were killed two months later on the banks of the Rio Grande River while once again trying to cross into Mexico; and a handful ended up for a time in Mexico, California, or Union-held New Orleans. And if any of them had any doubts about their aversion to the Southern cause, these had been thoroughly dispelled.

3

The Way of the Gun

OVER THE YEARS, INNUMERABLE GUNMEN and hoodlums have prowled the lonely roads and trails of the Lone Star State, preying upon those unfortunate enough to cross their paths and eventually enjoying similar fates themselves. Some of the most notorious have included outlaws John "King" Fisher, John Wesley Hardin, and the duo of Clyde Barrow and Bonnie Parker.

During the early 1930s, Bonnie Parker and Clyde Barrow became famous for their rampages throughout Texas and several other states, robbing banks, gas stations, and corner stores, and needlessly killing any number of people.

John "King" Fisher

During his brief and violent three decades on earth, John "King" Fisher wore the hats of rancher, lawman, and outlaw—sometimes all at once. He started his criminal career at the age of just fifteen with horse stealing and burglary and served four months in prison for the latter. Upon his release he established a ranch in the lawless and dangerous Nueces Strip of southwest Texas, where he became an accomplished gunman and the leader of a gang of hoodlums. Fisher carved out a livelihood based largely on cattle rustling, banditry, murder, and raids into Mexico. He cut a flamboyant figure, wearing an embroidered black Mexican jacket and hat and a scarlet sash, and bearing a pair of ivory-handled, silver-plated revolvers.

Fisher's illicit activities caused him to fall afoul of the Texas Rangers—especially the notorious Special Force led by Capt. Leander McNelly, which was eventually prompted to raid his bandit redoubt. He was also charged with murder, attempted murder, and a number of other crimes but managed to avoid being convicted for them.

Fisher was pretty burned out by his early twenties and, in 1876, abandoned the Nueces Strip, marrying and buying a new spread near Eagle Pass. Five years later he was even made deputy sheriff of Uvalde County and, in 1883, the acting sheriff.

Law enforcement might very well have turned out to be a good career for Fisher, but his violent past caught up with him in early 1884, during a trip to San Antonio. On the night of March 11, Fisher and his friend Ben Thompson went to the Vaudeville Variety Theater, where they were ambushed by some rivals in an elaborate battle that included the exchange of gunfire between theater boxes. Fisher and Thompson were both slain in the skirmish, and Fisher's career as a gunman was brought violently to an end.

John Wesley Hardin

John Wesley Hardin was one of the most violent and dangerous outlaws of the latter half of the nineteenth century in Texas, with a career that started at just age fourteen when he stabbed another boy in a schoolyard squabble. Not long afterward he shot a man in an argument, and over the ensuing year reportedly gunned down four of the U.S. Army soldiers seeking to arrest him.

Hardin worked as a cowboy for awhile in the early 1870s but that did not make him any less violent. He is believed to have shot to death at least ten people in 1871 alone. Upon his return to Reconstruction-era Texas he continued to work as a cowboy and rancher but joined the anti-government faction of the bloody Sutton-Taylor Feud of 1873–74 and killed a former captain of the Texas State Police (q.v.) named Jack Helm. He killed a number of other people during this period as well, including Brown County Deputy Sheriff Charles Webb.

After those murders, Hardin was a marked man in Texas, and after killing another half-dozen-or-so people, he took his family and fled to Florida. Texas Rangers caught up with him there, however, and captured him in Pensacola in July 1877. Upon his return to Texas, he was convicted of murdering Webb and sentenced to twenty-five years in prison. He studied law while in prison and, in 1894, was pardoned and admitted to the bar.

Hardin moved to El Paso and established a law practice there but was unable to go straight. After having an affair with the wife of one of his clients, he hired some rogue law enforcement officers to kill the man. He was slow to pay his contract killers, however, and one of them proceeded to gun down forty-two-year-old Hardin at a local saloon. Some thirty people or more who crossed him preceded him to the grave.

Bonnie and Clyde

During the early 1930s, Bonnie Parker and Clyde Barrow became famous for their rampages throughout Texas and several other states, robbing banks, gas stations, and corner stores, and needlessly killing any number of people. When they started shooting police officers, however—at least nine before they were done—a number of Texas lawmen took it upon themselves to track down and exterminate the murderous pair.

Beginning in February 1932, Bonnie and Clyde, often in conjunction with other criminal associates, committed more than a hundred felonies during a violent twenty-six-month spree that took them mainly across Texas but briefly into other areas as well. During this time, they had several close encounters with law enforcement personnel but managed to escape from them largely unscathed, although a number of their associates and police officers were killed.

In January 1934, Barrow coordinated a raid on the Eastham prison unit near the town of Crockett, freeing several of his associates and, in the process, embarrassing the Texas Department of Criminal Justice. The gang went double or nothing three months later in April, when they gunned down two highway patrol officers near Grapevine, an act that marked them for death and placed a short number on their days.

On May 23, 1934, a team of six law enforcement officers, four of them from Texas and two from Louisiana, ambushed Bonnie and Clyde while they were driving down a country road in Bienville Parish, Louisiana, about sixty miles east of the Texas state line.

"Each of us six officers had a shotgun and an automatic rifle and pistols. We opened fire with the automatic rifles. They were emptied before the car got even with us. Then we used shotguns," recalled Dallas County Deputy Sheriff Ted Hinton. "There was smoke coming from the car, and it looked like it was on fire. After shooting the shotguns, we emptied the pistols at the car, which had passed us and ran into a ditch about fifty yards on down the road. It almost turned over. We kept shooting at the car even after it stopped. We weren't taking any chances."

When the shooting stopped, twenty-five-year-old Clyde Barrow and twenty-three-year-old Bonnie Parker were dead, and then some, and their criminal careers were brought to an end.

4

The Death of
Ambrose Bierce

ON OCTOBER 2, 1913, WITH THE
border region between Mexico and the United
States engulfed in violence sparked by the Mexican Revolution, seventy-one-year-old Ambrose
Bierce departed his home in Washington, D.C.,
for the last time.

Everything in Bierce's prolific career, demeanor, and final correspondence suggest that he never intended to return from his final trip.

Despite suffering from declining health, the luminary author and journalist's stated goal was to make a tour of the Civil War battlefields on which he had fought a full five decades earlier and to then continue on into northern Mexico. There, Bierce said, he intended to cover the ongoing hostilities and attempt to obtain an interview with revolutionary leader Francisco "Pancho" Villa.

If he had lived a century and a half later he might have been a **Goth**.

Over a three-month period, Bierce worked his way southwestward, down to Tennessee and the killing ground at Shiloh, and then on through Louisiana and Texas. In November, he crossed the border at El Paso into Mexico. There, in Ciudad Juárez—today the most dangerous city in North America—Bierce joined Pancho Villa's army as an observer and in that capacity watched the November 23–24 Battle of Tierra Blanca, which the revolutionary forces won. A month later he was in the Mexican city of Chihuahua planning his next move.

"I leave here tomorrow for an unknown destination," he wrote to a close friend in his final letter, sent on December 26, 1913, from Chihuahua. And then he disappeared without a trace, consolidating his mark on literary history by becoming the subject of one of the most famous disappearances in America.

Legends in the state of Coahuila, Mexico, assert that Bierce was executed by a government firing squad in the town of Sierra Mojada and buried in an unmarked grave in the cemetery there. There is no firm evidence for this, however, nor for a number of other theories on the subject, including ones that assert the morose author had killed himself.

Many have, in any event, interpreted Bierce's final trip as being part of an ultimate death wish or attempt to commit suicide, and everything in Bierce's prolific career, demeanor, and final correspondence would suggest that this might indeed have been the case.

Often characterized as a misanthrope, Bierce was certainly a nihilist in the tradition of Solomon, his motto being "Nothing matters," and was broadly known as "Bitter Bierce." He was of a type with Edgar Allan Poe, who had preceded him by a generation, the major differences being that he was considerably more worldly and his works markedly grittier. If he had lived a century and a half later he might have been a Goth, and Goths who read literature would certainly be likely to respond to the works of Bierce.

The satirical author's worldview was the product of his grim and terrifying experiences during the Civil War, which he fought in as a member of the North's 9th Indiana Volunteer Infantry Regiment.

"War was the making of Bierce as a man and a writer," wrote biographer Richard O'Conner, who noted that from the author's grim experience he became "truly capable of transferring the bloody, headless bodies and boar-eaten corpses of the battlefield onto paper."

Bierce enlisted in 1861 and that year fought with his unit in western Virginia, participated in the Battle of Philippi, and fought bravely—rescuing a wounded companion while under fire—during the Battle of Rich Mountain. He was commissioned as a first lieutenant in February 1862 and, two months later, fought at the Battle of Shiloh. A little more than two years later, in June 1864, he was shot in the head by a Confederate sniper during the Battle of Kennesaw Mountain in Georgia and had to spend three months convalescing before returning to duty in the fall of that year. Four months later, in January 1865, he was discharged from the military.

Bierce settled in San Francisco after the war and drew upon his wartime experiences to establish himself as one of the most significant American editorialists, fabulists, journalists, and authors of his day. As a reporter for various newspapers and a veritable agent for publisher William Randolph Hearst, Bierce exposed corruption at the highest levels of government and became famous for such works as the short story "An Occurrence at Owl Creek Bridge" and the satirical lexicon "The Devil's Dictionary."

By the time Bierce embarked on his final journey to the West, he had been long divorced from his wife of many years, both his sons had predeceased him, and it was clear that his tenure on Earth was coming to an end. And, death being inevitable anyway, it is certainly possible that the macabre author would have relished the mystery that surrounded his end. Likewise, whether or not he would have expected his modern-day colleagues in the Fourth Estate to keep digging for the truth of what happened to him is an open question—but that is what happened.

In his 2010 book *Nothing Happened and Then It Did,* writer Jake Silverstein postulates a theory for Bierce's demise that could put this persistent mystery to rest. In early 2000, Silverstein was working as a reporter for the *Big Bend Sentinel* in Marfa, Texas, when he stumbled across a letter to the editor from a decade earlier that appeared to shed light upon the mystery and which thereafter prompted him to investigate it himself.

"Neither [Pancho] Villa nor his men had any involvement in the disappearance of Ambrose Bierce," the writer of this letter asserts. "Bierce died on the night of January 17, 1914, and was buried in a common grave in Marfa the following morning, in a cemetery then located southwest of the old Blackwell School and across from the Shafter road."

According to the writer, a California man named Abelardo Sanchez who had grown up in Marfa, in 1957 he had picked up an aging hitchhiker named Agapito Montoya who claimed to

Revolutionary leader Pancho Villa led the forces that Ambrose Bierce joined and followed through war-torn Mexico in late 1913 and early 1914.

One theory of Ambrose Bierce's death postulates that
he was buried in the west Texas town of Marfa.

have fought as a Mexican federal soldier during the revolution. After Villa routed the army he was part of during the Battle of Ojinaga in January 1914, he and three companions were making their way through the deep desert toward the village of Cuchillo Parado when they encountered an old American man.

This old gringo was very sick, apparently from a cold, and was trying to fix a broken wheel on his horse cart so that he could find the rebel army that Montoya and the other soldiers were trying to get away from. After camping together, the old American man changed his plans and the next morning offered to pay the soldiers to escort him across the U.S. border to Marfa, which they agreed to do.

"During the trip they heard of different books he had written, including one that my narrator recalled with the word 'devil' in its title," Sanchez continued in his letter. "He said his name in Spanish was Ambrocio. ... On the second day after crossing the Rio Grande they were captured by elements of the 3rd Cavalry, who were rounding up stragglers who had crossed the border. Bierce by this time had pneumonia and could hardly speak . . ."

By this time the old man was enfeebled and had lost his voice and neither he nor the federal soldiers could convince the U.S. Army cavalry troopers that he was indeed an American. Accordingly, they placed him in a wagon filled with dead and dying Mexicans, and he himself died soon after and was buried in a common grave in Marfa.

Silverstein was unable to locate the grave in question or to prove beyond a shadow of a doubt that the old gringo who breathed his last in Marfa in early 1914 was, indeed, Ambrose Bierce, but he was convinced that he was. It seems likely that this is the case—and, if so, then it appears that Bierce met his end not through the malice of Mexican soldiers but through the indifference of American ones.

5

Texas Ser-y'all Killers

TEXAS HAS CERTAINLY NOT BEEN immune from the brutal scourge of serial killers and has been home to some of the worst that have thus far been caught anywhere in the country. Some of the most prominent killers and their escapades are described on the following pages.

There are also a number of convicted serial killers who were born or lived in Texas for a time—including Judy Buenoano, Paul Durousseau, and Patrick Wayne Kearney—but who committed their crimes and were held accountable in other states, and are thus not included here. And, in addition to the ones listed here, there are many others who have killed multiple victims in the Lone Star State but are still not in the same league as those presented here—and innumerable others who have not yet or never will be caught.

One especially chilling thing to consider with most of these murderers is that the known lists of their victims is certainly not complete and likely should include more—sometimes many more—victims. Most also were never prosecuted, due to lack of evidence, even for murders law enforcement officials were confident they had committed.

Charles Frederick Albright
(Born August 10, 1933; "the Dallas Ripper," "the Dallas Slasher," "the Eyeball Killer")

Born in Amarillo, Texas, Charles Frederick Albright was raised by adoptive parents that included a strict and overprotective schoolteacher mother who drove him to graduate from high school by the age of fifteen. He was even more of a prodigy than she would have preferred, however, and launched his criminal career at age thirteen with thefts and an aggravated assault.

For the next four decades, Albright led a life marked by theft, forgery, fraud, and child molestation, serving a year in jail for one charge, six months for another, and probation for the rest. He attempted to live a seemingly normal life, creating false credentials in order to obtain work as a teacher; he also got married and raised a daughter, but he and his wife separated in 1965 and were divorced in 1974.

He married again in 1985 and, while being supported by his wife, took an early-morning paper route so that he would be out at opportune times to surreptitiously begin seeing prostitutes—and, eventually, killing them.

On December 13, 1990, the body of thirty-three-year-old prostitute Mary Lou Pratt was found lying face up in the Oak Cliff neighborhood of Dallas. She was wearing only a T-shirt that had been pulled up to display her breasts, had been shot in the back of the head with a .44-caliber bullet, and her eyes had been neatly removed.

Two months later, on February 10, 1991, prostitute Susan Peterson was discovered just south of Dallas, also wearing nothing but a pulled-up T-shirt, mangled by gunshot wounds to the top of her head, back of her head, and left breast, and with both of her eyes removed.

A month later, on March 18, 1991, prostitute Shirley Williams was found naked near a school, with facial bruising, a broken nose, gunshot wounds to her head and face, and both her eyes removed.

Four days later, police arrested Albright and charged him with those murders and nine others. His trial began on December 13, 1991, and, five days later, he was convicted on a combination of circumstantial and forensic evidence and was given eight life sentences. He is currently confined in the Texas Department of Criminal Justice's Bill Clements unit in Amarillo.

Joseph D. "Joe" Ball
(January 7, 1896–September 23, 1938; "the Alligator Man," "the Butcher of Elmendorf," "the Bluebeard of South Texas")

A boogeyman of Texas folklore, Joe Ball was a World War I combat veteran and bootlegger who, after Prohibition, opened a watering hole called the Sociable Inn in Elmendorf, Texas, just southeast of San Antonio. Beside it he built a pond where he kept five alligators, charging people to see them, especially during feeding times, when he threw them live dogs and cats.

Animals were not the only things he was feeding his reptilian pets, however, and from 1936 to 1938 he is believed to have killed more than twenty women and disposed of the remains of most of them in his pond. His apparent victims included his barmaids, former girlfriends, and even his wife.

On September 23, 1938, two Bexar County Sheriff's deputies went to Ball's bar to question him, and when they arrived, he pulled a pistol out of his cash register and fatally shot himself. Had he been tried and convicted, he almost certainly would have been executed in the electric chair.

Clifford Wheeler, a handyman who had been Ball's accomplice in some of his crimes, was arrested and led authorities to the bodies of two women, Hazel Brown and Minnie Gotthard, whom he had helped murder. Wheeler claimed that Ball had killed at least twenty other women and fed their bodies to his alligators.

Carroll Edward "Eddie" Cole
(May 9, 1938–December 6, 1985)

Born in Sioux City, Iowa, Carroll Edward Cole was as a child frequently beaten and terrorized by his mother, who forced him to watch while she engaged in sex acts with various men while his father was away fighting during World War II. He was also

Cole committed his **first murder** at **age ten** by drowning a classmate in a lake.

picked on by other children for having "a girl's name" and, in spite of having a high IQ, did poorly in school.

Cole committed his first murder at age ten by drowning a classmate in a lake, something that was thought to have been an accident until he admitted to it many years later. After finishing school, he drifted around, doing menial work, drinking heavily, and committing crimes that included arson, burglary, car theft, and vagrancy. He sporadically spent brief periods of time in jails, prisons, and mental hospitals, and in the latter institutions described fantasies about killing women and was diagnosed as a psychopath.

From 1971 to 1980, Cole killed numerous women in California, Texas, and Nevada, typically strangling them to death and dumping or hiding their bodies. On at least one occasion he drove around for a time with a corpse in the trunk of his car and periodically ate parts of his victims.

When Nevada authorities arrested him in late 1980 he confessed to killing at least fourteen women but said that, because he was usually drunk when he committed his murders, there may have been more. He refused to appeal his death sentence and was given a lethal injection on December 6, 1985.

Dean Arnold Corll
(December 24, 1939–August 8, 1973; "the Candy Man")

Dean Arnold Corll was a weak, sickly, introverted child with a strict father and an overprotective mother whose family moved from the Midwest to Pasadena, Texas, southeast of Houston, in 1950. Three years later, after divorcing, his mother remarried and took him to the little town of Vidor, Texas, and in 1958 they moved to Houston and opened a candy store. Corll lived in an apartment above the store and, before long, started making sexual advances on male employees.

Corll served ten months in the Army and, after receiving an honorable hardship discharge, returned to help run the candy company. Soon after, the company relocated to a spot across the street from an elementary school, and Corll began handing out candy to children—especially teenaged boys. In 1967, he befriended twelve-year-old David Owen Brooks.

The Corll Candy Company went out of business in June 1968, and Corll started working as an electrician at the Houston Lighting and Power Company. It was while employed there that he began his career as a killer.

From 1970 to 1973, Corll is known to have murdered at least twenty-seven people, all males between the ages of thirteen and twenty, and all but four were snatched in the Houston Heights neighborhood, a low-income area at the northwest end of Houston. After a point he was helped by one or both of his two younger accomplices—David Owen Brooks (whom he also subdued and repeatedly assaulted on one occasion) and Elmer Wayne Henley (whom Brooks procured as a victim but whom Corll subsequently recruited). He paid them $200 for each vic-

Corll began handing out candy to children—especially teenaged boys.

tim they procured. Several of the victims were friends of one of these partners, two were former employees of the candy company, and others were random victims, including hitchhikers. During this period, Corll frequently changed addresses in or around the Houston Heights area.

After abducting and subduing their victims, Corll and his helpers would typically torture and sexually assault them for up to a couple of days before executing them by strangulation or with a .22 caliber handgun. Then, after wrapping their bodies in plastic sheeting, they were disposed of in a variety of locations, including some woods near Corll's cabin on Lake Sam Rayburn, a beach in Jefferson County, a rented boatshed, and a beach on the Bolivar Peninsula. Corll sometimes forced his victims to write or call their parents to explain why they were missing.

In 1973, Corll moved back to Pasadena. Everything collapsed on August 8, 1973, when the seventeen-year-old Henley brought a victim to Corll's home—accompanied by a fifteen-year-old girl. Corll subdued and then threatened to kill them all but eventually freed Henley after he offered to help. At some point in the torture and sexual assault that followed, however, Henley got hold of the gun and shot Corll several times, in the head, shoulder, and lower back, killing him.

Henley called the police and confessed everything to them, although they did not initially believe him; he was ultimately convicted of six murders and, in June 1979, was sentenced to six consecutive ninety-nine-year terms. Brooks turned himself into the police and admitted knowing about some of Corll's activities but denied having anything to do with them; he was charged with one murder and received a life sentence. As of this writing, both are still in prison, Brooks at the Ramsey unit in Rosharon, Texas, and Henley at the Michael unit in Tennessee Colony, Texas.

At the time that they were revealed, what became known as the "Houston Mass Murders" were the worst case of serial killing in U.S. history. Police called off the investigation after finding twenty-seven bodies—despite claims from Henley that there were at least two more. Some forty-two boys and young men had disappeared in the Houston area since 1970, and there was evidence that Corll might have started his killing even earlier than this and may have been part of a larger slave ring catering to pedophiles.

Genene Anne Jones
(Born July 13, 1950)

From 1971 through the early 1980s, pediatric nurse Genene Anne Jones worked at what was at that time the Bexar County Hospital and is today the University Hospital of San Antonio. During this time, hospital administrators noticed that a statistically improbable number of the children she worked with in the pediatric intensive care unit were dying. Rather than investigate the strange situation, the administration simply allowed Jones to resign her position.

Jones promptly moved on to a job with a pediatric clinic in Kerrville, about sixty miles northwest of San Antonio, and took her aura of death with her. In 1984, the doctor who ran the clinic eventually discovered that Jones had been illicitly removing from a secure storage area drugs that caused symptoms similar to those suffered by some of the children under her care. He reported these findings to the authorities, and Jones was charged with murdering six children who had been treated at the clinic.

In 1985, Jones was sentenced to ninety-nine years in prison for killing one fifteen-month-old child and to a concurrent sixty-year term for killing another one. Because of a law designed to cope with prison overcrowding that was in place at the time of her conviction, however, she will serve only a third of her sentence.

Jones's motive seems to have been to create medical crises in which she could intervene in order to receive attention and admiration, but these attempts led to many fatalities; she also claimed to have been trying to draw attention to the need for an intensive care pediatric unit in Kerrville. It is believed that she killed at least eleven and perhaps as many as fifty children. Officials at the hospital she had worked at in San Antonio, however, apparently first lost and then destroyed records of her activities in order to avoid being targeted by lawsuits from grieving parents.

Jones is currently confined at the Carol Young Complex in Dickinson, Texas, and will automatically be paroled in 2017—if she is not released sooner by a parole board (but has been denied six times as of this writing).

Paul John Knowles
(April 17, 1946–November 18, 1974; "the Casanova Killer," "Lester Daryl Gates," "Daryl Golden")

From July 26 through November 17, 1974, John Paul Knowles killed at least eighteen people during a cross-country spree that took him through Texas. Knowles claimed to have actually killed nearly twice as many people as authorities were able to tie him to.

A product of foster homes and reformatories from an early age, Knowles had his first criminal conviction at age nineteen and thereafter was in and out of prison. In 1974, the twenty-eight-year-old Knowles was out on parole and seeking to marry a woman he had corresponded with while incarcerated. When she rejected him, Knowles went on a murderous, four-month rampage, killing people in Florida, Ohio, Nevada, Texas, Alabama, Virginia, and Georgia. Most of his victims were women or girls, many of whom he raped, strangled, and robbed.

On September 21, near Seguin, Texas, northeast of San Antonio, Knowles encountered a woman named Charlynn Hicks whose motorcycle had broken down. Knowles raped her, strangled her to death, and then dragged her body through some barbed wire.

Knowles was eventually caught and sent back to Florida. He attempted to escape while in custody, and the sheriff he was with shot him three times, killing him.

Henry Lee Lucas

(August 23, 1936 –March 13, 2001;
"the Confession Killer")

Convicted of eleven murders, evil redneck Henry Lee Lucas at one point claimed to have killed around six hundred people and was considered to be America's most prolific serial killer. He eventually recanted them, however, claiming that he was coerced by police.

The youngest of nine children, Lucas was raised in a one-room log cabin in Blacksburg, Virginia, by a pair of alcoholic parents. His prostitute mother was especially degenerate, dressing him as a girl, forcing him to watch while she had sex with various men, killing his pets, and once beating him into unconsciousness with a plank. At age ten, he lost his left eye in a fight with his brother and had it replaced with a glass one.

In 1950, shortly after his father froze to death in a snow drift while drunk, the thirteen-year-old Lucas dropped out of the sixth grade, ran away from home, and began his career as a drifter and criminal, engaging early on in theft, burglary, and bestiality. He also claimed to have committed his first murder, of a seventeen-year-old girl, in 1951 but later recanted this and it is unclear if it is true. In 1954, he was convicted in Richmond, Virginia, of more than a dozen burglaries and spent five years in prison.

In late 1959, Lucas went to live with his half-sister in Michigan. When his mother came to visit for Christmas, she objected to his plans to marry a woman he had corresponded with while in prison and insisted he come back to Virginia to care for her in her old age.

"All I remember was slapping her alongside the neck, but after I did that I saw her fall and decided to grab her," Lucas said of what transpired during their argument. "But she fell to the floor, and when I went back to pick her up, I realized she was dead. Then I noticed that I had my knife in my hand and she had been cut."

He was convicted of second-degree murder and given a sentence of twenty to forty years in a Michigan prison, but was released in 1970, after serving just ten years, because of overcrowding.

Lucas began drifting around the South and, in 1976 while in Florida, fell in with like-minded Ottis Toole and his twelve-year-old niece, juvenile delinquent Frieda "Becky" Powell, and had a sexual relationship with both of them. In 1978, the three of them began travelling around the state murdering what may have been hundreds of people.

Lucas and his accomplices eventually left Florida and ultimately ended up in Stoneburg, Texas, where they lived for a time at a religious commune. Ultimately, Lucas apparently killed Becky, and, once she was out of the picture, the two men once

He confessed to have been part of a cannibalistic Satanic cult, to

again went on the road and began killing people.

On June 11, 1983, Texas Ranger Phil Ryan arrested Lucas for unlawful possession of a firearm, and he was thereafter charged with killing both Becky and an eighty-two-year-old woman. Lucas confessed to the murders but later said the police had abused, isolated, and denied him counsel and that he had been coerced into making the statements he did. Despite this and dodgy forensic evidence, Lucas was nonetheless convicted of both murders and, during the trial, surprised the court by claiming to have "killed about a hundred more women."

Police and the media alike seized upon this claim, and before long Lucas was being flown around the country, in the custody of Texas Rangers, to meet with law enforcement officials who wanted to close out some of their unsolved murders.

By November 1983, Lucas was being held at the jail in Williamson County, Texas, and it was here that the controversial Lucas Task Force was formed with an eye to closing as many unsolved murders as possible in the state. This task force, which included Texas Rangers and county sheriffs, officially closed 213 open murder investigations based on Lucas's confessions. How many of these he was actually responsible for is unclear—the only thing for certain was that various members of the task force fed Lucas information that allowed him to make credible confessions about crimes he otherwise knew nothing about. Lucas later said that he went along with this because of the preferential treatment it gained him; he ultimately confessed, among other things, to have been part of a cannibalistic Satanic cult, to

have participated in **snuff films,** *and to have killed Jimmy Hoffa.*

have participated in snuff films, and to have killed Jimmy Hoffa, and there were many contradictions and inconsistencies in his claims.

Doubts about the veracity of his confessions kept Lucas from being charged with most of what he had admitted to, and some of the detectives who dealt with him began trying to trip him up. And in 1986 the Texas Attorney General's office issued a report that characterized the activities of the Lucas Task Force as a "hoax" perpetrated by law enforcement officials wanting to clear cases off their books.

Lucas was eventually tried for and convicted of eleven murders and sentenced to death for one of them, an unidentified woman that the attorney general said was almost certainly not actually killed by Lucas. There was, in fact, evidence that Lucas was in Florida at the time the woman was killed in Texas.

In 1998, then-Governor George W. Bush asked the Texas Board of Pardon and Parole to commute Lucas's death sentence to life imprisonment, and it complied—making it the only successful commutation of a death sentence in Texas since states were allowed to reinstate the death penalty in 1976.

On March 13, 2001, Lucas died in prison of heart failure. With his death went the certainty of whether he had killed three, three hundred, or some other number of people altogether.

Kenneth Allen McDuff

(March 21, 1946–November 17, 1998; "the Broomstick Murderer," "the Broomstick Killer")

A native of the central Texas town of Rosebud, Kenneth Allen McDuff had acquired a reputation as a violent thug even as a boy and was convicted on a dozen counts of burglary and attempted burglary in 1964. Despite receiving twelve four-year prison terms, he was paroled the following year and, although reincarcerated soon afterward for fighting, was soon let loose again.

On the evening of the first Saturday in August 1966, McDuff and his friend Roy Dale Green bought a six-pack of beer and drove to Fort Worth to visit a friend. Around 10 p.m. that night, the pair abducted eighteen-year-old Robert Brand, his sixteen-year-old girlfriend, Edna Louise Sullivan, and his sixteen-year-old cousin, Mark Dunman, who had been sitting in their car at a baseball field, forcing them at gunpoint into the trunk of their car. McDuff then drove off in the victims' car with Green following in his own.

Upon reaching an isolated area, McDuff and Green transferred the girl to their car and then shot the two young men. At a third area the pair raped Sullivan multiple times, after which McDuff choked her to death with a three-foot length of broomstick.

Green later claimed he had participated in the atrocities under duress, and he turned himself into the police. He received twenty-five years in prison for his role in the crimes, and McDuff received three death sentences. It came out at this point that McDuff had bragged to Green that he had previously raped and killed two other young women.

That should have been the end of the story, especially as McDuff was actually sent to the electric chair twice during his time on death row, getting last-minute reprieves in both cases. That bought him the time that he needed. In those days, a life sentence in Texas meant that someone had to serve just ten years before being eligible for parole, and in October 1989 the state parole board set him free. Within three days he had murdered again, this time a thirty-one-year-old woman in Waco, and even before he was linked to the killing had been returned to prison for making death threats against a young man in Rosebud.

In December 1990, Texas once again set him free. This is when he really got busy, launching a career as a drug dealer and armed robber and by October 1991 killing again, the first of ten victims he would murder over the six-month period that followed. Most of them were prostitutes or other vulnerable women whom he abducted, raped, and tortured before killing, in some cases with the aid of an accomplice.

McDuff kept one step ahead of law enforcement by committing his crimes in several different counties and by eventually relocating to Kansas City. It was while living there under an assumed name, however, that a coworker recognized him on the television show *America's Most Wanted* and reported him to the police. On May 4, 1992, the Kansas City Police arrested McDuff and sent him back to Texas.

McDuff was tried on one charge of capital murder and, on February 18, 1993, was once again sentenced to death. He sat on death row more than five years, filing appeals, writs of habeas corpus, and writs of certiorari to the U.S. Supreme Court, temporarily delaying his execution. Eventually, however, all avenues were closed to him, and on November 17, 1998, he was put to death by lethal injection.

McDuff did leave a legacy beyond the grief that he caused by his actions. In 1992, after he was arrested for murder a second time, Texas initiated sweeping reforms throughout its prison system to keep violent felons from receiving early parole. These measures, along with enhanced monitoring of violent parolees and expansion of prison facilities, are referred to collectively as the McDuff Laws.

The Phantom Killer
("the Texarkana Phantom," "the Phantom," "the Phantom Slayer," "the Moonlight Murderer")

Not all of the Lone Star State's serial killers have been caught or even identified. Like evil spirits, some have appeared, conducted their business for a time, and then disappeared for reasons unknown. For a period in 1946, Texarkana truly was the "town that dreaded sundown," as a mysterious hooded menace that became known as the Phantom Killer stalked and murdered several people over a three-and-half month period.

From late February until early May 1946, Texarkana's only known serial killer attacked a number of people in what became somewhat incongruously known as the Texarkana Moonlight Murders (i.e., none of them actually took place on moonlit nights).

Around midnight on February 22, the Phantom attacked twenty-four-year-old Jimmy Hollis and nineteen-year-old Mary Jeanne Larey, who were parked together on a street in Richmond, Arkansas, about twenty miles north of Texarkana. The Phantom pistol-whipped Hollis, fracturing his skull multiple times, and then sexually assaulted Larey with his firearm, but was scared off when he saw approaching headlights, allowing both his victims to survive. They were the only people ever able to provide a description of the killer, albeit it a sketchy one: He was six feet tall, wore a hood with holes cut out for his eyes and mouth, and was either a heavily tanned white man or a light-skinned black man.

On the night of March 23, twenty-nine-year-old Richard Griffin and his girlfriend, seventeen-year-old Polly Ann Moore, were slain by the Phantom Killer on a rural road outside of Texarkana. Both were shot in the back of the head with a .32 caliber handgun, and a blood-drenched patch of ground about twenty feet away implied that they had been executed outside of Griffin's vehicle and then placed back in it afterwards.

In the early morning hours of Sunday, April 14, the Phantom Killer murdered yet another couple, fifteen-year-old Betty Jo Booker and sixteen-year-old Paul Martin. Both had been shot multiple times and were found in separate locations some distance from where Martin's car was parked at Spring Lake Park, where they had apparently been abducted by the killer.

On May 3, a person believed to be the Phantom Killer shifted from parked cars to homes and attacked a farmhouse about ten miles outside of Texarkana in Arkansas. Standing outside of the house, the killer fired into it with a .22 caliber pistol, killing thirty-six-year-old Virgil Starks and severely wounding his thirty-five-year-old wife, Katy Starks. She managed to escape and make it to a neighbor's house, but by the time police arrived, the Phantom had managed to search the house and then disappear.

"Sex Maniac Hunted in Murders" was the headline slapped across the front of the *Texarkana Gazette* two days later, on May 5. That same day, the body of a man identified as Earl McSpadden was found on some train tracks north of Texarkana. Initially, there was some speculation that it was the Phantom Killer and that he had killed himself, but a few days later the coroner's report indicated the man had been stabbed to death before being dumped on the tracks. This led many to believe that he was yet one more victim of the Phantom Killer.

This unprecedented wave of violence had, in any event, terrified the citizens of Texarkana, and many responded by buying firearms, refusing to go out at night, and barricading themselves in their homes. Police began patrolling isolated streets and places frequented by couples looking for places to park together.

"This killer is the luckiest person I have ever known," Bowie County Sheriff Bill Presley said. "No one sees him, hears him in time, or can identify him in any way."

Police had one primary suspect in the case, a local ruffian named Euell Swinney, whose wife told them that the twenty-nine-year-old burglar, counterfeiter, and car thief was the Phantom Killer and that she had been with him when he had committed the murders. Police arrested Swinney on suspicion of the murders in July 1946, but his wife kept changing her story and could not provide authorities with what they needed to pursue a murder case against him. He was nonetheless convicted of car theft in 1947 and, as a repeat offender, was sentenced to life in prison. In 1973, however, his life sentence was overturned on appeal, and he was released and lived until 1994.

To this day, the case of the Phantom Killer has not been solved. Interestingly, a number of people subsequently noticed profound similarities between the Phantom Killer of 1940s Texarkana and the Zodiac Killer of 1960s and '70s San Francisco, so it is possible that this is a story that began in Texas but didn't end there.

Angel Maturino Reséndiz

(August 1, 1959–June 27, 2006; "the Railway Killer,"
"the Railroad Killer")

For twelve years, from 1986 to 1998, murderous Mexican hobo Angel Maturino Reséndiz illicitly rode the rails throughout Mexico, the United States, and Canada, killing at least thirty people in the course of his travels. He evaded law enforcement by living as an undocumented person, constantly moving around, and using dozens of aliases. For a short time he held a spot on the FBI's list of Ten Most Wanted Fugitives.

Most of Reséndiz's victims lived within striking distance of the railway lines that he traveled around on and were typically killed in their homes, although several were homeless people. He committed about half of his murders with blunt objects that included rocks, bricks, hammers, and statuettes and the rest with firearms, pickaxes, or other weapons. He raped a number of his female victims before killing them. After murdering his victims, Reséndiz would generally cover them up and then spend time in their homes, eating, perusing their effects, and stealing personal items and jewelry, much of which he gave to his wife in Mexico, who sold or melted it down. Cash, however, he often opted not to take. Many of his murders were committed in Texas, but some were also apparently committed in Florida, California, and Kentucky, and he admitted to killing at least seven people in Mexico.

Once authorities figured out who he was, they contacted Reséndiz's sister and convinced her to help them. She reluctantly agreed, and on July 13, 1999, accompanied by Texas Ranger Drew Carter, met with Reséndiz at an international crossing between El Paso, Texas, and Ciudad Juárez, Chihuahua, where the killer surrendered (albeit under the impression that he would be spared the death penalty by doing so).

Reséndiz was charged, tried, and sentenced to death for one murder. Despite actually being or simply portraying himself to be severely mentally ill and delusional, a Houston judge ruled that he was mentally competent to be put to death. He was housed at the Polunsky Unit in West Livingston, Texas, while awaiting death and, on June 27, 2006, was executed by lethal injection.

Tommy Lynn Sells
(Born June 28, 1964; "the Cross-Country Killer")

A native of Missouri, drifter Tommy Lynn Sells is believed to have committed his first murder in 1980, when he was just sixteen. Over the ensuing nineteen years he is believed to have killed numerous other people, perhaps as many as seventy, including a number of women and children—some of whom he sexually assaulted—and one entire family. He is believed to have committed many of these murders in Texas but possibly others in Missouri, New York, Illinois, and Kentucky.

On December 31, 1999, near Del Rio, Texas, Sells fatally stabbed a thirteen-year-old girl sixteen times and slit the throat of a ten-year-old girl. The younger victim survived, however, and helped provide a sketch that led to Sells' arrest.

Sells was convicted of capital murder, along with numerous other crimes, and as of this writing is on death row at the Allan B. Polunsky Unit near Livingston, Texas.

Carl Eugene "Coral" Watts
(November 7, 1953–September 21, 2007; "the Sunday Morning Slasher")

Carl Eugene Watts dispels the myth that there is no such thing as a black serial killer. Between 1974 and 1982, he is known to have killed a dozen women and believed to have possibly killed as many as hundred.

Watts was born in Killeen, Texas, while his soldier father was stationed at nearby Fort Hood. His parents separated when he was just two, however, and his mother moved to Michigan and in 1962 remarried. He was apparently an odd child and, possibly because of a bout of meningitis, was thought to have been mildly

Watts—in spite of being a **weird, retarded, sexual predator** *with poor grades—was given a football scholarship.*

mentally retarded; he did badly in school, where he was badly bullied. By the age of twelve he had begun to fantasize about torturing and murdering women and girls. By fifteen he is believed to have had slain his first victim and, in June 1969, was arrested for sexually assaulting a twenty-six-year-old woman and confined in a Detroit mental institution until November of that year.

Watts graduated from high school in 1973 and—in spite of being a weird, retarded, sexual predator with poor grades—was given a football scholarship to Lane College in Jackson, Tennessee. After just three months, however, he was expelled because of allegations that he had killed one woman and stalked and assaulted others. However, there was not enough evidence to convict him, and he was simply sent on his way and moved to Houston.

In 1974, at the age of twenty, Watts began his career as a serial killer. Most of his victims were young white women between the ages of fourteen and forty-four, and he typically abducted them from their homes and then tortured and killed them, typically bludgeoning, drowning, stabbing, or strangling them to death. Like many serial killers who evade detection for a long time, Watts committed his crimes in many jurisdictions and even different states, and because he did not generally sexually assault them and thereby leave behind biological evidence.

In May 1982, Watts was arrested for trying to kill two young women after breaking into their home in Houston. Authorities soon after linked him to several murders but, concerned that they did not have enough evidence to convict him, offered him immunity in exchange for providing information about his killings and pleading guilty to a charge of burglary with intent to murder. He accepted the offer, which came with a sixty-year sentence, and gave detailed confessions to twelve murders he had committed in Texas. He later claimed to have killed between forty and eighty women but would not provide sufficient details to link him to them. To this day he is still considered a suspect in as many as ninety unsolved murders.

An unforeseen legal technicality of the sort that has let more than one murderer walk free in Texas made Watts eligible for early parole, and he could have been released in May 2006. Authorities in Michigan, however, believed Watts to be responsible for the killings of at least ten girls and women in their state, but had not previously had enough evidence to successfully convict him. In 2004, however, prosecutors there pushed hard to pull together a case against him, and toward the end of that year he was convicted of one murder and was sentenced to life in prison. They subsequently charged him with a second murder, and he was convicted of it and sentenced to life in prison without the possibility of parole.

His life did not, however, last much longer. On September 21, 2007, fifty-three-year-old Carl Eugene Watts died from prostate cancer in a Michigan hospital.

6

The Ivory Tower of Death

ON TUESDAY, SEPTEMBER 28, 2010, nineteen-year-old sophomore Colton Tooley briefly ran amok across the University of Texas main campus in Austin, firing shots from an AK-47 assault rifle before retreating to the sixth floor of a school library and fatally shooting himself. The campus went into lockdown, and so many law enforcement personnel with bulletproof vests, automatic weapons, and armored vehicles responded to the scene that some students thought the Texas National Guard had been called out.

In August 1966, gunman Charles Whitman blockaded himself on the twenty-seventh floor of the UT Tower in Austin and began firing at people on the streets and campus below.

Before school shootings became a familiar—and, apparently, sometimes anticlimactic—occurrence, however, Charles Joseph Whitman set a gold standard for carnage on the UT campus in Austin that was not beaten anywhere in America for more than four decades. On August 1, 1966, twenty-five-year-old Whitman, a former Marine and an architectural engineering student at the university, launched a bloody rampage that left eighteen people dead and forty-two wounded by the time it was over.

Exactly what caused Whitman to snap when and in the way he did is not entirely clear, but it probably had a lot to do with the brain tumor that was discovered in the autopsy following his death. Severe headaches, amphetamine abuse, and a dysfunctional family life probably all played their role as well. Whitman's father had been a demanding, authoritarian perfectionist who was known to be both physically and emotionally abusive to the members of his family. The situation escalated in early 1966 when Whitman's mother left his father and, with Whitman's assistance, relocated from their home in Fort Worth, Florida, to Austin, Texas (a move that prompted his father to begin calling him several times a week to implore him to convince his mother to return to Florida). The dissolution of the family and the strains associated with it was, in fact, the primary subject of a discussion Whitman had with a psychiatrist six months before his attacks.

Whitman was also troubled by a number of failings that were indicative of emotional instability. These included receiving a court martial in 1962 for gambling, threatening another Marine, and keeping a personal firearm on base; loss of a scholarship to the University of Texas in 1963 for butchering a deer in his dorm room; and striking his wife, Kathy, on a number of occasions. It also bears mentioning, however, that Whitman had become an Eagle Scout at the almost-unheard-of age of twelve, scored highly on IQ tests, and was honorably discharged from the Marine Corps after a relatively uneventful enlistment.

By the summer of 1966, Whitman had hopped through at least four jobs since being discharged from the Marine Corps twenty months earlier, had visited five doctors and a psychiatrist over the previous year, and was doing poorly in school. He had reached his breaking point.

Shortly after midnight on August 1, Whitman went to his mother's house in Austin and killed her with a hunting knife he had bought just the day before (along with binoculars and some Spam). He then returned to his own home and stabbed his wife three times in the heart with the same weapon.

"I imagine it appears that I brutally killed both of my loved ones," he wrote in a note right afterwards. "I was only trying to do a quick thorough job ... If my life insurance policy is valid please pay off my debts ... donate the rest anonymously to a mental health foundation. Maybe research can prevent further tragedies of this type."

"I imagine it appears that I brutally killed both of my loved ones . . . I was only trying to do a *quick* thorough *job.*"

"I talked with a Doctor once for about two hours and tried to convey to him my fears that I felt [some] overwhelming violent impulses," Whitman continued later in the note. "After one visit, I never saw the Doctor again, and since then have been fighting my mental turmoil alone, and seemingly to no avail."

M-968150	SUPPLEMENTARY OFFENSE REPORT	APD 1-1-64-11

1. OFFENSE NO.
2. OFFENSE REPORTED
MURDER
3. CLASSIFICATION AFTER INVESTIGATION
4. ORIGINALLY CLASSIFIED AS
5. VICTIM'S NAME
OFF. BILLY SPEED
6. VICTIM'S ADDRESS
APD
7. DATE REPORTED
8-1-66
8. NARRATIVE:

Page 4.

GUNS FOUND AROUND BODY:

1. Remington Model 700 - 6MM, Bolt action #149037, with Leupold four power - M8-4X scope, cheek stock (serial #61384) and leather strap.

2. Sears 12 gauge 2-3/4 chamber automatic shotgun, barrel and stock, both sawed off

3. Remington 35 caliber model 141 pump #1859 rifle

4. U. S. Carbine 30 caliber M-1 Universal #69799 with Webb sling.

5. 357 Mag Smith and Weston 4½ barrel, chrome, Model 19 #K391583

6. 9MM Luger #2010

7. 6.35 MM Caliber Automatic pistol- Galesi-brescia #366869

One of the five pages from a police inventory listing the weapons and equipment Charles Whitman hauled into the UT Tower.

9. STATUS (CHECK ONE)   UNFOUNDED   CLEARED BY CITATION   10. FURTHER POLICE ACTION AND REPORT
CLEARED BY ARREST   EXCEPT. CLEARED   NOT CLEARED   REQUIRED: YES   NO

Report Made by Off.Ligon/313/crm/547   Time 5:00 P.M. Date 8-1-66   Indexed.
Approved by *Merleufeld 178*   Time 3:00 P.M. Date 8-2-66   Bulletin.
Austin 252 Franz 196   Time 3:00 P.M. Date 8-2-66   Recorded.
Moody 108
Cleared by: Arrest   Unfounded   Inactive   Excep. Cleared

Whitman then proceeded to load his service footlocker and a wooden crate with a sawed-off shotgun, a bolt-action hunting rifle equipped with a scope, an M-1 carbine, and a .35 caliber pump rifle; twelve boxes of ammunition and numerous clips, magazines, and loose rounds; and various other pieces of equipment,

In the end, Charles Whitman suffered the same fate as his victims and was gunned down in a hail of shotgun and pistol fire.

including food, camping gear, a machete, three knives, and a hatchet. On his person he carried three pistols, including a .357 magnum revolver, a 9mm automatic, and a 6.35mm automatic. Whitman had been fascinated with firearms since childhood and had been trained to use them by his father, and his experience as a hunter and a Marine had helped him to master his skills with them.

Transporting his arsenal on a handcart he had rented for the purpose, Whitman went to the UT campus, about three miles from his home, and proceeded to the university's tower, where he took the elevator to the twenty-seventh floor and then painstakingly hauled it by hand up the stairs to the observation deck. And then all hell broke loose.

Whitman started by butt-stroking the receptionist on duty with one of his rifles, knocking her unconscious (and causing her to die a week later). He then barricaded the stairway and, when a group of people tried to get past it, fired into them with his shotgun, killing two and severely injuring two more.

At that point, at 11:48 a.m., Whitman began firing with his sniper rifle at people on and around the campus below. Even people who heard the gunfire did not understand what was going on and several students were shot dead before anyone even called the police.

Once the situation was understood, every on-duty police officer in the city was dispatched to the campus, where they were joined by off-duty officers, troopers from the Texas Department of Public Safety, deputies from the Travis County Sheriff's Office, and a number of armed civilians. This armed assemblage began firing up at Whitman's position.

Impeded by the fire from below, Whitman was forced to take cover and to use the waterspouts at each corner of the tower as gun ports, severely limiting both his visibility and opportunity for targets.

As the firefight continued, the authorities called in a spotter plane with a sniper of their own, and it began circling the tower while the rifleman on board traded shots with Whitman. Turbulence made it difficult for the airborne police officer to get a good shot at the killer, and return fire from the tower struck the aircraft, driving it back to a safe distance, where it continued to circle until the incident was resolved.

Three police officers and a civilian stormed the tower and made it onto the observation deck, where they caught Whitman by surprise and engaged him at close quarters. One officer fired six shots from his .38 revolver at Whitman and another discharged his shotgun at him twice, killing him. Almost inexplicably, the other officer then grabbed the shotgun from his companion, rushed up to Whitman, and shot him again.

Ninety-six minutes after it began, the shooting spree was brought to an end. On the campus mall and Guadalupe Street below, dozens of people lay dead, dying, or injured.

Whitman's bloody campus attack was the worst in U.S. history up to that point, and was not eclipsed until April 2007, when a student at the Virginia Tech campus in Blacksburg, Virginia, killed thirty-two people and wounded twenty-five. Nine years after the UT campus attack, in 1975, it was commemorated in an NBC made-for-TV movie called *The Deadly Tower*, in which Kurt Russell played the deranged Whitman.

7

The Texas Chainsaw Massacre

FROM THE MOMENT IT HIT THE BIG
screens in 1974, *The Texas Chainsaw Massacre*
became the archetype for the slasher film and
supplanted *The Exorcist,* released the previous
year, as one of the most terrifying movies ever
made. It also quickly gained a reputation for
having been based on an actual incident that
had occurred somewhere in Texas.

There were certainly a number of factors that contributed to this impression. Director Tobe Hooper himself was a resident of Austin, Texas, where he had worked as a documentary cameraman and professor in the years prior to the filming of *The Texas Chainsaw Massacre,* so it seemed credible that he had based his seminal work on some real event that he had learned of.

The gritty, low-budget, documentary style of the film, its cast of unknowns, and its filming locations in rural Texas rather than stage sets or some recognizable back lot in California all reinforced the idea that there really had been—or was—a clan of cannibalistic degenerates murdering people along the back roads of the Lone Star State. *The Texas Chainsaw Massacre* was, in fact, filmed in an old farmhouse in Round Rock, about twenty miles north of Austin, on a site that is now part of the La Frontera "multi-use commercial business-retail-housing center." (In 1993, the Victorian-style farmhouse was disassembled and transported to Kingsland, Texas, where it was restored and turned into The Junction House, a restaurant affiliated with the Antlers Hotel and the town's historic railroad district.)

And, by all accounts, the idea that *The Texas Chainsaw Massacre* was based on a real series of gruesome murders was used as a device for marketing the film.

"This video cassette is based on a true incident and is definitely not for the squeamish or the nervous," the description on the original video release of the film reads. "The film is an account of a tragedy which befell a group of five youths, in particular Sally Hardesty. For them an idyllic summer afternoon drive became a nightmare when they were exposed to an insane and macabre family of chainsaw killers. One by one they disappear to be brutally butchered, each murder more horrendous than the last, with one victim being hung live on a meat hook, another trapped in his wheelchair as he is hacked to death, and the surviving member of the group making a frantic bid for escape in the horrific climax."

The idea of the story's veracity has been reinforced to one extent or another in the various sequels to *The Texas Chainsaw Massacre* and especially in the 2003 remake of the original film, which was explicitly touted as being based on fact. In the decades since the release of the film, however, Hooper and other people affiliated with it have come clean and acknowledged that there were several degrees of separation between the bloody movie franchise and whatever truth it might have been based on.

Actor Gunnar Hansen played the horrifying character Leatherface in The Texas Chainsaw Massacre.

"I was in the Montgomery Ward's out in Capital Plaza [Shopping Center in Austin]," Hooper told the *Austin Chronicle* newspaper in an interview in 2000. "I had been working on this other story for some months—about isolation, the woods, the darkness, and the unknown. It was around holiday season, and I found myself in the Ward's hardware department, and I was still kind of percolating on this idea of isolation and such. And those big crowds have always gotten to me. There were just so many people to go through. And I was just standing there in front of an upright display of chainsaws. And the focus just raced from my eyeball to the people to the saws—and the idea popped. I said, 'Ooh, I know how I could get out of this place fast—if I just start one of these things up and make that sound.' Of course I didn't. That was just a fantasy." Hooper also acknowledged early on to his collaborators in the film that the psychotic killer Leatherface and his family were inspired at least in part by serial killer Ed Gein. Gein was a Wisconsin farmer who in the 1950s killed at least two women and dismembered their corpses, robbed graves, made a wide variety of objects from body parts—including masks, clothing, bags, bowls, chairs, drums, jewelry, and lampshades—and is believed to have engaged in cannibalism and necrophilia. (Gein was also the inspiration for Norman Bates in *Psycho*.)

"But that's all," said Gunnar Hansen, the actor who played the chainsaw-swinging Leatherface. "The story itself is entirely made up. So, sorry folks. There never was a massacre in Texas on which this was based. No chainsaw either. And, in spite of those of you who have told me you remember when it happened, it really didn't happen. Really. Believe me. This is an interesting phenomenon. I've also had people tell me that they knew the original Leatherface, that they had been guards at the state prison in Huntsville, Texas, where he was a prisoner. Maybe they knew somebody who dreamed of being Leatherface. It is, I suppose, something to aspire to."

8

The Crime of the Century

ON MAY 29, 1979, HIT MAN CHARLES Voyde Harrelson made history when he killed U.S. District Judge John H. Wood Jr. in San Antonio, committing the first assassination of a federal judge in the twentieth century. What most people find at least as interesting, however, is that he was the estranged father of actor Woody Harrelson, who lost track of him for thirteen years, until he heard about his conviction in 1981. From that point onward, the actor visited his imprisoned father often until his death in 2007.

Throughout the '60s, the elder Harrelson made his way as an encyclopedia salesman, professional gambler, and armed robber. Then, in 1968, when his son Woody was seven, Harrelson abandoned his wife and three sons in Houston and moved up to drug trafficking and contract killing.

Harrelson "was handsome, in a rugged way, and enormously self-sufficient—an old-fashioned charmer who still opened doors for women and was quick to light their cigarettes," writes journalist Gary Cartwright in his book *Dirty Dealing*. "He dressed well and in expensive clothes, was almost obsessively neat, even meticulous, drank expensive Scotch and fine wine, and read a variety of books." He also had a taste for cocaine and women, marrying four times and having innumerable girlfriends.

In 1971, Harrelson was tried for the 1968 killing of grain dealer Sam Degelia Jr. in the border town of McAllen, Texas, apparently as part of a deal to cover the cost of a bundle of heroin he had lost a month earlier in Kansas City. The case ended in a mistrial, but two years later he was tried again, found guilty, and sentenced to fifteen years in prison. In keeping with the general Texas policy toward violent felons, however, he was released from prison just five years later, in September 1978.

Harrelson got back to work right away. Eight months after his early release, he accepted a commission to kill sixty-three-year-old Judge John H. Wood Jr., gunning him down in the parking area behind his San Antonio townhouse on May 29, 1979. Harrelson's client was Jamiel "Jimmie" Chagra, a major El Paso drug dealer whose family had been targeted by the overzealous federal judge who had become widely known as "Maximum John" because of the heavy sentences he imposed for drug charges.

Wood was descended from a prominent Lone Star State family whose lineage went back to the Texas Revolution. Except for a break when he served in the Navy during World War II, Wood was a lawyer with a key San Antonio law firm from 1938

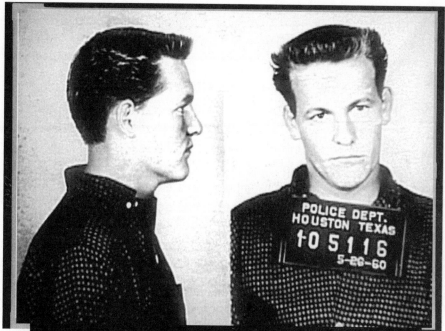

Contract killer Charles Harrelson is known to have murdered at least three people and probably killed many others as well.

until 1970, when President Richard M. Nixon appointed him to a seat in El Paso for the District Court for the Western District of Texas.

Wood was, by all accounts, a genuine son-of-a-bitch and often opined that he handed down the heaviest sentences he could—often decades-long—for drug-related charges because of his concern that freed defendants might end up getting killed. He also had a limited understanding of the law and made a practice not just of overtly siding with the prosecutors but also attacking, undermining, and humiliating defense attorneys. He maintained a heavy docket of cases, running roughshod over procedure and putting people away on even minor charges as quickly as

The Three Tramps

IN THE MINUTES AFTER PRESIDENT JOHN F. KENNEDY was killed in Dallas on November 22, 1963, police arrested a dozen or so people around Dealey Plaza. Three of them were a trio of men found hiding in a boxcar in the rail yard a few blocks west of the infamous "grassy knoll." These mysterious rail jumpers were cleaned up and relatively well dressed at the time, leading conspiracy theorists to speculate about some role they might have played in the assassination. The "tall tramp" has, in any event, been identified by some people as contract killer Charles Harrelson. Harrelson himself alternately denied and admitted to these suggestions, sometimes even bragging about his activities that day (and alluding to killing many other people over the years). Like so many of the things associated with the Kennedy assassination and the many conspiracy theories surrounding it, the truth may never be revealed. What is certain is that when a drug-addled Harrelson was arrested on suspicion of killing Judge John H. Wood Jr., he also confessed to murdering Kennedy.

he could, frequently noting that he could sentence people faster than the appeals process could free them based on errors that occurred in his courtroom. On top of everything else, he was also widely regarded as a racist.

Jimmy Chagra's brother, El Paso lawyer Lee Chagra, was one of the attorneys who had appeared before Wood any number of times defending clients charged with drug crimes, and essentially had his practice destroyed because of allegations the judge had made about him in court. He had been killed five months earlier

As if murdering a federal judge were not enough, contract killer Charles Harrelson also confessed to assassinating President John F. Kennedy and may have been one of the "Three Tramps" discovered hiding in a boxcar not far from the kill site.

in a drug-related robbery of his office. Jimmy's youngest brother, Joe, also practiced law in El Paso.

The investigation into Wood's murder—widely dubbed "the crime of the century"—was one of the longest, most detailed, and most expensive in the history of the United States and prompted U.S. marshals to provide indefinite security details for federal prosecutors and judges throughout Texas. Police eventually caught Harrelson through an anonymous tip and a taped conversation between Jimmy and Joe Chagra when the latter came to visit his drug-dealing brother in prison, and the assassin was ultimately convicted in large part because of this recording.

Harrelson himself was given two life sentences, and Joe Chagra received ten years for his role in planning the murder. Jimmy

Chagra was acquitted of his masterminding of the killing when his brother refused to testify against him and he made a plea deal admitting to his role in both it and the attempted assassination of U.S. Attorney James Kerr in San Antonio.

Harrelson was initially sent to the federal prison in Atlanta but, after he attempted to escape from it, was sent to ADX Florence, a supermax prison in Colorado. He succumbed to coronary artery disease in March 2007. But during his time in prison, his son Woody had unsuccessfully strived to have his father's conviction overturned so that he could be retried.

9

The Women of Death Row

OF THE 337 PEOPLE CURRENTLY ON death row in Texas, a mere ten of them are women, and just three of the 463 convicted killers that the state of Texas has executed since it reinstated the death penalty in 1982 have been women. They are no ladies, however, and are among the worst criminal offenders to have been caught and tried in the state. Pending their full range of appeals, no date has yet been set for any of their executions.

Their dates of birth are listed in parentheses, followed by a synopsis of their heinous crimes. While a few were career criminals, most did not have any prior convictions and were surprisingly young when they committed the crimes that landed them on death row. Most were also high school graduates but had no college education.

Suzanne Basso
(May 15, 1954; white; no prior prison record)

On August 26, 1998, Basso and five accomplices kidnapped a retarded fifty-nine-year-old man named Louis Musso and deliberately beat him to death with baseball bats, belts, steel-toed boots, hands, and their feet in a series of sessions at a suburban Houston home. Basso was the leader of the group and encouraged all the other members to torture Musso, whom she had promised to marry and had named her as the beneficiary of his insurance policy and his heir to other assets. Basso had lured the victim into leaving his family and friends in New Jersey and moving to Texas with the intent of killing him for financial gain. Musso's body was found in a ditch with injuries so horrendous that it was initially unrecognizable.

In October 2010, the U.S. Supreme Court refused to hear Basso's case, and earlier in 2010, the 5th U.S. Circuit Court of Appeals rejected her appeal, which was made on the basis that her trial attorneys had been deficient.

Linda Carty
(October 5, 1958; black; no prior prison record)

On May 16, 2001, Linda Carty, a native of St. Christopher, British Virgin Islands, and three associates—Chris Robinson, Gerald Anderson, and Carlos Williams—invaded the home of a twenty-five-year-old Hispanic woman in Harris County. After beating and tying up two other victims, they kidnapped the woman, along with her three-day-old baby, and hog-tied her with duct tape, taped a bag over her head, and stuffed her into the trunk of a car, whereupon she suffocated to death.

Lisa Coleman *(October 6, 1975; black)*

Lisa Coleman was convicted of her role in the death of nine-year-old Davontae Williams, the son of her codefendant and roommate, Marcella Williams. On July 26, 2004, authorities were called to Coleman's residence in Arlington, just south of Dallas, where they found the dead child. An autopsy of the victim revealed that he was severely underweight and malnourished, and the two women were found to have restrained and deprived him of food over an extended period of time. Williams, the mother, copped a plea and dodged death row, being sentenced instead to life in prison.

Coleman had previously been sentenced to five years in prison for possession with intent to deliver a controlled substance and two years for burglary.

Cathy Lynn Henderson
(December 27, 1956; white; no prior prison record)

On January 21, 1994, Cathy Lynn Henderson abducted and murdered a three-month-old boy, Brandon Baugh, whom she had been babysitting. Henderson claimed that the child had been killed after she accidentally dropped him on his head and that she had panicked and fled to her home state of Missouri, where police ultimately arrested her. She provided authorities with a map that led them to the shallow grave outside of Temple, Texas, where she had buried the child in a cardboard box. An autopsy confirmed that he had died of a fractured skull. Henderson had babysat him and his two-and-a-half-year-old sister, Megan, for about three months without incident.

She shoved a lamp pole more than five inches down the victim's throat.

Brittany Marlowe Holberg *(January 1, 1973; white)*

On November 13, 1996, Brittany Marlowe Holberg robbed and murdered an eighty-year-old white man in his home in Randall County, striking him with a hammer and stabbing him nearly sixty times with a paring knife, a butcher knife, a grapefruit knife, and a fork. She then shoved a lamp pole more than five inches down the victim's throat.

Holberg had a previous conviction for substance abuse.

Melissa Elizabeth Lucio
(July 18, 1968; Hispanic; no prior prison record)

On February 17, 2007, janitor Melissa Elizabeth Lucio was arrested for beating to death her two-and-a-half-year-old daughter, Mariah Alvarez, in Harlingen, Texas. Lucio had apparently beaten the child for months, as indicated by purple and green bruises discovered on her entire torso, head, face, and right shoulder, and the final attack inflicted fatal brain damage. Her live-in boyfriend and the father of the child, Roberto Antonio Alvarez, was charged as a codefendant in the killing.

Kimberly Lagayle McCarthy *(May 11, 1961; black)*

On July 21, 1997, Kimberly Lagayle McCarthy entered the residence of a seventy-year-old white woman in the Dallas suburb of Lancaster with the intent of robbing her. The two struggled, during which McCarthy stabbed the victim numerous times, killing her. McCarthy then stole and made use of the woman's vehicle and credit cards.

McCarthy's prior prison record included a two-year sentence

for one count of forgery, for which she was incarcerated about four months and on parole for eighteen months thereafter.

Chelsea Lea Richardson
(March 26, 1984; white; no prior prison record)

On December 11, 2003, Chelsea Lea Richardson and three associates—Andrew W. Wamsley, Hilario Cardenas, and Susanna Toledano—entered the Tarrant County residence of a couple, both age forty-six, and shot and stabbed them to death. Richardson, a laborer, was sentenced to death in August 2005.

Darlie Lynn Routier
(January 4, 1970; white; no prior prison record)

On June 6, 1996, Darlie Lynn Routier stabbed to death her two sons, six-year-old Devon and five-year-old Damon, while they slept in the downstairs family room of their home in the Dallas suburb of Rowlett. She did not harm her infant son, Drake, or husband, Darin, both of whom were asleep in their upstairs bedrooms during the attacks. Routier, who had wounds that the police said were self-inflicted, claimed that she had also slept through the attacks and woke up only to see the back of a man fleeing the home. She was arrested and charged after making inconsistent statements to the police. During her trial, the prosecution argued that her motive in killing the children was that they interfered with the lifestyle she wanted to lead.

Her **motive** in killing the children was that they **interfered** with the **lifestyle** she wanted to lead.

Women Executed by Texas

IN THE MORE-THAN-THREE DECADES SINCE THE U.S. Supreme Court lifted the ban on capital punishment, with its ruling on *Gregg v. Georgia* in 1976, twelve women have been executed in the United States—a quarter of them in the state of Texas. Their dates of birth and execution are listed in parentheses, followed by a synopsis of the crimes for which they were put to death. All were executed by lethal injection at the state death house at the state prison in Huntsville.

KARLA FAYE TUCKER
(November 18, 1959–February 3, 1998; white)

Karla Faye Tucker was convicted of murder in Texas in 1984 and executed four years later. She was the second woman to be executed in the United States since the reinstatement of capital punishment (the first being fourteen years earlier in North Carolina) and the first woman to be put to death in Texas since 1863.

The product of a broken and troubled home in Houston, Tucker was using drugs and working as a prostitute by age fourteen, after which she followed her mother as a groupie with the Allman Brothers Band, the Eagles, and the Marshall Tucker Band. By her early twenties, she was hanging out with bikers.

On June 14, 1983, Tucker and her boyfriend, Danny Garrett, broke into the home of some acquaintances with the intention of stealing a motorcycle and some parts for it. During the burglary, they murdered one of the residents. Tucker first helped restrain the victim while Garrett beat him

with a hammer and then, upset by the noises he was making, she attacked him herself with a pickaxe, after which her boyfriend finished him with the hammer. They then discovered a woman hiding under the bed and proceeded to kill her in a similar fashion.

While confined at the Mountain View Unit in Gatesville, Tucker made a jailhouse conversion to Christianity, prompting numerous people to appeal for a commutation of her sentence (among them one United Nations official, Pope John Paul II, Italian Prime Minister Romano Prodi, Congressman Newt Gingrich, televangelist Pat Robertson, the brother of the woman she helped kill, and her warden. The Texas Board of Pardons and Parole was, however, not swayed by these pleas, and she was put to death in February 1998.

BETTY LOU BEETS
(March 12, 1937–February 24, 2000; white)
Betty Lou Beets was the fourth woman in the United States executed and the second in the state of Texas after the reintroduction of the death penalty. A hearing-impaired waitress who had been sexually abused since age five, first by her father and subsequently by her various husbands, Beets was convicted of murdering her fifth husband, Jimmy Don Beets.

On August 6, 1983, Beets shot her husband twice with a .38 handgun, killing him. She and her son, Robert Branson, then hid the dead man's body in the front yard of their home in Henderson County, southeast of Dallas, and reported him missing. They then tried to make it look like he had drowned while fishing in nearby Cedar Creek Reservoir.

Two years later, the county sheriff's office received information that allowed it to investigate and arrest Beets on

Women Executed by Texas (continued)

June 8, 1985. A search of her home revealed not just the body of Jimmy Don Beets but also that of Doyle Wayne Barker, a previous husband, who had been killed with the same weapon (but for whose murder she was never tried). She was convicted on October 11 of that year for "murder for remuneration and the promise of remuneration," based on the fact that she stood to benefit from her husband's life insurance and pension.

After fifteen years of appeals, rehearings, and stays of execution, during most of which she was held in the Mountain View Unit, she was put to death in early 2000. At the time of her execution, Beets was sixty-two years old and had five children, nine grandchildren, and six great-grandchildren.

FRANCES ELAINE NEWTON
(April 12, 1965–September 14, 2005; black)
Frances Elaine Newton was the eleventh woman in the United States and the third in the state of Texas to be executed after the reintroduction of the death penalty in the nation.

Erica Yvonne Sheppard
(September 1, 1973; black; no prior prison record)

On June 30, 1993, Erica Yvonne Sheppard of Bay City, Texas, and her friend and codefendant, James Dickerson, saw a woman named Marilyn Sage Meagher carrying clothing from her car to her apartment in Houston and decided to steal her 1993 Mazda 626. They followed her to her apartment, where they tackled

She was convicted for the murders of her husband, Adrian (twenty-three), her son, Alton (seven), and her daughter, Farrah (twenty-one months).

After apparently shooting all three of her family members with a .25 caliber pistol she had obtained from a man she had been seeing, Newton claimed that they had been slain by a drug dealer. It was Newton, however, and not any drug dealer, who had taken out $50,000 life insurance policies on each of her three victims just three weeks before the murders, forging her husband's signature and naming herself as the beneficiary.

Despite the fact that the Houston police believed that Adrian Newton was indeed a drug dealer who was in debt to his supplier, reservations among jury members about information that had been withheld during her trial, evidence that her defense attorney was demonstrably incompetent, and other irregularities, Newton was sentenced to death. All subsequent appeals and writs of habeas corpus were denied by the Texas Court of Criminal Appeals, as were two appeals to the U.S. Supreme Court. Newton was put to death in September 2005.

her and, while she begged for her life, slashed her throat with knives five times, after which they wrapped her head in a plastic bag and beat her with a ten-pound statue. The killers fled back to Bay City in Meagher's vehicle, where they abandoned it. Both Sheppard—who did not have a previous police record—and Dickerson were sentenced to death for the murder.

10

A Fatal Attraction

BY THE AGE OF TWENTY-THREE, Mexican-American singer-songwriter Selena Quintanilla-Pérez—better known simply as Selena—had fourteen top-ten singles in the Top Latin Songs chart, half of them number-one hits and two the most successful singles of 1994 and 1995. She won Female Vocalist of the Year at the Tejano Music Awards in 1987, was subsequently named "Bestselling Latin Artist of the Decade" and "Top Latin Artist of the '90s," and was widely referred to as the "Queen of Tejano music." Her popularity was unprecedented, and she had a devoted, one might almost say fanatical following. And on March 31, 1995, one of those followers, jealous of her idol's success, shot the pop star to death.

Selena's family lost their home in the Houston area when she was young, and they moved to Corpus Christi, Texas, where she was raised. She had begun singing at the age of three, and her family staked many of their hopes on her success, performing with her at fairs, weddings, *quinceañeras,* and anywhere else they could. She released her first album when she was just twelve and signed a recording contract with label EMI Group two years after that. From that point onward, her fame and success grew almost exponentially, and she released album after album, performed throughout the Spanish-speaking world, and broke records that had never been approached by another female pop star.

In 1990, a fan by the name of Yolanda Saldívar approached Selena's father with the idea of forming a fan club, an idea to which he agreed, appointing her its president. Four years later, Selena went beyond music and started a clothing line, and when she opened two boutiques called Selena Etc. in Corpus Christi and San Antonio to support this venture, Saldívar was hired to manage them. In early March 1995, however, Selena's family discovered that she had been stealing money from the fan club and fired her.

Saldívar had held onto various business documents associated with the boutiques, and when Selena demanded them back, Saldívar requested that the singer meet with her at a hotel in Corpus Christi, where she promised she would hand them over. When they met there on the morning of March 31, however, Saldívar told Selena that she had just been raped. Selena drove her to a nearby hospital, but when physicians examined here there, they found no indication that she had actually been assaulted.

The two women returned to the hotel, and shortly before noon an irritated Selena demanded that Saldívar hand over the paperwork she had come to collect. The crooked manager responded by pulling a handgun out of her purse and brandishing it at her former idol and employer. When Selena turned and fled the room, Saldívar shot her in the back, severing an artery in her right shoulder, and then chased after the critically injured singer as she staggered toward the lobby. There, she identified Saldívar as her attacker to the clerk and then collapsed onto the floor as the crazed woman ran into the lobby and yelled, "Bitch!"

EMS rushed Selena back to the hospital to which she had brought her assailant only a short time before. There, about an hour and fifteen minutes after she had been shot, the popular singer died from blood loss.

Back at the hotel, Saldivar held police at bay for nearly ten hours before finally surrendering to them without incident. Seven months later, a jury in Houston convicted her of murder with a deadly weapon and, after deliberating for just two hours, sentenced her to life in prison. She is currently confined at the Mountain View facility of the Texas Department of Criminal Justice—where she is kept in isolation because of death threats— and will be eligible for parole in March 2025, on the thirtieth anniversary of Selena's death.

11

The Most Hated Woman
in America

MADALYN MURRAY O'HAIR MAY, in fact, have been the most hated woman in America at one point. She was certainly despised enough that in 1995, when she disappeared and it looked likely that she had been murdered, the police in Austin, Texas, pretty much just decided not to do anything about it.

In 1960, O'Hair was living in Baltimore, Maryland, and made history when she filed a lawsuit against the city's public school system, claiming it was unconstitutional that her son was required to participate in Bible readings at school. She noted in this suit that her son had been bullied because of his refusal to participate in Bible readings and that school administrators had ignored this.

In 1963, this case reached the U.S. Supreme Court, which voted 8–1 in favor of O'Hair. This ruling resulted in the banning of compulsory religious observations such as prayer and recitation of Bible verses in American public schools, setting a precedent that has held to this day. It also caused the intent of the Constitution with regard to separation of church and state to come under close and continuous scrutiny since then.

In the wake of the landmark decision, O'Hair more or less claimed to have single-handedly achieved the legal victory, although there had been a number of other similar lawsuits in the years leading up to hers, and even it was bundled with one other when it went before the high court.

O'Hair suffered such violent persecution in response to her actions that she was prompted to leave Baltimore and soon after relocated to Austin, Texas. There, she founded an organization called American Atheists, "a nationwide movement which defends the civil rights of non-believers, works for the separation of church and state and addresses issues of First Amendment public policy." O'Hair served as the president of the organization from 1963 to 1986, and her son, Jon Garth Murray, took over in this role from 1986 to 1995 (although O'Hair is believed to have retained much of the actual control).

O'Hair was the face of American Atheism throughout the 1960s and '70s, filing lawsuits to prevent the interaction of church and state, starting an atheist radio station and cable television show, and promoting her point of view through interviews with such high-profile venues as *Playboy* magazine and *The Phil Donahue Show*. By 1964, her activities had stirred up so much ire that *Life* magazine dubbed her "the most hated woman in America." In one particularly well-publicized episode in 1968, she sued NASA after the Apollo 8 astronauts read passages from the book of Genesis while orbiting the moon (although nothing came of this suit).

According to O'Hair, the hate people had for her manifested itself against her and her family in innumerable incidents of harassment, intimidation, and death threats.

O'Hair remained active throughout the 1980s—among other things, she wrote speeches for pornographer Larry Flint

Despite **clear signs of foul play**, the Austin Police Department opted not to pursue an investigation.

during his 1984 presidential campaign. Her abrasiveness drove away even the members of her own organization, however, and by 1991 all of the local and state chapters of American Atheists had split from the main organization or disbanded. From that point onward, the organization consisted of O'Hair, her son Jon Murray, her granddaughter Robin Murray O'Hair—daughter of estranged son William Murray—and a number of office staff. And, on August 27, 1995, O'Hair and her two relatives simply disappeared.

"The Murray O'Hair family has been called out of town on an emergency basis," a typewritten note apparently signed by Jon Murray stated. "We do not know how long we will be gone at the time of the writing of this memo." Breakfast dishes were still on the table, O'Hair's diabetes medication had been left behind, and no provisions had been made for their dogs.

A few days later, the three of them called various associates to say that they were on business in San Antonio. A few days after that, Jon Murray liquidated a trust fund and used it to purchase $500,000 worth of gold coins from a San Antonio dealer. Between then and September 27, Jon Murray and Robin Murray O'Hair made several more vague, strained phone calls

Waters talked about how much he **hated** her and wanted to **torture** her.

but provided no information about why they had left or when they would be back. Then, from September 28 onward, nothing more was heard from them.

Despite clear signs of foul play, the Austin Police Department opted not to pursue an investigation; apparently, that old saying "it's not a popularity contest" doesn't apply if you want the authorities to investigate your disappearance.

"Despite pleas from O'Hair's son William J. Murray, several briefings from federal agents, and solid leads developed by members of the press, [APD] sat on the sidelines of the O'Hair investigation," wrote Robert Bryce, a reporter for the *Austin Chronicle* newspaper. "Meanwhile, investigators from the Internal Revenue Service, Federal Bureau of Investigation, Bureau of Alcohol, Tobacco, and Firearms, and the Dallas County Sheriff's Office are working together on the case."

Early on, in any event, the presumption was that O'Hair and her family had been targeted by some religious fanatic who resented her atheistic activities. Eventually, however, investigators focused on a violent felon named David Roland Waters, who had worked for American Atheists until it was discovered he had stolen some $54,000 from the organization, a crime he had pleaded guilty to earlier in 1995. O'Hair had also publicly humiliated Waters after his thefts were revealed, and he had talked about how much he hated her and wanted to torture her.

Waters and two accomplices, a couple of hoodlums named Gary Paul Karr and Danny Fry, had in fact abducted Madalyn, Jon, and Robin, held them prisoner at a ranch outside of San Antonio, forced them to withdraw money from their accounts, and run up huge charges on their credit cards. On September 29, the kidnappers murdered their prisoners, dismembered them, and buried their pieces on the grounds of the ranch. Waters and Fry had a falling out soon after, and the former American Atheists employee killed his accomplice, hacked off his head and hands, and dumped the rest of his body into a nearby riverbed (burying his head and hands with the other victims).

Waters and his girlfriend, Patti Jo Steffens, then blew through $80,000 worth of the gold coins on a binge over a matter of just a few days. They had hidden the rest of them in a San Antonio storage unit, but when they returned to the unit to collect the balance of the coins in mid-October 1995, they discovered that they had been stolen by yet another group of criminals (who, police later learned, also burned through them relatively quickly; only one was ever recovered).

Waters was convicted of kidnapping, robbery, and murder and sentenced to twenty years in prison (plus sixty years for separate weapons charges), dying just a few years later, in January 2003, of lung cancer. Karr was convicted of extortion and sentenced to life in prison.

In the wake of O'Hair's death, there was little love lost for her.

"My mother was an evil person," O'Hair's son William said after her death. "Not for removing prayer from America's schools . . . She stole huge amounts of money. She misused the trust of people. She cheated children out of their parents' inheritance. She cheated on her taxes and even stole from her own organizations.

*"My mother was an **evil** person."*

She once printed up phony stock certificates on her own printing press to try to take over another atheist publishing company. . . . She was just evil."

12

(Bad) Mothers of the Year

A DISTURBING NUMBER OF TEXAS mothers have decided to end it all . . . for their unfortunate children (or, at the least, to injure them grievously). Medea herself would have been impressed with some of these filicidal matrons. Some of the most heinous cases of the last decade follow, but this list is more representative than exhaustive.

Debra Janelle Jeter

On June 5, 2009, thirty-two-year-old Debra Janelle Jeter took her two daughters, twelve-year-old Kelsey and thirteen-year-old Kiersten, to an abandoned farmhouse off of Route 77 in Hillsboro, Texas, about thirty miles south of Dallas. Jeter and her husband, Lee, were in the process of being divorced, and this was the first time she had spent unsupervised time with the girls since having a restraining order lifted.

After leading them inside the house, Jeter attacked the two girls with a knife. Kiersten tried to shield her younger sister with her own body, but the smaller girl was nonetheless fatally wounded and the older one critically so. Jeter then ordered her daughters to run around the house so that they would bleed out more quickly.

"I just killed my children," Jeter said in a 911 call she made at that point, adding "one of them is still alive, hurry . . . get an ambulance out here to save the one that didn't die." She also gave her location and said she had a knife.

"The first I found out what had actually happened, is the surgeon come out and told me that he had sewn Kiersten's neck back together and the surgery went well," said the father, Lee Jeter, in an interview with Nancy Grace in June 2010. "She was cut from one side of the neck all the way to the other. Her airway was cut and one of her main arteries were cut."

In May 2010, Debra Jeter pleaded guilty to one count each of capital murder and attempted capital murder and was sentenced to life in prison without the possibility of parole. She is currently confined at the Mountain View unit of the Texas Department of Criminal Justice in Gatesville.

Deanna Laney

On May 9, 2003, the beginning of Mother's Day weekend, thirty-eight-year-old Deanna Laney stoned to death and smashed the

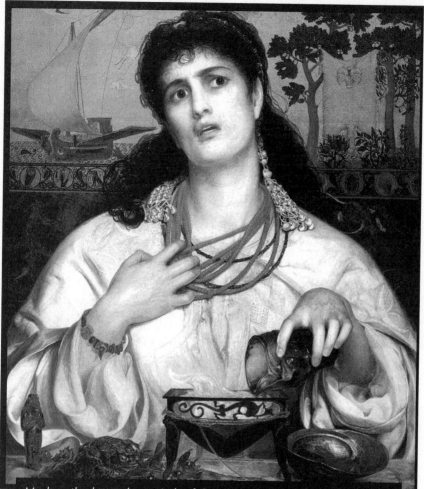

Medea, the legendary witch of Greek mythology, is the archetype of murdering motherhood but has actually been outdone by some of her sisters in the Lone Star State.

skulls of her two oldest sons, eight-year-old Joshua and six-year-old Luke in the front yard of their home in Tyler, Texas. She also beat and maimed in his crib her fourteen-month-old son, Aaron, who survived the attack.

Laney, who had home-schooled her children, reportedly showed no emotion during the attacks and claimed that she was acting on orders from God. She was an active member of the

"It was *graphic*, it was *horrific*, and it was *brutal*."

World Assemblies of God Fellowship, a Pentecostal evangelical denomination.

Mental health experts testified during the trial that Laney believed she was divinely chosen by God, as Mary was chosen to bear Jesus, to slay her children and then serve as a witness to the end of the world. In a videotaped statement played during the trial, Laney said that when she saw one of her sons play with a spear, hold a rock, and squeeze a frog, she took these as divine omens that she should kill her boys.

Prosecutor Matt Bingham wasn't having it.

"It was graphic, it was horrific, and it was brutal," Bingham said during the trial, "[Joshua] got strike after strike after strike on his head to the point that his brains were coming out of his head like liquid." And even if Laney thought she was following God's commands, Bingham said, she has to have known she was violating the laws of Texas and should be held accountable.

In April 2003, however, Laney was acquitted of killing her children by reason of insanity and was confined to a maximum-security Texas state mental hospital for an indefinite period of time. Five mental health experts, two provided by the defense, two by the prosecution, and one by the trial judge, all determined that she suffered from psychotic delusions. She would have automatically been given a life sentence had she been found guilty of capital murder.

Katherine Nadal

On the night of March 13, 2007, twenty-five-year-old Katherine Michelle Nadal, strung out on a cocktail of cocaine, methadone, and Xanax, used an unknown sharp object to cut the genitals off of her five-week-old son, Holden Gothia, at their suburban Houston apartment. The mutilated child survived the vicious attack but his genitals were never found.

Nadal's motivation may have been related to an ongoing argument she had been having with the child's father, her boyfriend, Camden Gothia, over whether to have their son circumcised, something she favored but he opposed.

During her trial, however, Nadal insisted that the perpetrator was the family's seven-pound dachshund, Shorty, and that she had merely "failed" her son. While that might have seemed plausible to someone with the psychology of a crack whore, prosecutors pointed out that the little dog could not have actually utilized the tool that had been used to affect the castration.

"You abused him when he was in the womb!" boyfriend Camden Gothia exclaimed during the trial, referring to Nadal's prolific prenatal drug use. She also had a number of drug arrests prior to the attack on her son.

The jury agreed with Gothia and the prosecution, finding Nadal guilty of severe bodily injury to a child and sentencing her to ninety-nine years in prison, of which she will have to serve at least thirty before being eligible for parole. She is currently confined at the Christina Melton Crain Unit in Gatesville.

Nadal insisted that the perpetrator was the family's seven-pound dachshund, Shorty.

Otty Sanchez

On July 26, 2009, thirty-two-year-old San Antonio mother Otty Sanchez killed and dismembered her three-and-a-half week old son, Scott Wesley Buchholz-Sanchez, chewing off three of his toes, removing his face, and eating his brain. The child's father, Scott W. Buchholz, had moved out of the home a week earlier.

When her sister discovered her with the mutilated remains of the child, Sanchez claimed that the Devil made her do it and had stabbed herself in the chest and neck.

"I didn't mean to do it! He told me to!" Sanchez screamed as her sister desperately pleaded with a 911 dispatcher to send help. Sanchez, who had previously been diagnosed with postpartum depression and schizophrenia, told police that voices had told her that killing her child was necessary to prevent an apocalypse.

Sanchez claimed that the Devil made her do it.

During her capital murder trial in July 2010, both the defense and prosecution pretty much agreed that Sanchez was nuts and agreed to waive a jury hearing for her. State District Judge Raymond Angelini found her guilty by reason of insanity and committed her to a maximum-security mental facility until she is deemed to no longer be a threat to herself or others.

Lisa Smith

On December 26, 1999, thirty-one-year-old grade-school teacher Lisa Marie Smith ate pizza and then opened presents with her two young sons, five-year-old William and three-year-old Tristen Smith, at her home in the Dallas suburb of Richardson. Then, after putting them to bed, she strangled them to death in their sleep with a scarf.

Smith's children were visiting her and lived with her ex-husband, Brit Smith, who styled himself a cowboy. The couple had divorced in 1998 after a tumultuous five-year marriage, and she was distraught that he had obtained permanent primary custody of the children just four days earlier. Brit Smith later admitted that his moves to take the children away from his ex-wife were "kind of sneaky" and that she probably felt isolated and abandoned. Lisa Smith had been diagnosed with depression and is believed by some to have suffered from a psychotic break at the time of the murders.

After killing the children, Smith spent a day-and-a-half trying to kill herself, taking more than one hundred Tylenol pills, cutting one of her wrists, and, finally, disconnecting the gas line leading to the stove and setting the house on fire. Firefighters responding to the scene found Smith lying on the floor next to her sons and transported her to the hospital.

At her trial, Smith pled guilty of two counts of capital murder as part of a deal that allowed her to avoid the death penalty and was sentenced to two concurrent life sentences. She is currently serving her time at the Christina Melton Crain Unit in Gatesville and will be eligible for parole in late 2039.

Dena Schlosser

When the police arrived at thirty-five-year-old Dena Schlosser's apartment in the Dallas suburb of Plano on November 22, 2004, they found her calmly sitting in the living room listening to hymns, covered in blood, and clutching a knife. A short time before, she had explained to a 911 operator that she had cut the arms off her eleven-month-old infant daughter as an offering to God. The child was still alive in her crib by the time EMS arrived at the scene but died soon afterward at the hospital.

Her two other daughters, aged six and nine, were at school when the attack occurred, and her husband was at work.

Schlosser, who had previously been investigated on allegations of child neglect and had a history of apparent psychotic episodes and postpartum depression, was charged with capital murder in the attack. She had reportedly seen a television news story about a boy being mauled by a lion shortly before the attack and interpreted the incident as a sign of the apocalypse.

Schlosser was charged with capital murder, but during her trial was found not guilty by reason of insanity and was remanded to the North Texas State Hospital for an indefinite period of time (where, for awhile, she shared a room with fellow committer of filicide, Andrea Yates [q.v.]). In November 2008, she was released to outpatient care and ordered to see a psychiatrist once a week, to take medication, to remain on physician-approved birth control—and, naturally, to not have any unsupervised contact with children.

Andrea Yates

When they were married in 1993, Andrea and Rusty Yates declared that they "would seek to have as many babies as nature allowed." For the next six years they stayed true to their promise, with Andrea bearing four sons and raising them in a succession of cramped trailers and motor homes while Rusty spent most of his time at work.

By June 1999, however, Andrea's role as breeding stock had begun to take a heavy psychological toll on her, and she began to suffer signs of severe postpartum depression and psychosis that were exacerbated by her fixation on the message of fire-and-brimstone preacher Michael Peter Woroniecki. She attempted to commit suicide twice and was committed to a mental hospital and prescribed antidepressants and the antipsychotic drug Haldol.

Rusty condescended to move the family into a small house at that point for the sake of his wife's mental health. By July, however, she had a nervous breakdown, made two more suicide attempts, and spent periods of time in two psychiatric wards, where she was diagnosed with postpartum psychosis.

Despite the urgings of her psychiatrist and warnings that doing so would "guarantee future psychotic depression," Andrea and her husband conceived their fifth child just seven weeks after her

"My children weren't righteous."

release from the hospital. She went off her medication soon thereafter, and her daughter was born at the end of November 2000.

As predicted, Andrea's mental state deteriorated rapidly and within a matter of months she had ceased talking, started mutilating herself, and stopped feeding her daughter. She had also taken to reading the Bible feverishly. Between April and June 2001 she became nearly catatonic a number of times and had to be hospitalized.

On June 20, Rusty Yates went to work an hour before his mother was scheduled to arrive at the house and left Andrea alone with the five children, ages six months to seven years, against the instructions of her psychiatrist.

"She drowned the four youngest children in the bathtub and placed them on a back bedroom bed and covered them with a sheet," the *Houston Chronicle* reported. "When the oldest boy walked into the bathroom and asked what was wrong with his sister, Andrea Yates told investigators she ran after him and then drowned him," leaving him floating in the tub.

Yates later claimed that she had killed her children in order to ensure their salvation.

"My children weren't righteous," she said. "They stumbled because I was evil. The way I was raising them, they could never be saved. They were doomed to perish in the fires of Hell."

Andrea's defense attorneys argued that she was not guilty by reason of insanity but, during her trial in March 2002, a jury rejected this and found her guilty of murder and sentenced her to life in prison with eligibility for parole after forty years. In January 2005, however, a Texas Court of Appeals reversed Andrea's convictions because one of the prosecution's expert psychiatric witnesses admitted to giving false testimony.

Yates was retried, and in July 2006, a jury found her to be not guilty by reason of insanity. She was initially sent to the North Texas State Hospital (Vernon Campus) but, in January 2007, was transferred to the low-security state mental hospital in Kerrville.

13

Cruel Justice

IN HER ROLE AS THE PRESIDING JUDGE of the Texas Court of Criminal Appeals, Sharon Faye Keller has never let trivial things like facts, compassion, or innocence prevent her from imposing the full weight of the law on a defendant. Descriptions by friends and coworkers and her own statements and actions paint a picture of a cruel and sanctimonious woman willing to put warped abstract concepts before the lives of other human beings—even ones she has every reason to believe are not guilty.

In a 2009 interview, *Texas Monthly* writer Michael Hall asked Keller if she felt bound to follow the law even if she knew she would be perpetrating an injustice by doing so.

"Absolutely," Keller answered. "Who is going to determine what justice is? Me? I think justice is achieved by following the law."

Friends and colleagues have also characterized Keller as "extremely religious." According to one colleague, "She believes strongly that God is on her side."

By all accounts, He has not been on the side of people whose fates have ended up in Keller's hands.

Keller was appointed to the Texas high court in 1994 and established herself as a hardliner early on. In 1996, she wrote the majority opinion in a 5–4 decision to deny a new trial to a laborer named Cesar Fierro, who had confessed to murdering a cab driver in El Paso after being implicated by a sixteen-year-old witness five months after the 1979 killing. Keller was aware that it had come out after the trial that police in Juarez, Mexico, had abducted and threatened to torture Fierro's mother and stepfather if he did not confess and that American detectives had perjured themselves during the trial. Based on these facts, both the prosecutor and the trial judge believed that the defendant deserved a new trial. Keller and four of her colleagues, however, opted to reject this.

"He told me if I signed, then they'd let them go, and if not, they were going to torture them," Fierro said El Paso detectives had told him.

Keller acknowledged that Fierro had likely been coerced and had false witness borne against him but dismissed these as "harmless" elements that did not affect the outcome of his trial and said it was up to the defendant to prove otherwise. Fierro has been imprisoned since 1980 and is currently on death row in the Polunksy unit of the Texas Department of Criminal Justice in Livingston.

In 1998, Keller got on board with a majority opinion to deny a retrial for mentally defective logger Roy Criner, a New Caney man who had been convicted on suspect testimony and very shaky evidence of aggravated sexual assault of a girl in 1986; she had also been murdered but there was not enough evidence to charge Criner with this. Criner was sentenced to ninety-nine years in prison. A decade later, however, he was subsequently exonerated by DNA evidence, but Keller dismissed this as "a technicality" in her 1997 decision to support overturning a district court recommendation for a retrial.

In subsequent interviews, Keller asserted that Criner had not unquestionably established he was innocent, turning on its head the fundamental basis of American justice, namely that a person is innocent until the state proves his guilt. She also dismissed the fact that critical evidence that might have exonerated Criner had not been presented to the jury during his trial.

Keller "offered a clumsy, embarrassing rationale of her decision on national television," the *Dallas Observer* reported. Justice Tom Price, Keller's colleague at Texas Court of Criminal Appeals, acknowledged that her opinion on Criner had made the court a "national laughingstock." And Judge Stephen Mansfield, who had initially sided with the majority in denying Criner a retrial, ultimately admitted that he had voted "the wrong way" and that he wished he could have been given "a chance to fix" his mistake. After the Texas Board of Pardons and Paroles recommended that Criner be pardoned, then-Governor George W. Bush—a man not known for his humanitarian ways—pardoned him in 2000.

In her two early high-profile cases, Keller had shown herself to be cruel and stupid, but it was not until the impending execution of convicted rapist and murderer Michael Wayne Richard that she revealed herself to be actually depraved.

Richard had been sentenced to death and was scheduled to be executed on Tuesday, September 25, 2007. That morning, the

Judged and Found Wanting

ON MARCH 30, 2009, THE DALLAS MORNING NEWS revealed that Keller had "failed to abide by legal requirements that she disclose nearly $2 million in real estate holdings."

Keller did not dispute what she claimed to be an error in her financial disclosure but protested that actually having to defend herself against the resulting civil and criminal charges against her would be "financially ruinous" and tried to have the complaints dismissed on that basis. (Wow! At least no one was trying to have her imprisoned or put to death.)

In April 2009, Keller corrected her personal financial statement to include more than $2.4 million in income and property she had previously neglected to mention. A year later, in April 2010, the Texas Ethics Commission fined Keller $100,000 for this oversight.

U.S. Supreme Court agreed to review a case called *Baze v. Rees* that challenged the constitutionality of the lethal injection protocol used in both Kentucky and Texas. Richard's legal representatives, Texas Defender Service, began to prepare the paperwork to request a stay of execution pending the Supreme Court decision.

Meanwhile, Keller left work early to meet a repairman at her home. TDS contacted the high court to request that the clerk's office stay open late so that they could file their motion and its general counsel, Edward Marty, called Keller to get this approved. She responded, however, by insisting that the clerk's office close promptly at 5 p.m. and TDS was thus unable to file the paperwork on behalf of its client. Richard was put to death that night. Talk about "a technicality."

Outcry against Keller was widespread. Hundreds of lawyers statewide responded by signing official judicial complaints about Keller's conduct, and the Texas Court of Criminal Appeals changed its policy to explicitly prevent an episode like this from happening again. And in February 2009 State Representative Lon Burnam filed a resolution calling for Keller's impeachment.

"It's one thing for a banker to close shop at five o'clock sharp," Burnam said. "But a public official who stands between a human being and the death chamber must be held to a higher standard." The attempt to have her impeached, however, was not successful.

Also in February 2009, the State Commission on Judicial Conduct charged Keller with five counts of misconduct, including dereliction of duty, incompetence in office, and denying the executed man access to the courts and voted to initiate formal proceedings against Keller that included a public trial.

Keller's trial started in August 2009 and revealed failings and sloppy or indifferent behavior on the parts of both the judge and the TDS lawyers on the case. The special master overseeing the proceeding, however, said that while "there is a valid reason why many in the legal community are not proud of Judge Keller's actions" she had not actually broken any laws and recommended no measures be taken against her.

In July 2010, the commission issued Keller a "Public Warning" and condemned her actions, saying that they cast "public discredit on the judiciary or the administration of justice" and constituted "willful or persistent conduct that is clearly inconsistent with the proper performance of her duties as a judge." In October 2010 a special court of review dismissed both the warning and the charges.

As of this writing, Keller remains the top judge for the Texas Court of Criminal Appeals.

14

A Texas Murder Trial

TEXAS JUSTICE HAS A REPUTATION for being harsh but that is mostly the case for blacks, Mexicans, and kids with small quantities of dope. Again and again, on the other hand, white people willing to talk about how Jesus is their lord and savior or who get friends from their churches to come in and testify on their behalf are given slaps on the wrist for the most heinous crimes. Enter Janice Marie Vickers. . .

Janice Marie Vickers stalked and brutally murdered eighty-three-year-old Shirley Lindenbaum, dumping her body on a darkened road and running over it multiple times with an SUV.

On the night of November 3, 2006, sheriff's deputies in Comal County, found the barefoot, mangled body of eighty-three-year-old Shirley Lindenbaum near 500 White Oak Drive in the Oaks subdivision of Startzville on the south side of Canyon Lake, about thirty miles north of San Antonio. A resident of the other side of the lake, forty-six-year-old Vickers, claimed to have run over her and then subsequently called 911 around 9:30 p.m.

The Comal County Sherriff's Office, in conjunction with the Texas Department of Public Safety and the Texas Attorney General's office, proceeded to conduct a two-year investigation of the incident. That led to the arrest of Vickers in December 2008 and a grand jury in early 2009 that determined she should be charged with intentionally striking Lindenbaum with the intent of killing her. Vickers pleaded not guilty to the charges.

After various delays, Vickers' murder trial began November 2, 2009, one day short of the three-year anniversary of the killing, in the 207th Judicial District court in New Braunfels, Judge Jack Robison presiding. The entirety of the first day of the trial was devoted to selection of the four-man, eight-woman jury.

Much of the initial proceedings on Tuesday, November 3, 2009, involved personal testimony from witnesses intended to establish the respective characters of both the defendant and the victim. The prosecution also presented crime-scene photos that many of the people present found to be horrific and disturbing. The entire top of Lindenbaum's head was removed when Vickers ran over it multiple times with her Chevrolet Tahoe, and the victim's body was so badly contorted that, witnesses testified, her breasts and buttocks were both facing in the same direction.

"I'll have nightmares for a long time," Mary Lindenbaum, daughter-in-law of the victim, told me when I spoke with her. Other family members and friends of the slain woman seemed equally shaken by the circumstances of her death.

On Wednesday, November 4, 2009, the prosecution showed the jury a two-and-a-half hour, videotaped interview of Vickers by the police the night of the incident, which began a little after 1 a.m. and continued until around 3:30 a.m.

During this interview, Vickers repeatedly changed her story of what happened at the scene of the apparent traffic fatality and ultimately gave several different, conflicting accounts of the incident. Her description clearly revolted courtroom observers on a number of occasions, as when she mimicked gurgling sounds she said Lindenbaum made while she was dying or—as in one version of the story she gave—when she said she had been driving around with the injured victim in her car but then panicked, opened up the door, and shoved her out onto the street at the site where she had originally claimed to have hit her. At one

"You don't **accidentally** run over somebody twice."

point she also claimed to have driven away from the scene and, upon returning to it, run over Lindenbaum again.

"You don't accidentally run over somebody twice," said prosecutor Ralph Guerrero, who, along with Wesley Mau, was one of two attorneys from the state Attorney General's office who had been deputized as Comal County assistant district attorneys for the trial. District Attorney Geoff Barr was also a member of the prosecution team.

Vickers said she had been in the neighborhood because her friend and Lindenbaum's neighbor, Jackie Ort, had asked her to check on her house while she was out of town. Vickers also asserted, again and again, that she had never met Lindenbaum and did not know who she was.

Jackie Ort testified that, when Janice Vickers had approached her about an investment scheme, she had directed her to Shirley Lindenbaum as one of the only people she knew affluent enough to participate in it. Blood is not visible on her hands in this photo ....

Over the following days, the prosecution proceeded to present its witnesses, many of whom gave testimony refuting claims made by Vickers in her statement. Many of these witnesses were law enforcement personnel involved in the initial or ongoing investigation, including Comal County Sheriff's Office deputies and detectives, a Texas Ranger, and Texas Department of Public Safety forensics experts. The prosecution subpoenaed a total of thirty-six witnesses for the trial.

Two non-law-enforcement witnesses, Ort and her daughter Lisa Castro, each characterized themselves as close friends of Vickers. Both testified that Vickers had driven to Houston the day before the killing for a professional conference and that Ort had accompanied her in order to pick up a used car from Castro. Both women said that Vickers had led them to believe she would be staying in Houston until Saturday, November 4, 2006, and that she would be following Ort back to Canyon Lake on that day. Ort further testified that she had never asked Vickers to check on her house and, when Vickers had approached her about an investment scheme, that she had directed her to Lindenbaum as one of the only people she knew affluent enough to participate in it.

Ort and Castro also gave testimony that conflicted with each other's—such as incompatible details of the trip to Houston—and which suggested that only one version, if either, could be true.

Throughout the proceedings, the prosecutors made a point of emphasizing the credentials and professionalism of the police officers and detectives involved in the investigation and the integrity of their investigative procedures, while defense attorney Mark A. Clark of New Braunfels attempted to draw attention to anything that might be interpreted by the jury as flaws in these things.

The relevance of some of the evidence presented or the point of some of the lines of questioning was not always made explicitly clear by the opposing attorneys. Vickers' financial data, for example, suggested she had monetary problems, but prosecutors drew no direct correlation between this and the killing. And, in an eye-glazing, hours-long cross-examination of Sergeant Michelle Stern, an investigator with the state attorney general's office, Clark asked question after question about the way cell phone calls were routed by towers and the procedure the police had used to determine his client's whereabouts at the time leading up to and during the killing.

Tensions in the courtroom mounted as the trial neared its conclusion, with numerous deputies present and the screening of spectators with a metal detector. The courtroom was filled to capacity the final day of the trial and unable to accommodate all the people who arrived to watch the proceedings.

The prosecution intensified its attack throughout the week, calling witnesses that included a number of forensics experts from the Texas Department of Public Safety in Austin—including two DNA analysts—and the chief medical examiner of Travis County, David Dolinak, who had reviewed the results of Lindenbaum's autopsy. He determined that Lindenbaum's fatal injuries were consistent with having been run over multiple times with a heavy vehicle.

The prosecution returned to the site of the killing in its final witness, Comal County Sheriff's Office Detective Sergeant Tommy Ward, the supervisor of the years-long investigation and the first senior police officer on the scene of the crime.

"I murdered her, I murdered her twice," Ward testified Vickers told him when he arrived at the scene of the killing and went to speak with her. He also revealed that an early suspect in the case was Phillip Russell Ort, son of Vickers friend and Lindenbaum neighbor Jackie Ort, and that the police had been prompted to investigate him because of comments provided by the defendant.

Prosecutors subpoenaed some three-dozen witnesses for the trial. They rested their case the morning of Thursday, November 12, 2009.

Vickers' attorney, Clark, immediately followed with his defense on the same day, presenting just two witnesses. One was a resident of the Canyon Lake area who testified to seeing Lindenbaum talking to an unknown dark-haired woman within a day or so of her death. The other was Sandy Parent, a DPS trace evidence analyst previously called by the state, who testified that marks on the victim's clothing could not be definitively matched to the tires on his client's vehicle. He rested his case after less than two hours.

Friday, November 13, 2009, was devoted to closing presentations, first by the prosecution, then the defense, and then, finally, a concluding commentary by the prosecution.

During its closing comments, the prosecution presented a theory of the crime that suggested Vickers had been granted access to the victim's property and home on some false pretenses. Once there, they said, Vickers had overpowered Lindenbaum, possibly injuring her in the process; forced the victim into the defendant's Chevrolet Tahoe; and taken her to a spot three-

"I murdered her, I murdered her twice."

tenths of a mile from her home, where Vickers pushed the older woman out onto the road and then ran over her, slowly and deliberately, multiple times with her vehicle.

During this phase, the prosecution also showed crime scene photos that had previously been partially obscured but now graphically depicted the full extent of the injuries inflicted upon the victim. These included having the entire top of her head removed and her body being so badly contorted that the upper front and lower rear of her body were both facing in the same direction.

"You don't accidentally run over somebody twice," prosecutor Guerrero reiterated numerous times in what became a virtual mantra for him during the trial.

The prosecution also presented a string of excerpts from Vickers' interrogation by police the night of the killing, each of which showed the defendant denying having ever met or even heard of the victim. A cornerstone of the prosecution's case was demonstrating through things like cell phone records and witness testimony that this assertion was untrue.

The defendant's attorney gave a spirited closing presentation on behalf of his client, during which he said the state had not met the necessary tests of evidence needed to convict Vickers of intentionally killing Lindenbaum.

"The state failed in their attempt to prove she used her car to kill Ms. Lindenbaum," Clark said, specifically referring back to his cross-examination of DPS forensics personnel who admitted they had never tested hair, fibers, or some of the other biological matter that had been identified on the undercarriage of Vickers' Tahoe.

"Are you kidding me?" Guerrero asked the jury in his final closing presentation, the last one given by either side during the trial. "Did she run over someone else we're just now hearing about?"

After closing presentations by the opposing attorneys, the court broke at around noon, and the four-man, eight-woman jury went into deliberation for about four hours. When it returned, it was with a verdict finding Vickers guilty of murder, which, according to the formal charge, is when a defendant "intentionally or knowingly causes the death of an individual." The jury could have instead found Vickers guilty of one of two lesser charges, manslaughter or criminally negligent homicide, or acquitted her altogether.

After the reading of the verdict, Vickers was taken into custody and not allowed to remain free pending sentencing, as requested by her defense attorney, Mark A. Clark, of New Braunfels.

"No sir, she is in custody," Judge Jack Robison said, explaining that Vickers had previously been allowed to remain free based upon the presumption of her innocence but now that was no longer the case and that her bond was revoked.

Friends and family members of the defendant cried and comforted each other until a bailiff took steps to clear the courtroom.

"Folks, this proceeding is over," he said. "She's gone."

262

This spot south of Canyon Lake, about a third of a mile from Shirley Lindenbaum's house, is where murderer Janice Vickers dumped her elderly victim one dark night in November 2006.

Much of Monday, November 16—the punishment phase of the trial and last day of the proceeding before sentencing—was devoted to testimonials from people who had been either negatively or positively affected by their interactions with Vickers.

The prosecution called five witnesses, among them two cheerleaders who said Vickers had menaced them after a mild altercation involving her daughter; amongst other things, one claimed Vickers had nearly run her over with her car, and the other said the defendant had made sexually suggestive comments to her. They also included a woman from Houston, Lydia Bustilloz, who testified that Vickers had stalked and harassed her after mistakenly

Doing it for the Children

VICKERS' DEFENSE ATTORNEY, MARK A. CLARK, GOT hit with some pretty serious legal problems of his own. The year after his murderous client got sent away, he himself was sentenced to a stretch in prison for the indecent liberties he was convicted of trying to take with a twelve-year-old girl. *See the chapter in the "Sex" section of this book titled "Mark of Shame."*

coming to believe that Bustilloz's husband had been involved with Lynn Jarviss, the Canyon Lake woman who had been the mistress of husband Jeff Vickers for about four months in 2004.

The defense called ten witnesses, mostly friends of Vickers who attended church with her or whose children had played sports with hers over the years. Most hesitated when asked by prosecutors whether or not the defendant should be punished for the crimes of which she was convicted, and several said nothing could convince them, not even the evidence that had been presented to and persuaded the jury, she was actually guilty.

"Please don't take our Janice away from us," a distraught Malibu Hart blubbered to the jury.

On Tuesday, November 17, the jury deliberated for about four hours, from 9 a.m. to around 2 p.m., with a one-hour break for lunch, before sentencing Vickers to seventeen years in prison. They could have imposed upon her a sentence of up to life in prison and a fine of up to $10,000.

Sentencing was immediately followed by the victim impact phase of the trial, during which the jury heard statements from Lindenbaum's friend Nancy Probst; her stepson Curt Lindenbaum, who showed some of the many paintings the victim had done; and his wife, Mary. All emphasized how much Lindenbaum had been loved, how much she was missed, and the good she had done during her life. Some of the spectators affiliated with the defendant snorted derisively and muttered amongst each other during this final phase of the trial.

Vickers was initially held in the Comal County Jail and was eventually turned over to the Texas Department of Criminal Justice. She is currently incarcerated in the Mountain View prison unit in Gatesville. Under Texas law, it is possible that with good behavior she could be set free by a parole board after just four-and-a-quarter years.

15

Joe Stack and the IRS

"**I SAW IT WRITTEN ONCE THAT THE** definition of insanity is repeating the same process over and over and expecting the outcome to suddenly be different. I am finally ready to stop this insanity. Well, Mr. Big Brother IRS man, let's try something different; take my pound of flesh and sleep well. The communist creed: From each according to his ability, to each according to his need.

The capitalist creed: From each according to his gullibility, to each according to his greed."

—Conclusion of Joe Stack's Suicide Letter

No one likes to pay taxes, but Andrew Joseph Stack III got worked up about it enough to actually commit suicide by flying a plane into an Internal Revenue Service field office in Austin, Texas, in February 2010.

By all accounts, software engineer Stack had been having tax problems for some time and neglecting to file state tax returns for at least sixteen years, and in 2004 the state of Texas suspended the business he started in 1995 because of this. As of early 2010 he was being audited by the IRS for failure to report income.

On the morning of February 18, Stack posted to his Web site a rambling suicide note that complained, among other things, about the government, bailout of financial institutions and airlines, politicians, Enron (q.v.), unions, drug and healthcare insurance companies, the Catholic Church, government indifference to and oppression of engineers like himself, President George W. Bush, the Federal Aviation Administration, and his longstanding problems with debt, taxes, and the IRS. It also included a call for revolution.

Sometime before 9 a.m., Stack set fire to his home in north Austin. He then drove about twenty miles north to Georgetown Municipal Airport where he kept his single-engine Piper Dakota in a rented hangar. There is evidence that he may have removed the seats from the plane so that he could jam extra drums of fuel into it.

Stack took off at about 9:45 a.m. and headed south, toward Austin. His target was Building I of the Echelon office complex at the north end of the city, where the IRS had a 190-person field office that performed audits, collections, investigations, and

The Echelon office complex in Austin shortly after Joe Stack flew his plane into it in February 2010.

seizures. A number of other state and federal agencies also had offices in the building.

It took Stack about ten minutes to reach his objective, and when he did, he descended at full speed and smashed into the four-story building. His plane exploded on impact, creating a huge fireball and sending debris raining down on Route 183 and the cars driving on it. The lethal impact incinerated Stack. It also injured thirteen of the people working in the building, two of them critically, and killed one other, sixty-eight-year-old IRS manager, Vernon Hunter.

Quick action on the part of a number of people in the vicinity of the crash site likely saved lives and reduced the damage Stack had inflicted. Glass worker Robin Dehaven witnessed the attack while on his way to work and used the ladder on his truck to rescue five people from the building. And the Travis County Hazardous Materials Team just happened to be conducting training right across the highway from the Echelon complex and responded to the crash immediately, battling the fire and conducting a search-and-rescue operation.

It was a good thing they responded as fast as they did—ironically, many of the firefighters who would have responded to the scene could not, because they were at that very moment battling the fire at Stack's house.

MAYHEM

in the
Lone
Star
State

1

The Texas Indian Wars

EVEN BEFORE THE ESTABLISHMENT of Texas as a republic in 1836, one of the most serious and persistent threats to the safety and security of settlers in the area was attacks by its hostile native inhabitants. Bad faith on the part of the whites as they explored and settled the new land and an almost incomprehensible savagery on the part of the Indians brought the two cultures into violent, continuous, and irreconcilable conflict.

As indicated by accounts from early visitors to the region, things did not start out badly between American settlers and the Indians.

"Though fierce in war they are civil in peace," wrote author Mary Austin Holley in her 1833 book *Texas*. "They call the people of the United States their friends, and give them protection, while they hate the Mexicans and murder them without mercy."

This mutual admiration was, however, neither universal nor long-lived. Many of the immigrants to the new land had no intention of sharing it with its indigenous peoples, among whom the Apache and Comanche were the most formidable. The Comanche in particular had dominated much of Texas for nearly four

Tribal leaders from the era of the Indian Wars included Little Plume, Buckskin Charley, Geronimo, Quanah Parker, Hollow Horn Bear, and American Horse, seen here in ceremonial attire around 1900.

centuries, especially its western plains, and had driven out Spanish, Mexicans, whites, and other Indians alike, and were thus not inclined to roll over for this newest invader. Historian John Howard Griffin wrote in his *Land of the High Sky*—

> . . . *the Comanche saw the frontiersman as an intruder on his lands [and] the frontiersman saw the Comanche as a subhuman fiend. He saw his and his neighbors' homes burned and their livestock stolen. He found white women scalped, brutalized, and mutilated. He buried the bodies of slain white infants, sometimes his own. . .*
> "*Exterminate the Indian*" *was soon heard throughout the Texas colonies.*

Mirabeau B. Lamar, second elected president of the Texas republic (1838–1841), responded to this call from his constituents and was particularly determined to suppress the Indians or exterminate them altogether. Among other things, he raised an army to prosecute the war against the aboriginal peoples and raised a force of fifty-six Texas Rangers specifically to fight the Indians. He also seized lands granted to the Cherokees in exchange for their neutrality during the Texas Revolution.

Lamar's campaign was not without a cost, however, and its palpable side effects included the inexorable destruction of any trust the Indians might have had for the whites and an increase in the debt of the new republic from about $1 million to $8 million (something that contributed to its failure as a nation and ultimate annexation by the United States). Sam Houston made great efforts to pursue a peace policy during his second term as president of Texas (1841–1844), but these were for the most part set aside once Texas became a U.S. state.

Kwahadi Comanche chief Quanah Parker was one of the most famous and effective of the leaders who led the struggle against the U.S. government during the Indian Wars.

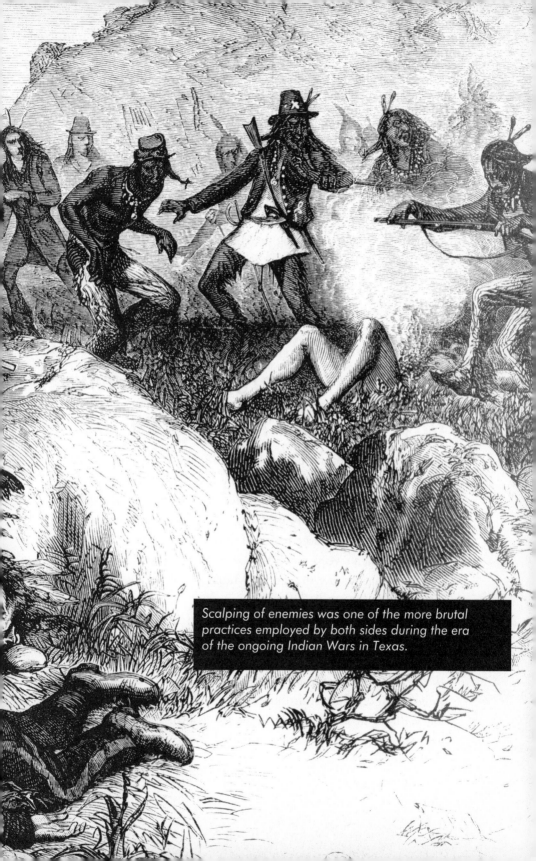

Scalping of enemies was one of the more brutal practices employed by both sides during the era of the ongoing Indian Wars in Texas.

Against this aggression the Comanche held their own in toe-to-toe warfare for a time. Even before Texas became the twenty-eighth state in 1845, however, the Indians had suffered heavy losses and, shunning direct battle with the settlers, had largely withdrawn to the high plains of the *Llano Estacado*. From that ancestral heartland in the western part of the state, they began resorting to savage raids against lone homesteads and small groups of travelers, avoiding or feigning friendliness with large or well-armed forces. Bands of Forty-niners, moving across the Texas plains en route to the California gold fields, were among those who suffered the depredations of the Comanche.

"The technique for scalping was to run a knife around the crown of a person's head, grab the

With the eastern boundary of their domain becoming more impenetrable to them, the Comanche also began turning their attentions southward, toward Mexico, which was a much softer target than aggressively held Texas, and made annual forays against it. Each fall, large bands of braves would gather in west Texas and then sweep down the Great Comanche War Trail—through what is now the city of Midland—and across the Rio Grande to kidnap, kill, and pillage.

In the face of these assaults, Mexican local governments became so desperate that they began to issue bounties for the scalps of hostile Indians and hire bands of mercenaries to collect them *(see the chapter titled "The Border Reivers" for more on this subject)*. And, while scalp hunters like John Glanton, Michael Chevaillie, and James Kirker were seen as little better than savages themselves, they were considered a necessary evil by the frontier settlers who were constantly menaced by Indian raids.

Scalping was, in any event, a grisly and barbaric phenomenon that supposedly did not originate with the Indians but was certainly embraced by them, and it became an almost iconic aspect of the endemic guerrilla warfare between whites and Indians.

"The technique for scalping was to run a knife around the crown of a person's head, grab the hair, place a foot on the victim's shoulder, and yank the scalp," wrote John Howard Griffin. This act was sometimes perpetrated against still-living people, and a number of them lived to tell the tale.

With the onset of the U.S. Civil War in 1861 and the departure of many white men for battlefields to the east, the situation on the frontier became increasingly desperate for the settlers. The sporadic attacks of the Comanche intensified as they tried to eradicate the whites from their lands once and for all.

hair, place a foot on the victim's shoulder, and yank the scalp."

Settlers responded by building "forts," picketed areas inhabited by from four to a dozen families where they could more easily look out for and defend each other; male inhabitants of such places were expected to spend about a quarter of their time on guard duty. Many of the men who remained behind also joined the Texas Rangers and spent ten days a month, more if called upon to do so, ranging along the frontier and conducting suppression operations against the Indians.

Battle between the Texas colonists and the Indians continued for a decade after the end of the Civil War, but by 1875 the natives had lost the war of attrition and were unable to continue any sort of organized resistance. The Indian Wars in Texas had come to an end.

The Murder of Lt. M.P. Harrison

DESPITE THE TENSIONS BETWEEN TEXANS OF ANGLO-
Saxon origin and the native Indian inhabitants of the region, some believed that the two peoples could live in peace together. Sam Houston, the first elected president of the new nation, was one of the most prominent voices in favor of amicable cohabitation with the Indians. His calls for tolerance, however, were largely ignored even in his lifetime.

One apologist of Houston's point of view was twenty-three-year-old Lt. M.P Harrison, an idealistic young U.S. Army officer who accompanied one of the first great journeys of exploration across the American Southwest. A grandson of both former President William Henry Harrison and explorer Zebulon Pike and brother of future President Benjamin Harrison, he was one of America's fair-haired children and, had he lived, might very well have achieved fame himself and influenced national policies toward the Indians.

In March 1849, Harrison had departed Fort Smith, Arkansas, under the command of Army Capt. Randolph B. Marcy and along with two other officers, twenty-six dragoons, and fifty infantrymen charged with escorting to Santa Fe, New Mexico, some two thousand emigrants bound for California.

On the return march to Arkansas, Marcy shifted south, hoping to find an easier route for travels and one suitable for the eventual establishment of a railroad, a journey that took them one thousand miles through uncharted territory. From the white-sand desert around Doña Ana—just north of what is now El Paso—Marcy and his eighteen-wagon party headed east, traveling much of the time through what was then designated as Indian Territory.

On October 6, 1849, the Marcy party pitched camp at a water-fed spot that they dubbed Big Spring, the name of the town that would eventually be established there. While there, Capt. Marcy ordered Lt. Harrison to scout a draw a few miles from the camp.

The next morning, on October 18, 1849, Harrison rode out of camp, armed with a Mississippi long rifle given to the party by another officer who had left the Marcy party in Santa Fe. As he worked his way up the draw, he was pleased to make the acquaintance of two other men, a pair of Comanche warriors. After exchanging greetings, Marcy and the Indians dismounted and sat together on the grass, where they smoked together and chatted for awhile.

During this interaction, the Indians admired the soldier's rifle, and when one of them asked to see it, the friendly Harrison obliged. Their prey disarmed, the two Comanche warriors attacked Harrison, beating him into submission and then tying him into his saddle before leading him away to a spot overlooking a river. There, they executed Harrison by shooting him in the back of the head with his own rifle and then scalped him, stripped him of his possessions, mutilated him horribly, and threw him over the cliff and onto the riverbank below.

When Harrison had not returned by the following morning, Marcy assumed he must have gotten lost and dispatched a search party, guided by the group's Delaware

The Murder of Lt. M.P. Harrison (continued)

Indian scout, to search for him. Before long, they discovered young Lieutenant Harrison's disfigured body and pieced together what had happened to him.

The incident was just one more in the growing list of atrocities committed by one side upon the other in the brutal clash of cultures. A voice of moderation had been silenced forever, and, ironically, the national attention the episode brought because of Harrison's family connections ensured the warfare between whites and Indians would only become more intense in the years that followed.

Comanche warriors like the one pictured here conducted savage raids, often on moonlit nights, against the homesteads of white settlers.

2

Crime and Punishment

TEXAS IS, BY ALL ACCOUNTS, MORE
violent and crime-ridden than the average state,
and it has a commensurate number of places
to keep its convicted criminals.

According to the latest statistics from the National Institute of Corrections, the annual crime rate in Texas is about 18 percent higher than the national average rate and is ranked tenth worse in the country. Violent crimes account for a little more than 11 percent of the crime rate in Texas, about 10 percent higher than that in other states. Property crimes account for the remaining 89 percent or so of the crime rate in Texas, some 19 percent higher than in other states.

The Lone Star State strives to hit back hard against its criminals, however, and statistics indicate that it has an incarceration rate that is 31 percent higher than the national average, with some 649 people out of every 100,000 members of the population jailed or imprisoned (only Oklahoma, Mississippi, and Louisiana have higher rates). The number of people on probation is 22 percent higher than the national average, some 2,401 people per 100,000. The number of parolees in Texas is a strik-

The yard of the state prison unit at Huntsville, Texas, as it appeared in the 1870s.

ing 46 percent higher than the national average, or 579 people per 100,000.

Statewide, there is a vast penal infrastructure for purposes of incarcerating and monitoring these criminals.

Texas opened its first prison on October 1, 1849, in Huntsville; it was originally open only to whites, the only punishments available to blacks in those days being whipping or hanging. Historically, this facility served as the administrative headquarters of

Texans do not spend more than they have to on convicts.

the Texas Prison System and the Texas Department of Corrections. The superintendent and other executive officers worked in the prison, and all of the central offices of the system's departments and its permanent records were located there. It is today part of the Texas Department of Criminal Justice's Region I and is also the site of the state's execution chamber, the most active in the country, with 423 executions between 1982 and 2008.

Texas opened a second facility, Rusk Penitentiary, in January 1883, and since then the Texas prison system has continued to expand. Today, the Texas Department of Criminal Justice operates fifty-one prisons and forty-five other incarceration centers, with a correctional staff of 38,238 overseeing some 171,249 prison inmates.

In addition, throughout the state's 254 counties there are 266 jails with a combined capacity of 79,515 detainees.

There are also a total of 122 Community Supervision and Corrections Departments within local judicial districts, which supervise 427,080 probationers.

While maintaining such a large prison and jail population is not without substantial cost, Texans do not spend more than

Siege at Huntsville

ON JULY 24, 1974, THREE PRISONERS—FRED CARRASCO, Ignacio Cuevas, and Rudy Dominquez—used pistols smuggled into the facility to take fifteen hostages and barricaded themselves in the prison library. This sparked what would become a desperate, eleven-day siege, one of the longest in U.S. history.

Carrasco, a south Texas drug lord serving a life sentence for trying to kill a police officer, was the ringleader of the operation. Eleven of the hostages were employees of the prison system and four were other inmates.

On the final day of the standoff, the three prisoners tried to make a break for it using the hostages, rolling chalkboards, and legal books to create a mobile shield to protect them while they made their way to a waiting vehicle. When the attempt failed, Carrasco shot to death one of the hostages, Elizabeth Beseda, and then turned his gun on himself. Dominquez was shot to death by law enforcement personnel. Cuevas killed another woman, Julia Standley, and was executed nearly seventeen years later, on May 23, 1991, for her murder.

they have to on convicts, and the annual cost per inmate in 2009 was $17,338, a full 40 percent lower than the national average that year of $28,689.

Texas State Prisons

MOST OF THE NEARLY ONE HUNDRED STATE-RUN prisons in Texas are organized into six large regions, with a number of minimum-security facilities being run by private companies under contract to the Texas Department of Criminal Justice. Locations of the headquarters of the various regions are given in parentheses.

Region I (Huntsville)

- Byrd Unit
- Duncan Transfer Facility
- Eastham Unit
- Ellis Unit
- Estelle Unit
- Ferguson Unit
- Goodman Transfer
- Goree Unit
- Holliday Unit
- Huntsville Unit
- Lewis Unit
- Polunsky Unit
- Wynne Unit

Region II (Tennessee Colony)

- Beto Unit
- Boyd Unit
- Coffield Unit
- Cole Unit
- Gurney Transfer Facility
- Hodge Unit
- Hutchins Unit
- Johnston
- Michael Unit
- C. Moore Transfer Facility
- Powledge Unit
- Skyview Unit
- Telford Unit

Region III (Rosharon)

- Central Unit
- Clemens Unit
- Darrington Unit
- Gist Unit
- Henley Unit
- Hightower Unit
- Jester I Unit
- Jester III Unit
- Jester IV Unit
- Kegans Unit
- LeBlanc Unit
- Lychner Unit
- Plane Unit
- Ramsey
- Scott Unit

Texas State Prisons (continued)

- Stiles Unit
- Stringfellow
- Terrell
- Vance Unit
- Young Medical Facility Complex

Region IV (Beeville)

- Briscoe Unit
- Connally Unit
- Cotulla Transfer Facility
- Dominguez Unit
- Fort Stockton Transfer Facility
- Garza East Transfer Facility
- Garza West Transfer Facility
- Glossbrenner Unit
- Lopez Unit
- Lynaugh Unit

- McConnell Unit
- Ney Unit
- Sanchez Unit
- Segovia Transfer
- Stevenson Unit
- Torres Unit

Region V (Plainview)

- Allred Unit
- Baten ISF
- Clements Unit
- Dalhart Unit
- Daniel Unit
- Formby Unit
- Jordan Unit
- Montford Unit
- Neal Unit
- Roach Unit
- Rudd Transfer Facility
- Smith Unit

- Tulia Transfer Facility
- Wallace Unit
- Ware Transfer Facility
- Western Region Medical Facility (Montford)
- Wheeler Unit

Region VI (Austin)

- Crain Unit
- Halbert Unit
- Hamilton Unit
- Havins Unit
- Hilltop Unit
- Hobby Unit
- Hughes Unit
- Luther Unit
- Marlin
- Middleton Transfer Facility

- Mountain View Unit
- Murray Unit
- Pack Unit
- Robertson Unit
- San Saba Unit
- Sayle Unit
- Travis County Unit
- Woodman Unit

Private Facilities

- Bartlett
- Bradshaw
- Bridgeport (Prison)
- Bridgeport (*Pre-Parole Transfer Facility*)
- Cleveland
- Dawson
- Diboll

- East Texas
- Estes
- Kyle
- Lindsey
- Lockhart (*Prison*)
- Lockhart (Work Program)
- Mineral Wells (*Pre-Parole Transfer Facility*)
- Moore, B
- Willacy County

The Holliday Unit in Huntsville is just one of the many prisons in Texas.

3

The Texas State Police

TEXAS WAS AS CHAOTIC AND
dangerous as it has ever been during the nine
years of Reconstruction that followed the end
of the Civil War, when much of the state was
occupied by U.S. military forces and ruled by
unpopular Republican politicians.

During the Constitutional Convention of 1868–69, a study by the Committee on Lawlessness and Violence found that at least 1,035 murders had been committed in Texas from 1865 to 1868—and this did not even include the entire state, as some counties did not provide information. Similarly, available sheriffs' reports for the period 1865 to 1871 indicate the commission of 4,425 crimes for which there were a mere 588 arrests and only a handful of convictions.

A number of factors contributed to this untenable situation, not the least of which is that only 82 of the 254 counties in Texas had jails, and many of these were easy to escape from. Many county sheriffs were also outnumbered and outgunned by criminals and unequipped to enforce the law of the vast land, and some were disinclined to arrest friends and neighbors for certain crimes (e.g., the murders of blacks by whites).

This level of anarchy called for a law enforcement organization that could operate statewide with no limits to its jurisdiction and arrest suspected lawbreakers when local law enforcement officials failed to do so. And so, on July 1, 1870, the state legislature passed the Police Act, which called for the formation of the Texas State Police. This force was directly answerable to Republican Governor Edmund J. Davis, quite possibly the state's most reviled politician, not least of which because of his attempt to have Texas partitioned into three separate states.

While the Texas State Police was authorized to have up to 257 officers, it never had nearly that many, and the total fluctuated from as many as 196 to as few as 166. Its members were a mixed bag in every sense, and included whites, blacks, Hispanics, veterans of both the Union and Confederate forces, dedicated lawmen, and outlaws. The one thing that most had in common was that they were Republicans.

From the start the Texas State Police was highly unpopular,

something that was probably inevitable no matter what it did, and memories of the organization are bitter to this day.

"The hated State Police, composed of black carpetbaggers, criminals, and psychos, was the governor's private force, and was used as a tool of repression," wrote Texas author Gary Cartwright. "When Conservative delegates to the state convention in Galveston in 1871 tried to protest the fraudulent nomination of two black Radicals, Davis' State Police cut off the gaslights and drove the convention out on the streets before the nominations could be overturned or questioned."

Some of its members certainly did provide a basis for criticism, and this started at the very top.

In September 1871, a disgruntled state policeman accused Adjutant General James Davidson, chief of the Texas State Police, of malfeasance in the procurement of supplies for the unit. This was never substantiated but appears as if it might have just been the tip of the iceberg . . .

Fourteen months later, in December 1872, Davidson accompanied Texas Secretary of State James P. Newcomb to New York City on a mission to sell state bonds. While there, officials in Texas discovered he had been embezzling funds from the state treasury that he was supposed to have paid to the officers under him. Davidson had no intention of returning to Texas to face the music and instead disappeared; although he was pursued by men from his own organization, he was never caught and is believed to have possibly settled in Belgium. The total value of his theft was eventually determined to be $37,434.67 (although this was offset to some extent by the seizure of his assets in Texas).

The worst of the bunch was certainly the bloodthirsty Jack Helms. In 1869, Helms, the sheriff of DeWitt County, became involved in the pro-Reconstruction faction of the bloody Sutton-Taylor Feud as one of the law enforcement officers widely known as "Regulators." This unpopular group of special officers terrorized Bee, DeWitt, Goliad, San Patricio, and Wilson Counties throughout the summer of 1869 and, according to the *Galveston News*, killed twenty-one people in July and August of that year, turning a mere ten rival feuders over to the civil authorities.

It was while embroiled in this long-running feud that Helms was appointed as one of the four captains of the Texas State Police. This did not curtail his involvement in the feud, however, and on August 26 he and his detachment arrested two members of the Taylor faction on a trivial charge and then shot them to death. These murders caused such public outrage that Governor Davis could not ignore it, and he responded by suspending Helms in October and then sacking him in December.

Helms continued to be a hazard for a few more months in his capacity as sheriff of DeWitt County, but, in April of 1873, he decided to get out while he was ahead and relocated more than 250 miles northwest to Albuquerque, Texas. Justice was not far behind him, however, and three months later, in July of 1863, two gunmen of the Taylor faction, Jim Taylor and John Wesley Hardin, shot him to death.

Other members of the Texas State Police were also accused of various crimes, and when the unit leadership became aware of them, these charges were typically dropped (although it is certainly likely that many of these accusations were spurious). The presence of blacks in a law-enforcement organization, however, probably stuck in the throats of many white Texans of the era more than anything and led to the ultimate dissolution of the organization. On April 22, 1873, the state legislature repealed the Police Act of 1870 and disbanded the Texas State Police, less than three years after it had been founded.

A few bad apples aside, much of the Texas State Police's unsavory reputation may have been unwarranted.

"Although in older studies the State Police have been described as politically oriented and corrupt, available evidence does not substantiate the charge," the Texas State Historical Association says. "More recent studies claim that earlier Texas historians of Reconstruction allowed bias against Republican organizations to influence their work."

And, far from being outlaws, many of the members of the Texas State Police were certainly dedicated law-enforcement officers with a record of service that speaks for itself. More than three dozen officers became Texas Rangers after the dissolution of the unit, among them the famous Leander H. McNelly. During its first month alone, the Texas State Police made 978 arrests (109 for murder and 130 for attempted murder); in 1871, it made 3,602 arrests; by 1872 it had made a total of 6,820 arrests (587 for murder, 760 for attempted murder, and 1,748 for other serious crimes); and the value of stolen property it recovered was $200,000. And, during the brief tenure of the agency, ten of its members were killed in action, all from gunfire.

4

The Marfa Ghost Lights

FOR AS LONG AS ANYONE AROUND the west Texas town of Marfa can remember, they have seen strange lights burning at night on the Mitchell Flat, an otherwise unexceptional stretch of desert that runs along Highway 90. There are one or two dozen reports of sightings most years, often around the halfway point to Alpine, which lies some twenty-six miles east of Marfa. What the cause of these light may be remains an open mystery that has been examined any number of times but never satisfactorily solved.

Highway 90 runs through Marfa, Texas, and leads out to the spots where many people have witnessed the famous "ghost lights."

Skeptics—including ones who have never investigated the phenomena themselves—have dismissed the Marfa lights in all sorts of predictable ways, typically as automobile headlights, swamp gas, and ranch lights. The fact that the lights don't move in ways characteristic of vehicles goes a long way toward discrediting the headlight explanation, and anyone who has ever driven through west Texas knows there is not enough standing water for a respectable swamp. And anyone familiar with the area knows that there aren't any ranches around where the lights are seen.

"'Oh, those are just ranch lights!'" people will say," said journalist Karen Russell Holmes, a native of the area who helped run Marfa's *Big Bend Sentinel* daily newspaper in the mid-1980s. "No, they're not. There are no ranches there and there are no ranch lights. Drive by during the day and you can see there is absolutely nothing there."

Less prosaic but more earnest explanations include static electricity, the extrusion of some sort of subterranean gas, an atmospheric effect, light glimmering off patches of mica, or even the spirits of the dead—perhaps those of Spanish conquistadors searching for gold—as suggested by the name of the occurrence.

294

Most people who have spent their lives seeing the lights, however, just accept them.

"I grew up in west Texas, and the Marfa lights have always been just part of life for us," said Holmes. "I don't even know that we even looked at it as something supernatural or anything like that; they were just there. They are actually really pretty and remind me of the aurora borealis, with their color and wavering. But for some people it's spooky, because you only can see them at night, and it's on a part of the highway that's a little obscure."

"In 1883 a young cowhand, Robert Reed Ellison, saw a flickering light while he was driving cattle through Paisano Pass and wondered if it was the campfire of Apache Indians," the Texas State Historical Association says. "He was told by other settlers that they often saw the lights, but when they investigated they found no ashes or other evidence of a campsite."

Writer Paul Moran wrote the first published account of the lights in "The Mystery of the Texas Ghost Light," an article

To some it is significant that the Marfa Lights appear in an area once occupied by the Marfa Army Airfield, shown here as it appeared during World War II.

for the July 1957 issue of the hip *Coronet* magazine. The lights have typically been described as bright, glowing, basketball-sized spheres that hover above the ground and which can be almost any color, including white, yellow, orange, red, green, and blue. They have been reported singly and in pairs, and are variously described as appearing and disappearing, remaining stationary, moving in regular patterns or shooting around, splitting apart and going in different directions, and merging together. They can appear any time of year and under any weather conditions during hours of darkness and can remain visible anything from seconds to hours, but disappear if anyone tries to approach them.

Anyone traveling through Marfa who wants to investigate the lights themselves can easily do so.

"Before, you just pulled off on the side of the road to look at the lights," Holmes says. "Now they have a whole nice area there with benches placed where you can stop and view them."

An observation platform that people can use to view the Marfa Ghost Lights is located nine miles east of the town on Highway 90.

5

The Aurora UFO Incident

MANY PEOPLE CONSIDER THE PHENOMENA of Unidentified Flying Objects to be relatively new occurrences that began with the famous 1947 incident in Roswell, New Mexico, an event that has been examined in innumerable books, movies, and television shows.

Beginning in the late 1880s, however, people throughout the United States began reporting seeing all sorts of flying machines in the skies over the country. These accounts varied somewhat in their particulars, describing aircraft of different sizes and characteristics, but a disproportionate number told of large, cigar-shaped flying machines that sound very much like dirigibles. And on April 17, 1897, a half century before the Roswell UFO incident, one of these mysterious airships apparently crashed in the little town of Aurora, Texas, located in Wise County, some twenty-eight miles north-by-northwest of Fort Worth.

This incident was revealed to the world in a newspaper story written by Aurora resident S.E. Haydon and published on April 19, 1897, by the *Dallas Morning News*:

> *About 6 o'clock this morning the early risers of Aurora were astonished at the sudden appearance of the airship which has been sailing through the country.*
>
> *It was traveling due north, and much nearer the earth than ever before. Evidently some of the machinery was out of order, for it was making a speed of only ten or twelve miles an hour and gradually settling toward the earth. It sailed directly over the public square, and when it reached the north part of town collided with the tower of Judge Proctor's windmill and went to pieces with a terrific explosion, scattering debris over several acres of ground, wrecking the windmill and water tank and destroying the judge's flower garden.*

This sandstone marker, etched with the likeness of a UFO, rests on a plot in the cemetery at Aurora, Texas.

The pilot of the ship is supposed to have been the only one on board, and while his remains are badly disfigured, enough of the original has been picked up to show that he was not an inhabitant of this world.

Mr. T.J. Weems, the United States signal service officer at this place and an authority on astronomy, gives it as his opinion that he was a native of the planet Mars."

Papers found on this person—evidently the record of his travels—are written in some unknown hieroglyphics, and cannot be deciphered.

The ship was too badly wrecked to form any conclusion as to its construction or motive power. It was built of an unknown metal, resembling somewhat a mixture of aluminum and silver, and it must have weighed several tons.

The town is full of people today who are viewing the wreck and gathering specimens of the strange metal from the debris. The pilot's funeral will take place at noon tomorrow.

This allegedly alien pilot was indeed reportedly buried the next day at the Aurora Cemetery, something which is briefly mentioned on a nearby Texas Historical Commission marker

"The pilot . . . was not an inhabitant of this world."

erected in 1976. This is particularly interesting in that official-dom generally prefers to ignore peculiar incidents of this sort rather than enhancing the attention they receive by commem-orating them. Amongst prosaic information about the earliest burials at the site, its provenance, notable people interred there, a yellow fever epidemic that ravaged Aurora in 1891, and the town's economic woes, there is a single straightforward sentence about the incident on the marker: "This site is also well known because of the legend that a spaceship crashed nearby in 1897 and the pilot, killed in the crash, was buried here."

Exactly where the ostensible Martian is buried in the eight-hundred-plus-grave site—reportedly "with Christian rites"—is, however, a little unclear. A 1973 investigation of the site and its legend by the Mutual UFO Network (MUFON) and *Dallas Times Herald* aviation writer Bill Case revealed a cov-ered marker that showed what appeared to be a flying saucer of some sort. Not long after the investigation, however, this marker disappeared.

During my own exploration of the site in May 2010, I dis-covered a small sandstone marker that also depicted what was apparently intended to look like a spacecraft of some kind. It looked pretty new, however, and did not seem to be too firmly planted in the ground, both of which suggest it has not actually been there very long (and may not still be there anymore). I also spoke with an older gentleman who was tending to some family graves and in the course of chatting him up asked him if he knew where the legendary grave was supposed to be located, but he said he had no idea where it might be (something, frankly, that

The Roswell UFO Incident

IN THE SUMMER OF 1947, SOMETHING HAPPENED near Roswell, New Mexico, that is believed by many to have involved the crash of an alien spacecraft and the death of its extraterrestrial crew. What became known as the Roswell UFO incident was one of the earliest such episodes of the modern era and since then has become the most famous and iconic of them and the subject of innumerable conspiracy theories and fevered conjectures. This incident also, naturally, has a Texas connection.

On July 8, 1947, the public information office at Roswell Army Air Field released a statement saying that personnel at the base had recovered a crashed "flying disc" from a ranch some thirty miles outside of Roswell.

The many rumors regarding the flying disc became a reality yesterday when the intelligence office of the 509th Bomb Group of the Eighth Air Force, Roswell Army Air Field, was fortunate enough to gain possession of a disc through the cooperation of one of the local ranchers and the sheriff's office of Chaves County. The flying object landed on a ranch near Roswell sometime last week. Not having phone facilities, the rancher stored the disc until such time as he was able to contact the sheriff's office, who in turn notified Maj. Jesse A. Marcel of the 509th Bomb Group Intelligence Office. Action was immediately taken and the disc was picked up at the rancher's home. It was inspected at the Roswell Army Air Field and subsequently loaned by Major Marcel to higher headquarters.

Within twenty-four hours, however, the service had retracted this report and claimed instead that the debris was that of a radar-tracking weather balloon. That was pretty much the end of the story until the late 1970s, when new claims from people involved with the incident drew attention to it once again. And the rest, as they say, is history (albeit a fantastic, lurid history that has included supposed firsthand accounts of alien autopsies).

One of the details of that history that is often overlooked, however, is that whatever crashed in New Mexico and was taken to the air base in Roswell was subsequently packed up and flown to Fort Worth Army Air Field in Texas. (This facility was soon after renamed Carswell Air Force Base and was known as such until 1994, when it was reclassified as Naval Air Station Joint Reserve Base Fort Worth/Carswell Field, the moniker it bears today.) Higher headquarters for the 509th Bomb Group in Roswell was the 8th Air Force, and when its commander, Gen. Roger M. Ramey, heard about the Roswell incident he ordered

The Roswell UFO Incident (continued)

the debris recovered from the crash site to be flown to his base in Fort Worth. It was accompanied by Maj. Marcel, the intelligence officer from Roswell who would eventually become one of the primary sources for the greater legend associated with the incident and characterize the materials as "nothing made on this earth."

Once the debris arrived in Texas, personnel there examined it, and subsequent information about it and its origins was disseminated directly by the headquarters for the 8th Air Force. Subsequent statements reiterated the story about it being a weather balloon and were accompanied by photographs supporting this that purported to show the remains of the wrecked object.

What ultimately happened to the items sent to the air base in Texas is somewhat obscure and has become part of the mystery surrounding the Roswell UFO incident. Some accounts state they were sent thereafter to Washington, D.C., and then on to Area 51, the infamous test facility in the deep desert one hundred miles north of Las Vegas in Nevada, while others claim they ended up at Muroc Army Air Field in California (better known today as Edwards Air Force Base).

to me did not seem very credible for a longtime resident who evidently spent lots of time in the cemetery).

In the course of its investigation of the site (featured in a December 2, 2005, episode of the television show *UFO Files* titled "Texas' Roswell"), MUFON got some peculiar readings with its metal detector, which seemed to jibe with accounts about material from the crash being buried with the spaceman. The group asked to exhume the gravesite but the cemetery association denied it permission to do so. The group was also not able to detect anything with subsequent use of its metal detector and figured that whatever metal had been buried there had been removed.

Examining the wreckage itself did not prove any easier to the MUFON investigators. It had ostensibly been dropped down a well near the crash site and, when a subsequent owner of the property had attempted to clear it out many years later so that he could use the well for water, he reportedly became ill as a result. In 1957, he is supposed to have responded to this by capping the well with a concrete slab and putting an outbuilding on top of it. He refused MUFON permission to unseal the well.

The MUFON investigators also interviewed two apparent eyewitnesses to the 1897 crash and its aftermath, one of whom had been fifteen at the time and the other of whom had been ten, and they corroborated many of the claims that had been made about it.

Finally, the MUFON's investigators discovered a piece of metal, purportedly from the crash, that analysis revealed to be 95 percent aluminum and 5 percent iron, with no trace elements, something that the group concluded could not have been terrestrial in nature given the technological capabilities of 1897 (but even the group acknowledges that the scrap might have been deposited where it was found anytime in the preceding one hundred years).

Perhaps needless to say, many people have dismissed the incident as a hoax, and have even gone out of their way to prove this was the case, including former mayor of Aurora Barbara Brammer, who postulated that Haydon's article was a desperate attempt to breathe life into what at that point was a dying town. The fact that neither the newspaper nor Haydon followed up on the story seems to support her supposition (but equally well supports conspiracy theories about cover-ups).

A 1979 article in *Time* magazine examined the legend and quoted some older residents of the town who said the story had been made up and that there had never actually been a windmill on the property in question.

This statement in particular, however, was refuted in a 2008 investigation by another show, *UFO Hunters,* a spinoff of the earlier *UFO Files,* in an episode titled "First Contact."

Many people have dismissed the incident as a *hoax.*

In a notable departure from earlier experiences, this group of investigators was given access to the well. Examination of it revealed high aluminum content in the water but no large pieces of debris, leading the members of group to suggest that it must have been removed by some previous owner of the property. They also discovered the remains of a windmill base right where one should have been.

The *UFO Hunters* group also investigated the cemetery. Similarly denied permission to exhume the grave, they used ground-penetrating radar to reveal an unmarked grave that appeared to be from the 1890s. The remains within it were so badly deteriorated, however, that they could not determine much about them.

So, whatever happened at Aurora in the last years of the nineteenth century remains a mystery to this day—the only apparent certainty being that something did indeed happen there and that more investigation is warranted.

6

Howard the Barbarian

"Barbarism is the natural state of mankind. Civilization is unnatural. It is a whim of circumstance. And barbarism must always ultimately triumph."

— Robert E. Howard, *"Beyond the Black River"*

Up until a few years ago, visitors to the central Texas prairie community of Cross Plains could still meet a handful of very old residents who remembered seeing author Robert E. Howard running around town wearing a cloak and carrying a sword. In our own era of Renaissance fairs, fantasy conventions, and ubiquitous black-clad Goths, the brilliant young

Author Robert E. Howard as he appeared in 1934.

writer would certainly attract much less attention (although probably he'd still be pretty well marginalized in a small Texas town). But in the Cross Plains of the 1920s and '30s, his behavior was nothing less than scandalous.

The imaginative mind that prompted him to act in ways inconceivable to the ranchers, farmers, and townsfolk he grew up with, however, also inspired him to create a seminal body of pulp fiction, conceive iconic characters like Conan the Barbarian, and become the father of the literary genre now known as

Howard achieved a modicum of success in his lifetime by having his stories published in a variety of pulp periodicals.

"Sword and Sorcery." And he accomplished all that by the time of his premature and tragic death at the age of just thirty.

Howard was born and raised in the Lone Star State and drew inspiration from the things he saw and experienced travelling around it and the Southwest in general. During a trip to Fredericksburg and the Texas Hill Country in 1932, he was stirred to create the harsh land of Cimmeria, home to his legendary hero, Conan. A bodybuilder and amateur boxer, the hulking Howard cultivated within himself some spark of the rugged heroes he relished writing about from an early age.

While his protagonists could survive encounters with wizards, warriors, and monsters of every type, Howard could not prevail against the toxic bonds forged between him and a clingy, terminally ill mother, Hester. Even before she met travelling physician Isaac Mordecai Howard and had a single child with him, she had been diagnosed with tuberculosis and spent the entirety of her son's short life fading away before him. She also derided, fought with, and attempted to drive a wedge between her son and his father, whom she looked down on.

But the intellectual Hester also did much to instill in her son

Robert E. Howard's home in Cross Plains, Texas, is now operated as a museum dedicated to his life and works.

a love of literature and poetry and was one of the forces that set him on the path he chose. Storytelling was also a prominent feature of the society in which Howard grew up. And life in rural Texas—where he heard stories from just the generation before

The town of Cross Plains is today proud of its association with the famous fantasy author, as indicated by this mural on the side of a downtown building.

of gunfights, feuds, and Indian raids, saw injuries treated by his father, and encountered toughs and bullies in both the school-yard and the somewhat seedy and dangerous boomtown that Cross Plains became when oil was discovered there—supplied his hardboiled worldview and the seeds of much that he wrote about in his fantasy, Western, and horror stories and poems.

"I've seen whole towns debauched by an oil boom and boys and girls go to the devil wholesale," Howard wrote to friend H.P. Lovecraft in 1930. "I've seen promising youths turn from respectable citizens to dope-fiends, drunkards, gamblers, and

One of the items at the Robert E. Howard Museum in Cross Plains, Texas, is the author's typewriter, which contains a copy of his suicide note.

gangsters in a matter of months." Violence, theft, gambling, prostitution, and even banditry plagued Cross Plains beginning in 1920, when oil was discovered and the population exploded from fifteen hundred to ten thousand in the course of just a few months.

Howard's stories incorporated such personal observations, his love for history and the Southwest, and elements of the macabre, the supernatural, social decay, and the esoteric.

Life as a freelance writer can be harrowing in any age, and despite his many successes, Howard had suffered through many menial and short-term jobs while trying to establish himself; the ongoing struggle had taken a toll on him. By the summer of 1936, he had been widely published in *Weird Tales* and several other magazines, was on the verge of having his first novel published, and, during the Depression, earned more than anyone else in Cross Plains. But payment for his work was always slow and never enough, many of his closest friends—including his sole girlfriend—had moved on with lives that did not include him, and his mother required an increasing amount of attention that kept him from his writing.

And, on top of everything else, his mother's final demise was too much for Howard to handle, and he would not survive it. In the weeks leading up to his mother's inevitable death, there is evidence that he had begun to plan for his own.

On June 11, 1936, Hester Howard slipped into a coma for the last time. When he was told that she would never again awake, Robert E. Howard walked out to his car, took a borrowed automatic pistol out of the glove compartment, and fatally shot himself in the head.

Author Robert E. Howard is buried beside his parents in a cemetery in Brownwood, Texas.

In many ways, of course, Howard lives on in his work and in the minds of those he has entertained and inspired in the more than eight decades since his first words were published. And those who wish to can visit the home in Cross Plains where he lived and died, which has now been restored by a local organization as the Robert E. Howard Museum, or the gravesite in Brownwood, where he rests beneath a headstone that also bears the names of his father and mother.

7

The Paperclip Swastika

IN THE YEARS FOLLOWING WORLD War II, an obscure office of the Joint Chiefs of Staff illegally relocated some sixteen hundred Nazi war criminals to the United States and placed them in sensitive scientific and industrial positions throughout the country. Unbeknownst to many, a significant number of these unreformed fascists ended up in the vicinity of El Paso and elsewhere throughout the state of Texas.

Less than two weeks after Germany surrendered to the Allied Powers in May 1945, the Joint Intelligence Objectives Agency (JIOA) brought the first of these Germans to the United States under the aegis of what would become known as Operation Paperclip. Most of them were rocket scientists, chemists, nuclear physicists, and physicians whose expertise the United States hoped to exploit initially in the war with Japan and then in its ongoing arms race with the Soviet Union.

Toward the end of that year, three groups of rocket scientists arrived at Fort Bliss, Texas, and nearby White Sands Proving Grounds, New Mexico, where they were classified as "War Department Special Employees." There were ultimately more than a hundred German war criminals employed at Fort Bliss alone, and many of these people and their families resided in nearby El Paso. Their presence there turned the sleepy Southwestern town into a Cold War hotspot on par with cities like Berlin, with communist spies both seeking to gain information from and

about them. These intelligence agents also helped maintain a line of communication between the Paperclip scientists and former colleagues who had been captured by the Soviet Union and employed in its weapons research laboratories.

It was not until more than a year after the JIOA had begun importing war criminals into the country that President Harry Truman actually authorized Operation Paperclip. In doing so, he ordered that the project prohibit anyone who had "been a member of the Nazi Party, and more than a nominal participant in its activities, or an active supporter of Nazi militarism." This would have excluded most of the scientists the JIOA wanted to channel through the program—not to mentioned those it already had—so it went to great efforts to cover up and expunge the actual wartime work and political histories and replace them with revised and whitewashed versions. These efforts violated not just

Taken in 1946, this photograph shows 104 German scientists, many of them Nazi war criminals brought illegally into the United States, who worked on weapons projects at White Sands Proving Grounds and Fort Bliss, Texas. Those pictured here include Wernher von Braun, Ludwig Roth, and Arthur Rudolph.

U.S. laws but also agreements the United States had made with its fellow Allied Powers.

"By 1955, nearly a thousand German scientists had been granted citizenship in the United States and given prominent po-

Their presence turned the sleepy Southwestern town into a Cold War hotspot.

sitions in the American scientific community," author Jim Marrs writes in *The Rise of the Fourth Reich*. "Many had been longtime members of the Nazi Party and the Gestapo, had conducted experiments on humans at concentration camps, used slave labor, and committed other war crimes." Many of them had also been involved in the development of weapons systems like the infamous V-2 rocket and had been classified as a "menace to the security of the Allied Forces."

A number of the Paperclip scientists ended up elsewhere in Texas, and one of the most prominent of these was physician Hubertus Strughold, the originator of the term "space medicine." In 1948, he became the first and last "Professor of Space Medicine" at the School of Aviation Medicine at Randolph Air Force Base in San Antonio, and the following year, he was appointed director of the school's Department of Space Medicine (now the U.S. Air Force School of Aerospace Medicine at Brooks City-Base in San Antonio).

Strughold held many other positions of responsibility and was honored for his numerous accomplishments right up until his death in 1986, to include having the aeromedical library at Brooks named after him. In the 1990s, however, documents from the Nuremberg War Crimes Tribunal revealed that Strughold had conducted medical experiments on prisoners at the Dachau concentration camp and that many of them had been tortured and killed in the process. Suffice it to say, the library at Brooks no longer bears his name.

Many of the other Paperclip scientists were outed for their wartime activities earlier than that, and in the years following their arrival in the United States, a number were deported, tried for their crimes, or otherwise disgraced. Many more, however, escaped justice altogether and enjoyed fruits bought at the expense of the victims of World War II during the nearly half a century that Operation Paperclip was conducted in one form or another.

"The project continued nonstop until 1973—*decades* longer than was previously thought," writes former CNN investigative reporter Linda Hunt in her *Secret Agenda: The United States Government, Nazi Scientists, and Project Paperclip, 1945 to 1990.* "And remnants of it are still in operation today."

8

The Texas City Disaster

EARLY ON THE MORNING OF APRIL 16,
1947, the French cargo vessel SS *Grandcamp*,
heavily laden with highly explosive ammonium
nitrate fertilizer, caught fire at its berth in the
Galveston Bay port of Texas City.

Almost the entirety of the local fire department, some twenty-six firefighters with all the available equipment, including four trucks, responded in an attempt to douse the blaze. At 9:12 a.m., however, the vessel exploded in a massive fireball that annihilated the entire dock area, the Monsanto Chemical Company plant, and numerous other structures. It also showered massive pieces of iron shrapnel and flaming debris thousands of feet in every direction, destroying buildings and igniting fires throughout the city and generating a fifteen-foot tidal wave.

All the firefighters and spectators were killed in the explosion, and another fertilizer-packed ship, SS *High Flyer,* was set on fire. Workers managed to tow it one hundred feet away from the ruined docks but could not extinguish the blaze, and sixteen hours later, at 1:10 a.m. on April 17, it, too, exploded. With no firefighters and equipment available to fight them, fires raged

Nearly six hundred people were killed in the explosions and fires caused by the Texas City Disaster, making it the worst industrial catastrophe in U.S. history.

Plumes of smoke from the explosions and ensuing fires at the Texas City wharfs could be seen from miles away.

unchecked throughout the city until volunteers could be mobilized and factory disaster plans set in motion.

"Damage to property outside the dock area was widespread," the official report on the disaster reads. "Approximately 1,000 residences and business buildings suffered either major structural damage or were totally destroyed. Practically every window exposed to the blast in the corporate limits was broken. Several plate glass windows as far away as Galveston (10 miles) were shattered. Flying steel fragments and portions of the cargo were found 13,000 feet distant. A great number of balls of sisal twine, many afire, were blown over the area like torches. Numerous oil tanks were penetrated by flying steel or were crushed by the blast wave which followed the explosions. Drill stems 30 feet long, 6

More Industrial Mayhem

DESPITE THE MAGNITUDE OF THE 1947 DISASTER, Texas City recovered fairly quickly, and its docks, warehouses, and chemical plants were rebuilt within three years. Today, the port of Texas City is the ninth largest in the United States and the third largest in Texas in terms of tonnage shipped through it. That level of activity, however, has continued to make it a venue for industrial mayhem.

In October 1987, a crane at the Marathon Oil refinery accidentally dropped a load of equipment on a tank of liquid hydrogen fluoride, releasing thirty-six thousand pounds of highly toxic hydrogen fluoride gas, which spread out over the city in a plume three miles long and a mile wide. Some three thousand residents were evacuated from a fifty-two-block area, and critics later claimed that more than twenty times as many people had been endangered and should have been removed.

In March 2005, an explosion rocked a BP oil refinery, killing fifteen people and injuring more than a hundred. With more than two thousand people employed at the refinery, this disaster could have been much worse, and the implications are only hinted at when one considers that it is the third-largest petroleum refinery in the country, processing some 460,000 barrels of crude oil and about 4 percent of national gasoline consumption each day.

3/8 inches in diameter, weight 2,700 pounds, part of the cargo of the SS *Grandcamp* were found buried six feet in the clay soil a distance of 13,000 feet from the point of the explosion."

The exact number of people killed in the disaster is unclear but is probably around 581—some 398 of whom were identified, the balance being unidentified or presumed missing. Part of the uncertainty was caused by the destruction of the Monsanto personnel and payroll records. As many as five thousand people were injured. Estimates of property loss soon after the disaster were around $67 million (a staggering $640 million in adjusted 2011 dollars!). Lawsuits against the governments of France and the United States continued into the 1960s, and reforms in the way chemicals were manufactured, stored, and shipped were called for.

More than six decades after it occurred, the Texas City disaster remains the worst industrial catastrophe in U.S. history and, deregulation and shoddy corporate practices by companies like BP notwithstanding, has yet to be surpassed.

The massive explosions of two vessels at the port of Texas City in 1947 scattered debris thousands of feet in every direction and caused widespread destruction throughout the area.

9

Mistreating the Treaty Tree

IN MARCH OF 1989, A FORTY-FIVE- year-old heroin addict and farm equipment salesman named Paul Stedman Cullen dumped two containers of a powerful herbicide on a five-hundred-year-old live oak in downtown Austin, Texas, as part of a black magic ritual. The victim, known as the Treaty Oak, had sprouted about the time Christopher Columbus was setting sail for the New World, and by the time it was attacked, its branches had spread to an impressive 127 feet.

The Treaty Oak in Austin, Texas, which was old centuries before the first people of European descent began to settle in Texas, was severely damaged by a vicious attack in 1989.

Located on the east bank of the Colorado River in a park named for it, the majestic tree was the last remnant of a fourteen-tree grove called the Council Oaks that had been used as a sacred meeting place by the indigenous Comanche and Tonkawa Indian tribes. There, they would plan variously for war or peace and brew a protective potion from honey and the acorns of the holy trees.

According to local legend, in the 1830s, Stephen F. Austin, the "Father of Texas," met with Indian leaders at the grove to negotiate and formalize Texas' first boundary treaty, and, three decades later, Sam Houston reputedly rested beneath the great oak after being removed as governor at the start of the state's involvement in the Civil War.

By the late 1920s, the Treaty Oak was the final surviving member of the historic grove, but was thriving in its solitude: the American Forestry Association declared it the most perfect specimen of a tree anywhere in North America and inducted it into its hall of fame in Washington, D.C. A decade later, the city of Austin purchased the land the tree was growing on and made it into a small municipal park. It became a popular site for people to picnic, for children to climb, for young men to propose to their girlfriends, even for weddings.

When Cullen attacked the gnarled and ancient Treaty Oak, he did so with enough of a powerful hardwood defoliant called Velpar, according the experts, to kill one hundred normal trees. By Memorial Day of 1989, about two months after it had been poisoned, people began to notice the effects of the poisoning and it became apparent that the great old tree—which had withstood flood, drought, insects, pollution, and all sorts of other hazards for some five centuries—was dying. By June, it had lost all of its leaves, and every time it grew a new set, it shed them soon after, something that would eventually sap its resources and kill it.

Cullen's crime sparked an overwhelming emotional response, not only in Austin or Texas as a whole, but throughout the country and even internationally. Children sent get-well cards that were hung on the fence around the park, people wept and prayed for the tree's recovery or called for the perpetrator to be hung from its branches, industrialist and one-time Reform Party candidate for president Ross Perot wrote a "blank check" to finance the efforts to save it, and Velpar manufacturer DuPont donated $10,000 as a reward for the capture of the poisoner. Toward the end of June, the city flew in eighteen experts on live oaks and hardwood herbicides to formulate a plan for saving the tree.

Extreme efforts to save the famous tree included replacing the contaminated soil around it; installing a system to mist it with water as an antidote to the extreme heat of summer; truck-

"I bet he rues the day he decided to go at that tree."

ing in sixteen thousand gallons of spring water a week for the misters; setting up sixty-foot-high shades to protect it from the sun; wrapping its trunk in plastic; using charcoal and microbes to break down the poison; and injecting sugar, saline, and other nutrients into its root system.

Cullen was eventually caught after bragging to a friend about poisoning the Treaty Oak as part of casting a spell intended to destroy his love for a woman who worked at the methadone clinic he went to and to protect her from another man. He also wanted to avenge himself against the state for outdoor work he had been compelled to do while serving time on a conviction for felony burglary. Unable to afford his $20,000 bond, he spent nearly a year in jail before being tried.

"The guy could have killed two to three people in downtown Austin . . . He could have blown up a building that nobody had heard of and not be in this much trouble," Sgt. Gary L. Richards of the Austin Police department said of Cullen. "I bet he rues the day he decided to go at that tree."

Cullen was, in fact, convicted of felony criminal mischief in State District Court in Houston, and on May 10, 1990, he was sentenced by a jury to nine years in prison and fined $1,000. He got off easy, by all accounts, as his previous felony conviction meant that he could have been sentenced to life in prison.

Despite the severity of the vicious attack, and contrary to expectations, the Treaty Oak survived. It did not do so unscathed, however, and some two-thirds of the historic tree died, and more than half its crown had to be pruned away. In 1997, however, the tree produced its first crop of acorns since being poisoned, which the city gathered, germinated, and distributed throughout Texas and other states. Today, the tree survives, maimed and truncated but once again healthy—as fitting a symbol as any for the resilience of Texas and its people.

10

Legend of the Chupacabra

FOR THE PAST SEVERAL YEARS, THE boogeyman that has haunted the Texas darkness has been the chupacabra, a creature that many dismiss as a legend but which an increasing number of people hold accountable whenever something goes bump in the night or happens that they cannot readily explain.

Since at least 1995, there have been reports throughout the Spanish-speaking world and beyond of creatures bearing the name chupacabra, but these have had widely varying characteristics, contributing to a breakdown of rational discussion on the subject. The creature to which that name has been attributed in Puerto Rico, for example, has been described as a sometimes-winged chimerical monster with spines running down its back and attributes of humanoid, reptile, and vampire.

Chupacabra, in fact, can roughly be translated as "goat sucker," referring to the blood-drained livestock that this creature has been blamed for killing. So, when someone—often a local news reporter—invokes the word chupacabra, some people pay greater attention, but a lot of people stop paying attention at all.

What ranchers and law enforcement personnel have reported seeing in Texas, however, is a verifiably real beast and does not have the supernatural or alien characteristics of creatures bearing the same name in Argentina, Bolivia, Brazil, Chile, Colombia, the Dominican Republic, El Salvador, Honduras, Mexico, Nicaragua, Panama, Peru, the Philippines, Russia, and throughout the United States. The Texas chupacabra is nonetheless still pretty weird and looks like a canine with characteristics that include longer-than-usual legs, exceptionally large teeth, a rank odor, and a gray, mostly hairless hide that is sometimes described as "mangy."

"We're certainly not dealing with a domestic dog," Dr. Eileen Johnson, an anthropologist with Texas Tech University, said on an episode of the National Geographic television series *Paranatural* after examining the mangled remains of a suspected chupacabra that had been run over by a car. "And we're not dealing with a red wolf."

Some experts have suggested that the creature known as a chupacabra in the Lone Star State might be a crossbreed between a coyote and some sort of dog, or a coyote or a dog with a xolo, a type of hairless Mexican wild dog. Others say it is likely a genetic hybrid between a coyote and a gray wolf or Mexican wolf (which does not, however, explain why such creatures would be hairless).

Over the past decade, there have been dozens of reported sightings of actual or supposed chupacabras throughout Texas.

In July 2004, for example, a rancher in Elmendorf, near San Antonio, killed an apparent chupacabra that had been attacking his livestock, and three months later the bodies of two similar beasts were found. DNA testing indicated that the creatures were, at least in part, coyotes.

In 2006, a farmer in Coleman captured and killed a strange creature matching the description of a chupacabra and turned it over to the Texas Department of Parks and Wildlife officials for identification. Soon after, however, the remains of the creature disappeared, and an official identification was never tendered.

In August 2007, a rancher in the south Texas town of Cuero whose chickens were being killed and drained of blood found the carcasses of three strange doglike creatures, and scientific examinations of them revealed both coyote DNA and physical characteristics associated with chupacabras.

In August 2008, a DeWitt County deputy sheriff used his dashboard camera to film a hairless, doglike creature with a long snout and exceptionally long back legs running along some back roads near Cuero. This footage has subsequently become some of the most famous associated with the chupacabra and has appeared in numerous programs about the creature.

Then, in August 2009, following the lead of a KSAT 12 news reporter, a national media furor erupted when a taxidermist in the Hill Country town of Blanco, about fifty miles north of San Antonio, claimed to have a chupacabra in his workshop. CNN picked up the story, and the following day a Telemundo news crew showed up outside the taxidermy shop in Blanco, and taxidermist Jerry Ayer started getting invitations to appear on talk shows. Ayer was not interested in the publicity, but he did preserve and mount the chupacabra and then sell it for an undisclosed sum to the Lost World Museum, a creationist institution in Phoenix, New York.

Sightings, shootings and trappings, discovery of strange carcasses, and the like have continued pretty much unabated since, and the word chupacabra has sometimes been thrown around pretty indiscriminately.

In January 2010, for example, news reports broke of an ostensible chupacabra that had been found dead on a golf course in the north Texas town of Runaway Bay, and the *Wise County Messenger* said the "brown, earth-colored creature is hairless with oversized canines and elongated padded feet with inch-long toes tapered with sharp, curved claws. The creature also had long hind legs." A careful examination of this monster, however, revealed it to be a raccoon that had been rendered hairless by mange.

Runaway Bay, however, remained true to its devotion to the chupacabra legend, and in May 2010, lack of a real sighting notwithstanding, its city council voted to make the creature the official mascot of the community.

This doglike creature, which was identified as a chupacabra in August 2009, is shown here skinned and being prepared for mounting in a taxidermy shop in Blanco, Texas.

11

Zombies Ahead!

EARLY ON THE MORNING OF MONDAY, January 19, 2009, commuters in the state capital of Austin were surprised to see the dire warnings "ZOMBIES AHEAD" and "Zombies ahead! Run for your lives!" on two large electronic signs. The messages had been posted sometime the night before.

Subsequent statements by officials claimed that the construction zone placards at the intersections of Lamar Boulevard with West Fifteenth Street and Martin Luther King Boulevard—near the University of Texas at Austin—had, in fact, been hacked by pranksters. They made no reference to the presence of any actual zombies.

Officials responded to the apparently spurious messages with a characteristic lack of humor, noting that tampering with the digital signs endangers the public and is a class C misdemeanor in Texas, punishable by fines and possibly jail. Padlocks securing the signs had been cut and the password-protected computers that control them had been overridden.

The precise motivation for the hackers, beyond a selfless desire to warn fellow citizens about an outbreak of the undead, was unclear. Speculation included the episode being a response to the recent release of various zombie-oriented video games and films.

"Even though this may seem amusing to a lot of people, this is really serious, and it is a crime," said Sara Hartley, a representative for Austin Public Works. "We want to make sure our traffic on the roadways stays safe."

Many local residents, however, were indeed amused by the incident.

"I thought it was pretty funny," one University of Texas student said in an interview with local media. "We wondered who did it."

Officials wondered, too, and in the wake of the incident vowed to make it harder for troublemakers to suborn the traffic signs.

"The big problem is public safety," said Hartley. "Those signs are out there to help our traffic on the roadway to stay safe and to know what's coming up."

Officials did not, however, have anything to say about how they planned to respond in the event of an actual zombie attack.

12

Let the Bad Times Roll

YOU CAN'T SPELL "ABUSIVE" WITHOUT "bus," something riders on VIA Metropolitan Transit, the public transportation system of San Antonio, were well aware of by the summer of 2010, when the system had become so plagued by violence that it received national attention.

"One of the major reasons people say why they don't ride public transit is because of fear. They think something will happen to them," said VIA CEO Keith Parker at a press conference around that time.

Such concerns were, by all means, not without a legitimate basis, as disturbing images captured by onboard cameras on VIA buses revealed. Those images were made public in September 2010, when WOAI Channel 4, the local NBC news affiliate, investigated the situation and aired footage from onboard bus cameras that it had obtained. Some of the images were so striking that they ended up both getting shown on CNN and getting dispersed across the Internet.

In one incident depicted in the videos, a group of teenagers assaults a girl talking on a cell phone, throws her to the floor, and begins stomping on her. Another incident shows a four-person brawl in which, after a passenger and his assailants are thrown off a bus, the operator closes the door and then drives off as the ejected passenger is beaten. Others show large groups of young people rioting as the buses roll down the street.

In one of the most iconic and horrifying/amusing episodes, the mothers of two newborns begin pounding each other, a baby hanging from the chest of the one throwing the first punch; as other travelers rush in to break up the fracas, the hapless baby of the one woman can be seen bouncing around on her chest, and the other can be seen lying behind its mother, ignored during the melee.

People interviewed by local media have also described incidents that include people being menaced by knife-wielding hooligans. Where does the fun end?

The mothers of two newborns begin pounding each other.

Things had reached such epidemic proportions by mid-2010 that VIA decided to get tough and laid down the law by . . . publishing a code of conduct on September 1 of that year. Uh huh. A perusal of this extensive and colorful list of prohibitions reveals some of the shenanigans to which riders have been exposed (and is a fun read in and of itself).

One has to wonder, of course, just how effective a published code of conduct is going to be in swaying the behavior of people inclined to do the sorts of things it proscribes. Who, for example, is going to scroll through the various prohibitions, get to item 12—which prohibits "Spitting, urinating, defecating or exposing one's anus, breasts, or genitals"—and, duly impressed, think, "Huh! Well, I *was* going to expose my anus, breasts, or genitals, but I guess that just isn't allowed so I had better not."

A big proportion of the things banned by the code are, in any event, simply against the law in Texas or anywhere else with a modicum of civilization and thus serve only to request people not engage in behavior that is always criminal in nature, on or off a bus (e.g., to "Illegally possess, use, distribute, or sell any controlled substance").

According to the head of VIA, however, the problems on the system are not that bad, especially where compared to those on other urban transit systems, and giving riders some rules to live by will likely do the trick.

"Our goal is to get that very small percentage of folks who don't behave properly . . . into compliance," Parker said. "Now after trying that, if they don't, we will do whatever necessary to remove them from our services and ask them to find a ride somewhere else."

In the meantime, anyone who could find a ride somewhere else had likely already done so.

VIA Code of Conduct

IT IS A VIOLATION TO COMMIT THE FOLLOWING ACTS
on a VIA vehicle, VIA facility or VIA property:

1. Smoke or expel the residue of any tobacco product including chewing tobacco on a VIA bus or other VIA vehicle or at a VIA facility or on VIA property, except as allowed in designated areas.

2. Consume any alcoholic beverage or possess an open container of any alcoholic beverage on a VIA bus or other VIA vehicle or at a VIA facility or on VIA property.

3. Eating on a VIA bus or other VIA vehicle unless medically necessary.

4. Drinking beverages on a VIA bus or other VIA vehicle without using a spill-proof or screw-top container.

5. Engage in disruptive, disturbing behavior including: loud conversation, profanity, rude insults, or operating any electronic device used for sound (radio, MP3 player, etc.) without an earphone(s).

6. Take any animal onto a VIA bus or other VIA vehicle unless the animal's purpose is to assist a person with a disability, or unless the animal is in training to assist a person with a disability, or unless the animal is secured in a container sufficient to contain the animal.

7. Carry or possess any illegal weapon.

8. Possess or transport any explosive, flammable liquid, combustible material, or other dangerous substance such as gasoline, kerosene, or propane.

9. Litter.

(continued on next page)

VIA Code of Conduct (continued)

10. Vandalize any VIA bus or other VIA vehicle, VIA facility or VIA property by writing, marking, scribbling, defacing or causing destruction to the bus, vehicle, facility or property in any manner.

11. Beg, solicit, or panhandle from another person.

12. Spitting, urinating, defecating or exposing one's anus, breasts, or genitals.

13. Illegally possess, use, distribute, or sell any controlled substance.

14. Engage in any horseplay or fighting.

15. Ride a VIA bus or other VIA vehicle without evidence that the proper fare has been paid.

16. Unauthorized presence on a VIA bus or other VIA vehicle, VIA facility, or VIA property after hours of operation.

17. Unauthorized use of a VIA bus or other VIA vehicle, VIA facility or VIA property.

18. Interfering with the operation of a VIA bus or other VIA vehicle.

A person who violates one or more of these regulations may be warned and/or ordered to leave the VIA bus or other VIA vehicle, VIA facility, or VIA property immediately by a VIA Police Officer or a VIA Bus or Paratransit Supervisor. Situations where a person refuses to leave a VIA bus or other VIA vehicle, VIA facility or VIA property after being ordered to do so may be handled by VIA Police or other appropriate law enforcement agencies.

13

Gangland Texas

NUMEROUS GANGS REIGN OVER THE criminal underworld of Texas, prowling its urban streets and rural highways, and wreaking violence on anyone who would challenge their control of lucrative concessions like the drug trade, prostitution, and various rackets. Many of these groups' activities spill over into other states and even into the war zone that is the border with Mexico.

Some of the most dangerous gangs operating in Texas or along its border with Mexico were founded by or use deserters from various special-forces units.

"Approximately 5,297 gangs with nearly 111,000 members are criminally active in the Southwest Region," the FBI's National Gang Intelligence Center said in a 2009 report. "According to interviews with local law enforcement officers, gangs are responsible for as much as 60 percent of crime in some communities in the Southwest Region (Texas, Arizona, Colorado, New Mexico, Oklahoma, and Utah). The most significant gangs operating in the region are Barrio Azteca, Latin Kings, Mexikanemi, Tango Blast, and Texas Syndicate."

Most of the following gangs are currently active in the Lone Star State, although a few enjoyed their heyday in decades past. A few are also active primarily in the Texas Department of Criminal Justice prison system.

Bandidos Motorcycle Club (aka Bandido Nation)

Established in San Leon, Texas, in 1966, the Bandidos Motorcycle Club is a "one-percenter" outlaw motorcycle gang and organized crime syndicate with an estimated twenty-four hundred members in ninety chapters in the United States. It also has more than a hundred international chapters and numerous support clubs that it uses as fronts for both legal and illegal activities. Its symbol is an obese Mexican *bandido* brandishing a pistol and machete, and its slogan is "We are the people our parents warned us about."

Historically, the Bandidos have been active in drug running, prostitution, enforcement, and contract killings, and are believed to have been involved in the attempted assassination of U.S. Attorney James Kerr in San Antonio (called for by drug kingpin Jimmy Chagra, who contracted the hit on federal judge John Wood III; see "The Crime of the Century" in the "Murder" section).

"I don't have no remorse."

Founder Donald Eugene Chambers ended up serving eleven years in prison for his role in the 1972 murder in El Paso of two drug dealers who sold the Bandidos baking soda on the pretense that it was methamphetamine.

"First, the Bandidos and their old ladies tortured the brothers a few days," journalist Gary Cartwright wrote in his book *Dirty Dealing*. "Then they hauled them to an isolated spot in the desert and made them dig a common grave," where they executed them with a sawed-off shotgun and then buried them.

Violence remained an important part of the Bandidos' way of life. On August 2004, gang member Richard Merla was convicted for stabbing to death International Boxing Federation super flyweight champion Robert Quiroga.

"I don't regret it," Merla said. "I don't have no remorse. I don't feel sorry for him and his family. I don't and I mean that." This was a bit much even for the Bandidos, and they expelled Merla (who is currently serving his sentence at the Alfred Hughes unit in Gatesville and will likely be released in 2047).

In March 2006, the police in Austin announced that Bandidos were the primary suspects in the slaying of Anthony Benesh, a forty-four-year-old motorcyclist who had been trying to start a local Hells Angels chapter. He was assassinated with a high-powered rifle during the same weekend as the Bandidos were celebrating the fortieth anniversary of their founding.

Barrio Azteca

According to the FBI, the Hispanic Barrio Azteca criminal gang "has approximately six hundred active members who engage in murder, assault, extortion, human and drug trafficking, and other crimes. Many of the members are in U.S. and Mexican prisons and benefit from the gang's illicit profits by having funds placed in their prison commissary accounts."

Eduardo "Tablas" Ravelo, leader of the violent street and prison gang, became the 439th addition to the FBI's famous Ten Most Wanted Fugitives list, and the agency is offering a $100,000 reward for information leading directly to his arrest. Crimes he is charged with include possession of cocaine and heroin with intent to distribute, money laundering, and racketeering. And, while he has not been charged with murder as of this writing, he and other members of Barrio Azteca are believed to have committed numerous contract killings for the Vicente Carrillo Fuentes drug cartel of Mexico.

"From everything our intelligence sources tell us, Ravelo is a ruthless killer who has absolutely no respect for human life," FBI Special Agent Samantha Mikeska said. He is believed to be living just across the border from El Paso in the war-torn city of Ciudad Juarez, where he is protected by a paramilitary force of gang members equipped with armored vehicles.

"They are well organized," Mikeska said, "and they are dangerous."

Dixie Mafia *(aka Southern Mafia)*

Perhaps the epitome of vicious white trash, the Dixie Mafia is a criminal organization based in Biloxi, Mississippi, that reached its peak in the '70s and '80s, gaining fame by battling larger-than-life Tennessee Sheriff Buford Pusser.

The Dixie Mafia got its start in the late 1960s as a loose group of itinerant hoodlums engaged in burglary, robbery, and theft, thereafter moving into trafficking of drugs, bootleg liquor, and stolen goods. They spread throughout the south, including Texas. Its affiliates included Darrel Ward, a Clarksville, Texas, thug who is believed to have controlled bootlegging and organized crime throughout Texas, Arkansas, Louisiana, and Mississippi and to have connections with the Giancana crime family.

Tools employed by the Dixie Mafia have included bribery, intimidation, and murder, and it has specialized in operating in small communities and rural areas lacking a strong law-enforcement presence, where it could more easily prey upon the local populace. The group's motto is "Thou shall not snitch to the cops," and much of the prolific violence it has perpetrated over the years, to include contract killings, has been against members who could not stick to this code. Other victims included circuit court judge Vincent Sherry and his wife, a Biloxi political figure.

Hammerskins *(aka Hammerskin Nation)*

A white supremacist skinhead group, "the Hammerskins first appeared in the late '80s as the Dallas-based Confederate Hammerskins and spread to Georgia, Tennessee, and Florida," a Southern Poverty Law Center report said in 1999. "More namesakes followed: the Northern Hammerskins in the Great Lakes region, the Eastern Hammerskins in Pennsylvania and New Jersey, and the Western Hammerskins in Arizona and California." At one

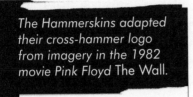

The Hammerskins adapted their cross-hammer logo from imagery in the 1982 movie Pink Floyd The Wall.

point, it was considered to be the country's most well-organized white racist gang.

The primary focus of the group, which idealized Nazis, Vikings, and other heroes of the Aryan race, was producing and promoting white-power rock music, and many bands playing such music were affiliated with the gang, as was the record label 9% Productions. The group organized several concerts each year, including Hammerfest, an annual event held both in the United States and Europe. Its slogans were "Hammerskins Forever, Forever Hammerskins" and "Hail the Crossed Hammers." Its logo was adapted from fascist imagery in the 1982 movie *Pink Floyd The Wall* and depicted a pair of crossed claw hammers.

Many Hammerskins members were convicted of crimes that included assault, harassment, and murder. The gang also established "Crew 38" support chapters and numerous international chapters, and some of its groups in Texas are even known to have had German and British affiliates active in their ranks.

Within a decade or so of its founding, however, a number of splinter groups split off from the Hammerskins, including the volatile Outlaw Hammerskins, and the group began to fall apart and lose members. Today, little is left but local affiliates and its Crew 38 support group.

Mexican Mafia *(a.k.a. El Eme, La EMI, Mexikanemi)*

Founded in California as a prison gang in 1957, by the 1990s the Mexican Mafia was "the most dominant of the prison-spawned gangs operating in Texas," according to the FBI; its membership was estimated at seven hundred in 1992, around fifteen hundred in 1998, and is even larger and still growing today.

The Texas branch of the gang, founded in a Huntsville prison unit of the Texas Department of Criminal Justice in 1984 by Heriberto "Herbie" Huerta, identifies itself as La EMI or *Mexikanemi,* "Soldiers of Aztlan." Huerta wrote the twelve-point constitution adopted by the Mexican Mafia and collected and managed revenue generated by the gang's criminal activities; in 2002, his prison bank account held $8,000 derived from the 10 percent tax on drug revenues earned by the Mexican Mafia on the outside.

The headquarters of *Mexikanemi* is in San Antonio—where it is believed to be responsible for one in ten killings committed in the city—and its members are active throughout Texas, notably in Corpus Christi, Dallas, El Paso, Houston, and the central and southern portions of the state.

"The Mexican Mafia operates on a paramilitary structure, complete with a president, vice president, and numerous generals, captains, lieutenants, and sergeants," InsidePrison.com says. "Below these high-ranking members are soldiers, also known as *carnales,* as well as suppliers and associates, all of whose activities are overseen by the generals. Only one general operates in the federal prison system, while another one operates in the state prison system. The state general appoints a committee of lieutenants and captains who command prison units across the entire state."

According to a prosecutor in a 2005 San Antonio trial of a gang member, "the Mexican Mafia is a criminal organization that works in any criminal aspect or interest for the benefit and advancement of *Mexikanemi* [and deals] in drugs, contract killings, prostitution, large-scale robbery, gambling, weapons, and everything imaginable."

Overton Gang

The Overton Gang was "an Austin-based, white-trash mafia syndicate and perennial headline-maker in the 1960s," according to author Jesse Sublett, who has investigated and written extensively about the group. "They were white guys, old-school thugs. Safecracking and prostitution were their mainstays, but they also had a hand in various other criminal opportunities abundant during that era in the River City. . . . They were involved in drug smuggling, murder and arson for hire, massage parlors, a plot to assassinate the sheriff, and violent junkyard feuds."

The group took its name from its bare-knuckled leader, Timmy Overton, a native of Austin's working-class eastside neighborhoods, who landed a football scholarship and used the two years he managed to stay in college to engage in burglary, drug dealing, and whore mongering.

Jerry Ray James of the Overton Gang and kingpin Jimmy Chagra both served time together in the U.S. penitentiary Leavenworth. What Chagra didn't know was that James was going to snitch on him to the FBI.

A Federal Snitch

JERRY RAY JAMES, AN UNREPENTANTLY VIOLENT career hoodlum who was an affiliate of the Overton Gang, ended up being friends with drug kingpin Jimmy Chagra while they were both serving time in Leavenworth. This was not a coincidence, as James was working as an informant for the FBI, providing testimony that helped convict Chagra and contract killer Charles Harrelson for the assassination of federal judge John Wood III (see "The Crime of the Century" in the "Murder" section).

Overton went on to become, as Sublett puts it, "Austin's white trash godfather," and by the early '60s had become a major player in the Austin underworld.

"Wherever he went, he trailed an entourage of usual suspects," Sublett says. "Burly thugs, hookers, used-car salesmen, domino hustlers, paper-thin junkies, and the cleverest, crookedest barristers that UT Law School ever turned out."

In 1968, the Overton Gang's penchant for burglarizing banks prompted the federal government to come down on it, and Timmy Overton was sent to Leavenworth for a few years. That in itself would not likely have been enough to finish the gang off, but in December 1972, exactly two months after Overton's release from prison, a fellow thug executed him for reasons that remain obscure but which likely involved a contract.

Police turned their attention to the Overton organization as late as August 1976, when two junkie hoodlums believed to have been associated with the group were gunned down within hours of each other. Neither of them turned out to have been killed as a result of gang activity, however, and the era of the Overton Gang had apparently come to an end.

Texas Syndicate (aka Syndicato Tejano)

In the 1960s, Texan prisoners at Folsom Prison in California founded the Texas Syndicate to protect themselves from the predations of other gangs, especially the Aryan Brotherhood and Mexican Mafia (q.v.). Many of its members have been Mexican immigrants, "border brothers," rather than U.S.-born Hispanics.

The Texas Syndicate currently has more than eight thousand members in prisons throughout Texas, notably at the Coffield Unit near Tyler and the Allred Unit near Wichita Falls. There are probably more than twice that many in other states. On the streets they are especially active in Austin, Corpus Christi, the Dallas-Fort Worth area, and the Rio Grande Valley. Ten percent of the gang revenue generated by un-incarcerated members—known as "the dime"—is provided for the use of the gang in prison.

The Texas Syndicate is among the gangs that the Los Zetas Cartel has hired to carry out murder for hire on its behalf.

Los Zetas Cartel

In the late 1990s, the head of the criminal Gulf Cartel drug trafficking operation recruited a rogue officer and thirty deserters from the Mexican army's special forces, Grupo Aeromóvil de Fuerzas Especiales, for use as enforcers and assassins. Many had been trained by the U.S. military in aerial assault, ambush, small unit tactics, intelligence gathering, counter-surveillance techniques, marksmanship, prisoner rescues, rapid deployment, and sophisticated communications for use in counterinsurgency and anti-narcotics operations. Their activities were soon expanded to include debt collection, securing drug trafficking routes, and conducting military operations against rivals.

The badge of Grupo Aeromóvil de Fuerzas Especiales, a Mexican special forces unit, members of which deserted to become enforcers for the Gulf Cartel.

In 2003, when the current head of the Gulf Cartel, Osiel Cárdenas Guillen, was arrested, Los Zetas negotiated for a more prominent role in the organization and went beyond enforcement and into actual drug trafficking as well. The group thereafter expanded its ranks to include corrupt former local, state, and federal law enforcement officers and former members of the Guatemalan special forces and established paramilitary camps for training its recruits.

Then, in February 2010, Los Zetas broke off from the Gulf Cartel and established itself as an independent criminal enterprise. This split led to a violent battle for the control of border areas both wanted to control and the virtual destruction of entire towns and the establishment of alliances between Los Zetas Cartel and the Juárez and Tijuana Cartels.

Today, Los Zetas Cartel is led by Heriberto "El Lazca" Lazcano and, as the most violent and well-trained paramilitary group in Mexico, has helped transform the border region into the increasingly dangerous war zone that it has become (which has only been exacerbated by the decision of other cartels to also establish highly trained and heavily armed paramilitary units for use against rivals and law enforcement personnel). Its armaments include fully automatic assault rifles, submachine guns, heavy machine guns, grenade launchers, surface-to-air missiles, explosives, armored vehicles, and helicopters, as well as bullet-proof body armor.

Los Zetas Cartel is active throughout Mexico and Texas, and possibly other U.S. states and Italy, and has expanded its operations to include contract killing, extortion, kidnapping, money laundering, oil siphoning, and human trafficking. In the face of the threat the group represents, Texas Governor Rick Perry announced the "Operation Border Star Contingency Plan," which includes the use of military forces to protect the border against the Zetas and in the event of "the possible collapse of the Mexican State."

Bibilography
and Resources

This section contains lists of all the sources used in the research for this book and additional resources that readers can use to learn more about the topics covered in *Texas Confidential* and to go beyond them altogether. In particular, two official online tie-ins to this book contain material associated with it:

Texas Confidential Online (**texas-confidential.blogspot.com**). This online supplement includes new write-ups of historic and breaking episodes of sex, scandal, murder, and mayhem; addenda, expansions, and updates to chapters in the book; additional photos and graphics; and reviews, interviews, lists, links, tips, and other features designed to complement the book.

Michael O. Varhola's TravelBlogue (**varhola.blogspot.com**). Among other things, this site contains travel and event information tying in with many of the sites associated with the chapters in *Texas Confidential*.

Books

Anderson-Lindemann, Brenda. *Spring Branch and Western Comal County, Texas.* Omni Publishers Inc., 1998.

Bellesiles, Michael A. *Arming America: The Origins of a National Gun Culture.* Alfred A. Knopf, 2000.

Chamberlain, Samuel. *My Confession: The Recollections of a Rogue.* Harper and Brothers, 1853.

Cartwright, Gary. *Galveston: A History of the Island.* MacMillan Publishing Company, 1991.

Cartwright, Gary. *Dirty Dealing: Drug Smuggling on the Mexican Border and the Assassination of a Federal Judge—An American Parable.* Cinco Puntos Press, 1998 (2nd Edition).

Deaton, Charles. *The Year They Threw the Rascals Out.* Shoal Creek Publishers, 1973.

Durham, George. *Taming the Nueces Strip: The Story of McNelly's Rangers.* University of Texas Press, 1962.

Davis, Jeff C. and Fisher, Ovie C. *King Fisher: His Life and Times.* University of Oklahoma Press, 1966.

Fanning, Diane. *Through the Window: The Terrifying True Story of Cross-Country Killer Tommy Lynn Sells.* St. Martin's True Crime, 2007.

Griffin, John Howard. *Land of the High Sky.* The First National Bank of Midland, 1959.

Hunt, Linda. *Secret Agenda: The United States Government, Nazi Scientists, and Project Paperclip, 1945 to 1990.* St. Martin's Press, 1991.

Kinch, Jr., Sam and Procter, Ben. *Texas Under a Cloud: Story of the Texas Stock Fraud Scandal.* Jenkins Publishing Company, 1972.

Lynch, Dudley. *The Duke of Duval: The Life and Times of George B. Parr* (Texian Press, 1976).

Marrs, Jim. *Rise of the Fourth Reich: The Secret Societies That Threaten to Take Over America.* William Morrow, 2008.

McCarthy, Cormac. *Blood Meridian: The Evening Redness in the West* (Vintage International, 1992).

McCarthy, Cormac. *No Country for Old Men* (Vintage International, 2006).

Neal, Bill. *Sex, Murder, and the Unwritten Law: Courting Judicial Mayhem*, Texas Style.

Silverstein, Jake. *Nothing Happened and Then It Did: A Chronicle in Fact and Fiction.* W.W. Norton and Company, 2010.

Stephens, A. Ray. *Texas: A Historical Atlas.* University of Oklahoma Press, 2010.

Wright, James C. *Reflections of a Public Man.* Madison Publishing, 1984.

The Texas Prison Museum in Huntsville. See more about Texas prisons in the chapter "Crime and Punishment."

Newspapers

The Austin Chronicle (**www.austinchronicle.com**)

The Dallas Morning News (**www.dallasnews.com**)

The Hilltop Reporter (**hilltopnewspaper.com**)

Houston Chronicle (**www.chron.com**)

New Braunfels Herald Zeitung (**herald-zeitung.com**)

San Antonio Express-News (**www.mysanantonio.com**)

Web sites/Online Resources

American Serial Killers (**americanserialkillers.com**)

Congressional Badboys.com (**www.congressionalbadboys. com**)

The Handbook of Texas Online/Texas State Historical Association (**www.tshaonline.org/handbook**)

Michael O. Varhola's TravelBlogue (**varhola.blogspot.com**). Contains travel information about many of the sites in Texas Confidential.

Office of the Secretary of State (**sos.state.tx.us**)

Texas City Firefighters Local 1259 (**local1259iaff.org**)

Texas Confidential Online (**texas-confidential.blogspot.com**) New write-ups of historic and breaking episodes of sex, scandal, murder, and mayhem, and more.

Texas Department of Criminal Justice (**www.tdcj.state.tx.us**)

Texas Monthly (**www.texasmonthly.com**)

TPMMuckraker (**tpmmuckraker.talkingpointsmemo.com**)

truTV (**www.trutv.com**)

UFO Casebook (**www.ufocasebook.com**)

Wikipedia (**www.wikipedia.org**)

WorldNetDaily (**www.wnd.com**)

Newspaper, Magazine, and Online Articles and Reports

"Texas City, Texas, Disaster, April 16, 17, 1947" (Fire Prevention and Engineering Bureau of Texas and the National Board of Fire Underwriters, 1947).

"Battle of the Nueces" (*Handbook of Texas Online,* Texas State Historical Association).

Humphrey, David C. "Prostitution" (*Handbook of Texas Online,* Texas State Historical Association).

Kaderli, Elizabeth. "Veteran's Land Board Scandal" Handbook of Texas Online (*Handbook of Texas Online,* Texas State Historical Association).

Metz, Leon C. "John Wesley Hardin" (*Handbook of Texas Online,* Texas State Historical Association).

"Americana: Close Encounters of a Kind" (*Time,* March 12, 1979).

"The Founder" (*Time,* February 15, 1971).

Michael O. Varhola

About the Author

Michael O. Varhola is a writer, editor, publisher, and journalist who lives in the Hill Country north of San Antonio, Texas. He has authored or co-authored ten nonfiction books, including *Texas Confidential, Life in Civil War America, Ghosthunting Maryland, Ghosthunting Virginia, Shipwrecks and Lost Treasures: Great Lakes,* and *Fire and Ice: The Korean War, 1950–1953.*

Varhola studied at Metropolitan State College in Denver, Colorado, and at the American University of Paris before earning a B.S. in journalism from the University of Maryland, College Park and is an eight-year veteran of the U.S. Army. Varhola also has an active online presence, notably through his Travel Blogue, Facebook, and on a variety of other blogs, forums, and sites.

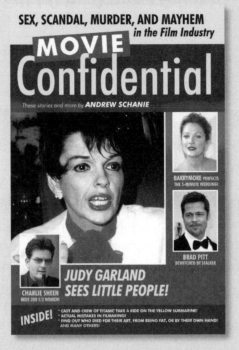
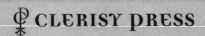

Check out this other great title from
— Clerisy Press! —

OHIO Confidential

by John Boertlein
ISBN: 978-1-57860-299-5

$15.95, 1st Edition
288 pages, 6x9, Trade paper

Ohio Confidential exposes—then scratches—the seamy underbelly of the Buckeye State as it's never been done before!!!

The Great State of Ohio has produced many wonderful people who have achieved many wonderful accomplishments, and their stories have been told in many wonderful books. This isn't one of them.

In *Ohio Confidential* you'll read about the most notorious, scandalous, salacious, murderous, and just plain nuttiest Buckeyes ever to fall from our fair state's hallowed limbs. From adultery to treason, crimes of the heart to heartless brutality, this book offers a mesmerizing stroll through Ohio's Hall of Infamy.

With a sharp sense of history and a sharper sense of humor, author John Boertlein is your tour guide, presenting more than thirty stories guaranteed to explode the myth that Ohio is a bland and boring place full of nice, God-fearing folks.

Thoroughly researched and packed with photos, *Ohio Confidential* is the perfect book for buffs of history, lovers of licentiousness, mavens of murder, and voyeurs of villainy, not to mention amateur sleuths, fiendish gossips, teachers, students, librarians, researchers, and anyone else looking for a wild, rollicking read.

⳨ CLERISY PRESS